Franchising: Fact Fraud & Fallacy

By Danielle Baillieu

Published by Streetwise Publications
A Division of Streetwise Franchising Ltd.

First published in 1990 by Streetwise Publications
A Division of Streetwise Franchising Ltd.
Lincoln House, 661 High Road,
London N12 0DZ

Photoset by DT pro, Norwich.

Printed and bound in Great Britain by
Galliard (Printers) Ltd. Great Yarmouth, Norfolk.

British Library Cataloguing in Publication data

Baillieu Danielle
Franchising: Fact, Fraud & Fallacy
1. Franchising
I. Title
658.8708

ISBN 0-9516682-0-X

TO JAMES

Contents

Acknowledgements

I would like to thank the many franchisors who gave me so much of their time in discussing the ingredients of success and in particular Moshe Gerstenhaber and Andrew Quail (Kall Kwik) Roy Bishko(Tie Rack) and Derek Mottershead (Prontaprint).

This book would not have been possible if existing franchisees with problems or successful franchisees had not shared their experiences with me or used Streetwise Franchising to conduct negotiations with the franchisor. As a consequence I am indebted to them for information that I would never have otherwise received but which can be used to benefit potential franchisees and promote ethical franchising.

In addition many thanks to Melvyn Markus (City editor - Observer newspaper) for the use of their research facilities, Professor John Adams and Professor John Miller, Richard Eccles of McKenna Solicitors, Ray Cannon (Peters & Peters solicitors) Steven Kenton and Nicholas Kissen (Kenton Brandman solicitors), The British Franchise Association, Bob Riding of Franchise World Magazine, Dr. Dennis Chaplin and the many other professionals and franchisors who have been so supportive of my views and in particular the need for disclosure requirements.

In particular I would like to thank William Baillieu for his constant support, Sheila Baillieu for her devotion and assistance with the most important thing in my life, and Alfred Hughes for his humour and understanding, all my family for giving me the values to respect every persons right to know the truth. Thanks also to Sue Campbell, Jean Wylde, Peter and Martin Briggs for their friendship and caring and Anna Dacey for being a real brick and giving me real Streetwise advice.

Thanks also to Gorden Tomkins for assisting with the book cover and he and his wife Grace for their affection and friendship and last but not least my secretary and friend Alyson Whall who has burnt the candle at both ends on so many occasions to meet hair raising deadlines that her family are beginning to think she has left home and moved in with me (to her horror !).

FOREWORD

by

Professor John Adams

"Barrister and Academic".

I first met Danielle Baillieu when she was doing research for her book 'Streetwise Franchising', and setting up her advisory company FACTO (Franchise Advice and Consultancy Trade Organisation). She impressed me at the time as an energetic and capable person who was turning her own personal experience as a franchisee to good advantage.

FACTO assisted many franchisees to sort out their problems, and renamed **'Streetwise Franchising'** is assisting franchisors too.

This is not 'joining the enemy' but rather a reflection of the fact that franchising is a partnership, and that problems when they arise often confront both sides equally.

If, however, prospective franchisors and franchisees were to pay attention to the advice given in this book before starting out, such problems would be less likely to arise.

The case studies especially are instructive. I hope that this book will be read by anyone thinking of becoming involved in this industry. It can also be read with profit by those already running franchise businesses.

Introduction

If you know the problems you can avoid the pitfalls and achieve success in franchising.

"Look after the downside and the upside looks after itself"; this is a motto that ***Hanson Trust***, the leading industrial holding company uses. The origins of Hanson Trust go back to a small public company originally valued at less than £1 million. It has an unbroken twenty year record of annually increasing profits. Since 1984 Hanson Trust has been one of the thirty constituents of the Financial Times Industrial Ordinary Share Index.

The author adopts this motto and shows how proven and accepted business principles apply to franchising; gone is the myth that franchising is a strange creature set apart from other businesses.

No more an enigma, this business method is taken for what it really is - a unique distribution option that if handled correctly and applied in the right circumstances makes a profitable slave; but if abused paves the way to financial ruin for both franchisor and franchisee.

By exploring the failures and successes in franchising the recipe for success is discovered. What rules are there in this game of success versus failure?

One thing is clear - successful franchise companies display all the characteristics of other non-franchised successful companies. The difference lies in the extra skills a franchisor must possess before taking the fate of inexperienced individuals into their hands.

If any business is to succeed it must achieve excellence in several areas. If that same business then franchises, what it needs is "super-excellence" in all those areas and an ability to rapidly change with market forces.

This book investigates a sample of companies - successful, unsuccessful and those which have experienced the good and the bad in franchise practice. There are many important lessons to be learnt from their experiences.

The author has relied on published material and information provided by networks of franchisees who have suffered as a result of a franchise collapse. In some cases the franchisor companies have gone into liquidation. In other cases the companies have realised where they are going wrong and avoided failure by a change in policy. It is these companies that were obviously more willing to talk about their previous failings.

An awareness of problems, and what can go wrong in a franchise relationship, provides for the first time a unique insight into business format franchising success - and not just for the potential franchisee who wants to invest in a good business but also for the entrepreneur who wants to expand quickly.

Unsuccessful franchises lack some or all the characteristics of success. This book will show you how to spot them a mile away. At the end of the day there is no substitute for expert independent professional advice - but this book will show you how to think objectively when assessing a franchise opportunity, rather than letting your heart rule your head.

If you are already a businessman or indeed a franchisor you can gain insight into why some franchises are doomed to failure while others destined for stardom. What sets them apart? How do good franchisors handle problems?

Research of both successful and failed franchisor companies show that there are ***10 critical areas*** which dictate the fate of the franchise.

10 Golden Rules

(1) Management:

Unsuccessful and failed franchise operations tend to have an ineffective management structure. They are usually not respected by either the employees of the company, or by the franchisees.

Dick Garrett, a Hanson Trust executive, once said ***"a badly managed company is like a boiled egg. You can't eat it until you've whipped the top off. Underneath there is usually some excellent management".***

This applies just as well to franchising - if anything it's more important because franchisees are not like employees who can be sacked if they don't do what they are told. They are investors running their own businesses with their own money, albeit under the corporate and business format umbrella of the franchisor. Such investors cannot and will not respect management who don't pull their weight, don't keep promises, and use dogmatic and divide-and-rule tactics to keep them in line.

In one case the author dealt with, the franchisees didn't have a hope - their franchisor's method of negotiation was to shout, intimidate and hurl abuse at them whenever they wanted to discuss a problem. Communication ceased and a number of franchisees had to cease trading.

In the case of ***Avis Rent-A-Car*** in 1989, a number of franchisees complained that it was practically impossible to communicate with the management of the franchisor company, who continually failed to respond to them. In addition they felt that the management did not even communicate between themselves. When asked to negotiate on behalf of a group of Avis franchisees, the author was requested by them to write by recorded delivery to every executive director and non-executive director. There was no trust in the management and the franchisees did not know who to communicate with. There appeared to be no visible leadership.

Another common sign of poor management is that they fail to set realistic goals for the business, and are frequently negligently optimistic about the future projections and number of outlets that will be opened. They forget one of the golden rules of business - to behave like a horse-trainer and start with the low fences first - and never ask other people, namely the franchisees, to try to accomplish goals that are unrealistic.

(2) Red Tape:

Most unsuccessful franchises try to adhere strictly to bureaucratic form-filling when they can see that the system just doesn't work. Instead of taking the approach that they will devise a more workable system they determine to sit on their laurels unmoved by common sense. Most of the unsuccessful companies also employ ineffective personnel, especially in the area of franchise managers/ trainers. Many franchisees complain that when they have a problem they get fobbed off by ***"some lackey who doesn't know half as much about the business as they do."***

In contrast it is clear that successful franchise companies move heaven and earth to minimize bureaucracy, and their franchisees know exactly who to contact within the organisation to solve the problem.

(3) Control:

Nearly all unsuccessful franchises do not use the controls they have in place properly. There is no effective monitoring of the business. That doesn't mean they don't keep tabs on what's going on - quite the contrary - they're usually buried under a mountain of accounting information.

The problem is that they don't seem to know what the information means. When faced with operations having problems, the first thing I ask is **what is the cash-flow of the business; what did it make last week; what is the break-even point; what are the losses to date; and what were you supposed to make?** Do I ever get a simple answer? No. They usually provide an enormous file of accounting data and projections that have served no purpose except gather dust.

Compare that with the successful franchise operator, who will have all the relevant answers at his finger-tips, and will tell you before you ask.

Most unsuccessful franchises have poor business planning. There is usually negative cash-flow, and the business is on red-alert all the time. And if they are lucky enough to get some cash, they are usually stupid enough to spend it on the wrong thing, like lavish promotions. (To attract new franchisees ?)

(4) Quality:
Every successful franchise has an eagle's eye for detail. Customer satisfaction, excellent quality and good value are the foundation of any successful operation, and no more clearly depicted than McDonald's hamburger chain. Sacrifice these, and you might as well say good-bye to the business.

(5) Involvement:
Most of the unsuccessful franchises that the author has come across adopt a divide and rule policy. They are petrified that franchisees will get together and discuss together the problems they are experiencing.

By employing the ***Divide and Rule policy*** the franchisor can fob off complaints by saying that only that particular franchisee is experiencing them, and that everyone else is doing OK. So it must be that the franchisee is doing something wrong....

This myopic view only leads to great resentment and mistrust because inevitably franchisees within a network do talk to each other, if only in a desperate attempt to discover what they are doing wrong. It's hardly surprising that they are then angered by the discovery that the franchisor has been lying and nearly everyone in the network is having the same problem.

In such cases the franchisor's reluctance to address the problems inevitably means that the situation goes from bad to worse. Some franchisors fear franchisee associations so much that they threaten franchisees not to set them up. One franchisor actually told his franchisees that any meeting they arranged would be illegal. They were sufficiently intimidated and did nothing until in desperation contacted the author who advised them on their position.

Successful franchisors on the other hand encourage regular franchise meetings usually via a franchisee association. Problems can be aired and good business tips passed on. Often additional information is shared by newsletters.

(6)Flexibility:
Practically every good franchisor is supportive and flexible if things are not going to plan. The reason being that they can afford to be. They usually don't have continuous cash-flow problems and therefore if a particular franchisee isn't doing

well they can afford to provide financial support in the form of deferring royalties and providing management support.

In too many cases the franchisor does not have the resources to take such action. Their employees are usually ineffective trouble-shooters and the franchisor demands royalties that the franchisee cannot afford to pay.

If the franchisee is delaying payments for supplies and royalties to the franchisor, he is of course in breach of the franchise contract - and he has little choice but to inject more money into his franchise (which he normally doesn't have), or cease trading. In such cases an unscrupulous franchisor will continue making impossible demands, terminate the contract for breaches by the franchisee, and re-franchise the same area to the next gullible investor who inevitably always comes along.

Even worse, some such franchise tyrants have refused to allow a failed franchisee to mitigate losses by ceasing to trade by threats that they will sue the franchisee for future royalties for the remainder of the franchise contract. In the author's experience ethical franchisors are more sensitive, and if a franchisee has to cease trading then they are only too aware that the franchisee has lost money and do not pursue them for lost royalties for ceasing trading.

(7) Training:

One of the most important aspects of franchise operations is the training of inexperienced individuals to become successful businessmen in a relatively short period of time.

Hence ***McDonald's*** **University Of Hamburgerology** and the ***Tie Rack*** **School**. Good franchisors recognise that training is crucial if franchisees are to reflect the high standards the franchisor must maintain. Only by training franchisees to achieve excellence can the good name of the franchise continue.

All too often the training provided is inadequate and disappointing. Probably because training costs time and money - two commodities that the unscrupulous or badly managed franchisor just doesn't care about.

The **operation manual** - is supposed to be the franchisees' life-line, setting out all the operation procedures; but in the case of most unsuccessful franchises it is a conglomeration of literary rubbish thrown together in a piece-meal and irrelevant fashion. In several cases the author dealt with franchisees had never received an operations manual.

In a few cases unsuccessful operations have paid attention to a vigorous training programme, but whether the training is effective in relation to the whole business is another matter. If the franchisor hasn't got his act together in relation to training issues and on-going training, then the resources committed to training are wasted. This is probably what happens in most unsuccessful franchise operations.

(8) Market Orientation:
The market place is a constantly changing sea of activity. The tides can be for you one moment and against you the next. The only way to survive is to move with the tide. A battle against it is likely to be fatal.

One of the most important attributes of a franchise is the **" brand name".** If a franchise company doesn't have a good product with strong brand recognition then they should not be asking for a high initial fee. The whole point of buying a franchise is to invest in a well known and proven product or service.

Most of the unsuccessful franchises have a poor product or service, and it is wise to remember the dictum ***that all the advertising in the world won't sell a rotten product more than once.*** Market research is an essential tool for any business. All successful franchisors know their market inside out.

(9) Direction:
Successful franchisors not only have an eye for detail, a fetish for quality control, and a sense of fair play, but most importantly they never lose sight of their objectives.

Unsuccessful franchisors often not only lose their way but forget the basic fundamentals of good business practice.

Successful franchisors in one field have tried diversification - only to their cost. This will be explored later in detail in the case of ***Prontaprint*** who tried to diversify into ***Fudge Kitchens*** and ***Poppies.*** All that happens in such cases is that the management ends up putting their time into the ailing limb to the whole group's detriment. Rather than testing the water with their toe, they've taken the plunge, and usually ended up drowning - unless they act quickly and untie the leaden weights.

Unsuccessful franchisors are slow to react when they've made a mistake. Either they don't grasp that the mistake has been made or expect everything to work out by some miracle. Franchising or for that matter any business, is not that simple.

A classic *non - franchised business example is the board of* **Woolworths,** who knowing that customers had a poor opinion of the stores took no action to improve the quality of goods and service. Instead they made matters worse by trying to improve their image by advertising ***"The Wonder of Woolworths"***. Customers just didn't see it. But now after new management and a change in name to Kingfisher PLC, the company is at last adjusting to consumers tastes.

Franchisors, probably more so than other businesses, make a habit of using hype to the extremes. Examples of these will be looked at later. A typical example was ***Rainbow International*** who continued in 1989 to use the slogan ***"Be a part of our Success"*** together with a photo of a franchisee, who in fact had failed and ceased trading.

(10) Innovation:
No business, no matter how successful, can afford to turn a blind eye to new ideas.

Most unsuccessful franchisors forget that it is the person on the shop-floor - the franchisee, who is in daily contact with customers and who is directly involved in the day to day running of the business, and who will have hands-on experience not only of complaints and problems, but also what the customer wants.

In such cases, when franchisees communicate this essential feedback, the franchisor tends to ignore them. This type of situation arises particularly when the business is performing badly. Then, franchisees want to try new ideas which might boost sales. A successful franchisor is usually more understanding, although he will still want to maintain a uniform product and image.

A good franchisor should keep an open mind. It's worth remembering that **McDonald's 'Big Mac'** was invented by a franchisee.

A combination of these 10 qualities together with integrity are a recipe for success in franchising.

Since experience is the best teacher and those who face adversity the quickest learners (unless they die first) it is the author's intention that by looking at real examples of what has gone wrong and how some franchisors have solved their problems, potential and existing franchisors and franchisees, and their professional advisors, can ensure they can recognise the danger signs before it is too late.

1

What Is Franchising all about?

The word 'franchising' apparently comes from a French word meaning "to be free from servitude". It involves ownership rights belonging to a system so that such rights are free if you operate within the system. Feudal Lords and Kings charged citizens royalties (taxes) to live free within their system or area.

Today, franchising is simply a business system whereby the franchisor company grants you a licence to operate a "clone" business. This is called Business Format Franchising. Forget all the fancy jargon you hear and all the rubbish about "**being your own boss**". As a franchisee you are a hybrid animal - neither your own boss nor an employee. Franchising works if you do it the way the franchisor has proved the method to work. If you want to do it all your own way, franchising is not for you.

Rags to riches stories are few and far between. So, rather than have your head in the clouds let's assume you are like the man on **"the Clapham Omnibus"**, average, hard-working with some hard earned money (that you're not in a hurry to lose) to invest.

The whole idea about taking up a franchise is that you pay an initial fee for the expertise gained from a proven concept and use of the trade name. The franchisor should have tested that the system works by the operation of pilot operations in at least two to three totally different areas. He should also have carried out a market research programme that should be made available to you.

In a number of cases an ongoing franchise fee called a royalty or service management fee is also payable. This is usually based on turnover. If products are being supplied then a mark-up may be charged. There is nothing wrong with this because the franchisor has a business to run as well. But you do need to know exactly how much extra is being charged. If the franchisor claims there is no mark-up, then you should verify this in writing so that there is no confusion at a later date.

Franchising cannot make a silk purse from a sow's ear. A good franchise sells itself and by the time you have read this book you should be pretty competent at separating the good from the bad and the ugly.

A franchisee - franchisor relationship is a partnership. Both parties should be working for the benefit of the whole chain. Everybody should be making money. If they're not, there is something seriously wrong. A franchisor should treat you with respect. If you feel you are being looked down upon, think carefully. Is this the type of partner you will get on with?

As one client said: **"we had an interview with one well known franchisor who treated us as if we were applying for a £5,000 per annum job, not looking to invest £70,000. The franchisor then added insult to injury by wanting to interrogate us using some special test but seemed totally unaware of our past working achievements. They clearly had read nothing of the details we sent in"**. Not surprisingly, my clients did not go ahead with this franchise even though it is a fairly big name. At the end of the day you have to get on with your franchisor.

You need to ensure that your franchisor can give you the support and back-up that he promises and that if you experience difficulties, he can do something to help. Good ethical franchisors do exist and they go to great lengths to assist in every way possible including deferring royalties. Don't waste your time with a franchisor who isn't prepared to give you this type of commitment. If a franchisor can't afford to help you in such ways should you need it then he's in it for the wrong reason, ie., "expansion at your expense". The last thing you need if you're having teething problems with the business is a franchisor breathing down your neck with threats of breach of contract and termination. It happens, so look out.

If you go into franchising knowing what you can and cannot expect, that's half the battle. I get some franchisee clients coming to me who are totally to blame. They go into franchising without good professional advice. They don't do anything according to the operations manual and their franchisor is usually a nervous wreck trying desperately to assist. I never hesitate to tell such clients that they are in the wrong. Going into business is tough. But you can make it easier on your own if you know exactly what to expect from day one. It helps to understand the franchise contract and of course to use a solicitor who knows more than conveyancing houses and divorcing spouses.

On the other hand, I get clients who have believed everything the franchisor has told them and are conned into entering a contract by inducements that are never fulfilled. Again, good professional advice would have helped.

Research is the most important ingredient in achieving success in any business and especially franchising. Spending a few hundred pounds on initial research could save you thousands later. Streetwise Franchising's own Franchise Advice Centre has a slogan for encouraging people to invest in reports: **" If You Think Research Is Expensive, Try Ignorance."** It says it all.

Many good franchise opportunities exist. If you don't expect too much, realise you do actually have to work at it and if you're clued up about the problems, then there is no reason why you can't find a good franchise to invest in. So, let's plug on.

2

Franchising Today And Tomorrow

The data in the following diagrams was taken from the National Westminster Bank / BFA 6th Annual National Survey of franchising in Britain in 1989 and compiled by M.C. Power Research Associates.

Size band (franchised operating units)	*% of franchisors in membership*
Over 50	60%
11-50	40%
1-10	22%

Yes, it's official. According to **Euromonitor's 'Franchising in the European Economy' report**, *"franchising has become big business"*. It is estimated that in the UK alone there are some **16,600 business format franchised** outlets. This year the annual turnover from UK franchises stands at about **£4.5 billion**, a figure predicted to more than double by the early 1990s.

Franchising

Franchisors and Gross Franchised Turnover

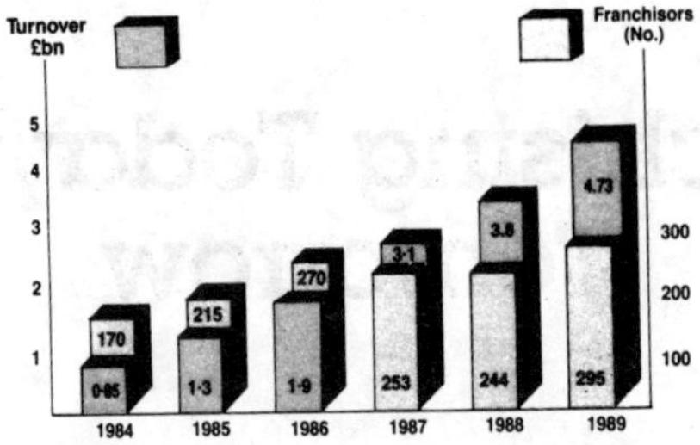

There are about **400 franchises** in existence in the U.K. and by 1991 it is predicted that one in every 35 businesses will be franchised. Of the 16,600 units now in operation, 11,900 use a full business format system. The average turnover of the 11,900 business format units is now £361,000, a 188% increase over the five years since 1984. The range of turnover is wide and varies from £5,000 to over £10m :

Franchisees

Growth and Average Turnover

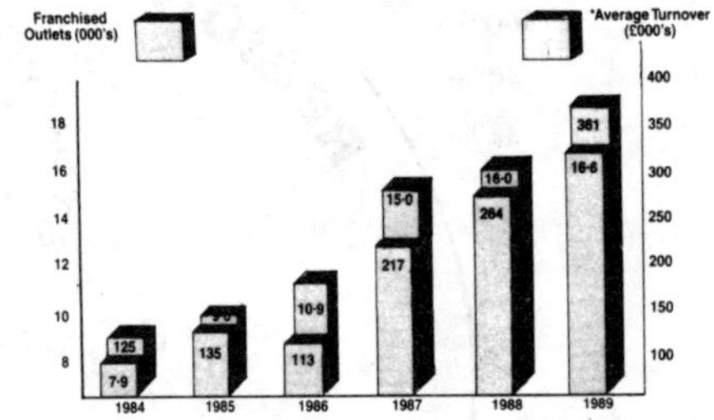

What is even more important is that franchising keeps a lot of people in work - in the current decade, a third of a million people are supposed to be employed via this business system. Within the 16,600 franchised outlets there are estimated to be 4,800 joint franchisees :

Employment in Franchising

Total numbers directly employed

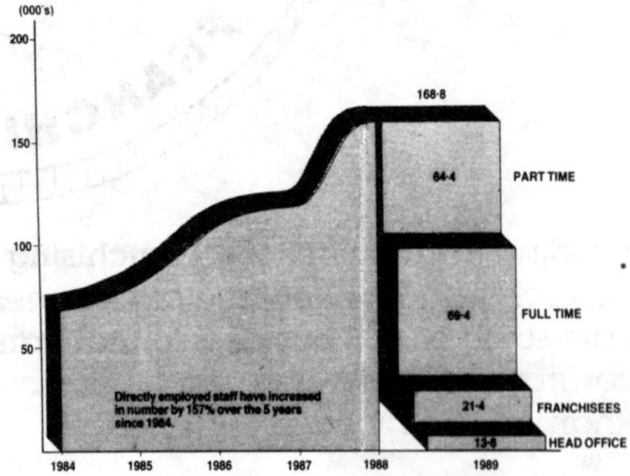

* Within the 16,600 franchised outlets there are estimated to be 4,800 joint franchisees.

BUSINESS SUCCESS

What's the big deal with franchising ? Well, basically, franchising has a lower failure rate than traditional methods of entering business according to the **Natwest/ BFA** survey and diagram.

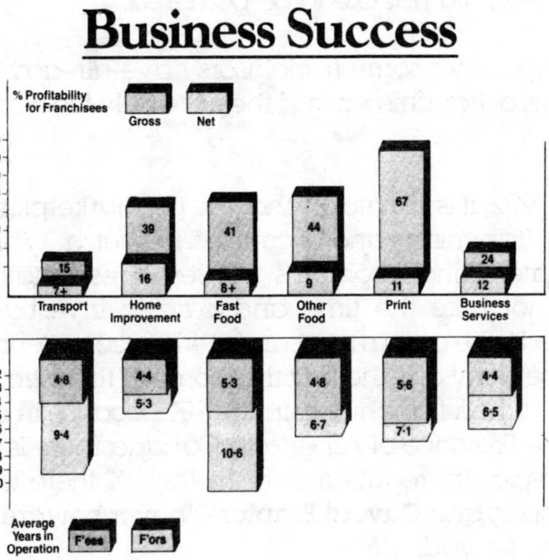

The failure rate isn't as low as some people will have you believe. If we are to accept that in a traditional business start-up the failure rate after the first year is between 85-95% then my own research in conjunction with reported "franchise problems" through Streetwise Franchising and franchise litigation in general shows that in a franchise set-up the failure rate is between 30-40 %. Some franchise authorities say the figure is between 2-5 %. Don't be fooled. Their figures just don't stack up.

Most of the current problems in franchising stem from the fact that people are misled into thinking that franchising is an easy option that is relatively problem-free. Not so. You will experience most of the problems found in a traditional business. The difference is that in franchising, you should have someone to hold your hand and guide you - the franchisor. Most franchisees eventually outgrow this parent-child relationship as their confidence and experience develops, but the initial support is vital to the success of the business. It is one of the main selling points - inducements if you like - in marketing a franchise opportunity, and one of the main areas of misrepresentation, as my research has indicated.

The figures that get bandied about in franchising should be taken with not a pinch but abag of salt. They are like any statistics - you can get them to speak any language, fit any pre-conceived picture. They're like a bikini - they reveal a lot, but hide the most interesting parts. There are no thoroughly researched figures available and research projects carried out so far have been on limited samples of franchise operations. The big problem is to get franchisors to reveal details of their franchisees. While ethical franchisors will have no objection to doing this, it is anticipated that the last thing some franchisors want is Streetwise Franchising or anybody else to contact their franchisees regarding the franchisor's good and bad points. More than one franchisor Streetwise Franchising have contacted for information have staunchly refused to give details of franchisees. One actually stated their franchisee's did not like to be bothered.

What is encouraging is that some franchisors have already furnished Streetwise Franchising with lists of franchisees and they are only too happy to fill in the forms sent to them.

With the advent of 1992, it is inevitable that the UK marketplace will become more attractive to foreign franchisors and of course vice versa. While this will make our high streets more interesting, problems will result, especially where franchisors from overseas do not take the time and care to investigate the UK market. Franchisees will need to be even more careful when considering such investments. Another aspect to be wary of is the fact that some of these franchisors will in effect be "let off the leash" when franchising in the UK because in some other countries like the USA and the Province of Alberta in Canada there is franchise legislation and specifically, disclosure requirements. In the UK there is nothing except the common law principles and **Caveat Emptor - 'buyer beware'**. As a UK franchisee you have to look out for yourself.

In **France**, even before disclosure requirements came in, there was a practice called the **"Three:Two rule."** This stipulated that ideally, a franchisor should only franchise if he has at least three franchise operations which have been operating for a period of two years. The French Government proposed legislation to prevent abuses in franchise relationships. Implementing regulations were drafted and the information included in the disclosure document includes points such as: see page for more details.

1) Information about the franchisor including the owners, the history of the businesss etc.

2) Addresses of existing franchisees.

3) The registration number of the franchisor's trademark registration.

4) The franchisor's bank references.

5) Financial statements for the franchisor's two most recent years of trading

6) List of principal suppliers of products that are an integral part of the franchise.

This is the type of information that Streetwise Franchising requests from franchisors and is actively lobbying for Disclosure legislation in the U.K.

Currently, the twelve EEC member states all have different national laws regarding franchising. This particular situation isn't going to change in 1992. Unification of franchise laws in Europe is not part of the 1992 project. But there will be a "mutual recognition" of each member's regulations. This means that in practice, if a franchisor complies with the regulations of one member state, this will allow him access to the other member states without the need for further authorisation. Of course the obvious will happen - franchisors will choose the most attractive body of law - or a "no law" country.

There are many important lessons to be learnt from the American experience of disclosure requirements. And while some sort of protection is needed by the British public, it is equally clear that disclosure must not be a hangman's noose for the franchise concept. In the States, where it is generally agreed that disclosure requirements are too onerous, it is at least refreshing to see that the developement of franchising has not been hampered.

In Western Europe, franchising is worth about ***$50 billion*** according to **Euromonitor.** There are about ***3,500 active franchisors in Europe***. The future of franchising certainly has a rosy glow - and quite rightly so. But tomorrow's franchising will not be trouble free - indeed, things will get more complicated. The important issue to bear in mind is that franchising can offer you a chance to go into business which may never otherwise come your way.

Important changes have already taken place in the last few years in the UK to ensure that only ethical franchising is promoted. More people are openly speaking of their experiences. Franchisees experiencing problems are beginning to speak up after a long time of being silenced under a kind of ***'divide and rule' strategy*** practised by franchisors. With the encouragement of concerned franchise authors and journalists, they are being coaxed out into the open to reveal the extent of the problems in franchising and draw attention to factors which should, if properly handled, educate and guide the next generation of franchisees to avoid making the same mistakes. It is rather like the pre-legislation movement in the States and is a healthy sign.

As a business system, franchising is certainly worth protecting. Tomorrow's franchising in the UK is ***'The Franchise Revolution'***. The aim is to promote ethical franchises and to ensure that the public are protected from the sharp practices, fraud, incompetence and under-capitalisation of some franchisors.

Earlier this year a report was prepared by **Chater Associates** - a firm of management consultants. The purpose of the report was to provide an analysis of the performance of 100 franchising companies which had the highest number of outlets within the UK. It was based on records filed with Companies House at January 1st 1990.

The companies in the report fell into 4 categories:-

1) Semi-autonomous franchise operations which were part of a larger group. This included some companies that were dormant. For example, Hertz and Home Tune.

2) Businesses where franchising was just one distribution option being used. Example, Holiday Inns, Thornton Chocolates.

3) Free-standing franchise operations. Example, Body Shop and Tie Rack.

4) Master Franchises where the concept had probably been developed abroad. For example, McDonald's, Kentucky Fried Chicken and PIP Printing.

The results of the survey certainly gave food for thought:-

27% were making losses.

17% were trading as £100 companies.

10% were insolvent (and therefore possibly trading illegally)

9% were operating at dangerous levels of liquidity (below 35%)

6% had recently gone into liquidation or receivership.

Also disturbing was the fact that a number of small and medium sized companies were taking advantage of **section 247-249 of the Companies Act 1985** - a loophole which allows them to limit the amount of information they need to reveal in relation to their results. The report states ***"if a franchisor does this he is clearly signalling to "would be" franchisees that there may be a problem with his operations".***

The report reaches some interesting conclusions and as far as it goes, the financial information is presented clearly. However, the report does not emphasise enough:

1) that the amount of information filed with Companies House can be very limited, especially for smaller companies. So much so, that any analysis based on that information alone has very limited value.

2) for bigger companies more detailed information may be filed and financial information may be available from other sources. This means that when preparing comparisons and setting out tables the analysis is not always comparing like with like.

3) Analysis of Franchisor Companies only where the franchisor is a subsidiary of a trading group of companies. But with smaller/less well known franchisor companies, it would have been useful to show the consolidated accounts for the group as well.

4) Analysis did not make the point that sometimes the Franchisor company is a shell company only. The franchisee's contract is with a shell company, through which all monies are channelled to other companies within the group of which the Franchisor Company is a part.

5) Some companies have recently floated on the Unlisted securities market eg Alan Paul Hairdressing, but no mention is made of this. This illustrates that the analysis has been limited.

However the report does make some very pertinent comments, and the conclusions are good.

Small and medium sized companies are generally allowed to file modified accounts (ie very limited financial information is filed) with the Registrar of Companies. Some categories of Company have been unable to make use of these exemptions in the past. These categories will now be as per Companies Act 1989. So full accounts have to be filed by:

(1) Public companies whether U.K. or overseas Companies. (ie p.l.c's - whether quoted or not).

(2) Banking and insurance Companies.

*(3) Companies authorised under the Financial Services Act 1986.
eg FIMBRA, LAUTRO, TSA

(4) Companies which are members of groups including Companies in any of the above categories - new S246 of Companies Act 1985 - S13.
(Previously shipping companies were also included as an additional category).

Comment

As many if not most franchise companies abuse the right of the franchisee to disclosure. Surely there is a good case to be made out for campaigning for Franchisor Companies to be included in this list? Certainly until we get disclosure requirements...

3

Franchise Associations & Advisory services

The British Franchise Association (BFA)
ADDRESS:
FRANCHISE CHAMBERS
THAMES VIEW
NEWTOWN ROAD
HENLEY ON THAMES
OXON

TEL: 0491 578049

The BFA has come under much criticism over the last few years - not only from the author but from many of its own members. The main problem has been that many perceive the BFA as an incestuous and nepotistic organisation geared towards the old boy network. In all fairness they are trying to remedy this since their new director Brian Smart took over at the beginning of 1990.

The BFA is an organisation for franchisors who pay a membership fee to join. A number of excellent franchisors including McDonald's and The Body Shop however are not members. Equally there are franchisors who are members who should perhaps not be. This is particularly illustrated by the fact that there have over the last few years been a number of BFA member failures.

Some franchisors hide behind the respectability and credibility that the BFA has built over the years, but at the BFA's expense. No one is probably more aware of this than the BFA. Consequently they have recently announced radical changes in Membership Criteria.

Under the new rules Members must allow access to confidential information by an authorised BFA staff member.

The previous "Associate Member" category has been revised in accordance with the Full Membership criteria. Applicants must fulfil Full Membership requirements but don't have to demonstrate the extended trading and franchising track record of Full Members. Consequently Associate Members can no longer use the BFA logo.

The previous Early Development Category has at last been abolished. Streetwise Franchising had found that franchisors with a "bright idea" were franchising overnight when in fact they could not give franchisees backing or support and were underfunded. So, in this case the BFA has made a wise move.

Now the BFA will be offering a range of services to companies who wish to franchise. These will be operated on a commercial basis and the intention is to eventually get the franchisors into a membership category. Services are to include training workshops, a preliminary contract check and access to advice and guidance.The obvious critisicm is that new franchisors will use the BFA services just to get in as a member rather than obtain the best advice from independent sources who may not be BFA members or associates.

The BFA appear to be trying to pull up their socks but everything is geared to making money. While there is nothing wrong with this there is something wrong when someone tries to give the impression that they only wish to promote ethical franchising. However, one of the biggest problems remains; the author and others have frequently referred to the BFA as a "watchdog without teeth". This does not appear to have changed. There are no real sanctions against members who breach the BFA code of ethics. The only sanction the BFA has is to withdraw membership. Unfortunately this isn't much of a sanction.

The BFA Arbitration Scheme

This has now been in operation for a couple of years. Its aim was to promote solving problems outside litigation with the franchisor sharing costs. There are mixed feelings about its effectiveness. Ask the BFA, and it works. Ask some of the franchisees who have used it and they tell a different tale.

Under the scheme if the franchisee loses he only has to pay one third of the costs. If he wins the franchisor pays all the costs. Administration of the scheme is by the Chartered Institute of Arbitrators. A franchisee having a problem fills in a Request for Arbitration form and pays a deposit of £150-00. The franchisor then agrees to arbitration by filling in the form. Once the arbitrator is appointed the franchisee has 28 days to submit evidence in support of his claim and then the franchisor has another 28 days to respond.

The problems that have arisen are:

1) the BFA is not thought of as an independent professional body. Its members are franchisors, and franchisees quite rightly feel that they will not get a fair hearing. Matters are not helped by some franchisors who intimidate franchisees by an attitude of "We are BFA members so we are OK". Unfortunately in some of these cases the BFA probably does not know what is going on.

2) In the past some franchisees who have sought assistance from the BFA with a view to invoking the arbitration process have had their correspondence passed onto the franchisor who has then sued them for libel. One such case was defended by the franchisee on the basis of qualified privilege. The BFA should not have passed on documentation but more importantly should have had some control over the franchisor involved.

The author has raised this matter with the BFA and has been assured that the above will not happen again.

The public have long memories and much of the damage has been done - especially when franchisees lose homes and life savings. The BFA will have to do more than just give reassurances to win back confidence.

3) The franchisor involved may not be a BFA member and therefore may decide not to partake in the arbitration proceedings.

4) Some contracts are appearing which state that franchisees will in the case of dispute use the BFA arbitration scheme. Franchisees are signing the contracts because the franchisor will not negotiate but when it comes to disputes do not want to use the arbitration scheme because they feel they will not get a fair hearing.

Matters could be complicated as to whether such a clause is valid or whether there was an unequal bargaining position between the two parties and the franchisee agreed under duress.

Streetwise Franchising Ltd
ADDRESS :
LINCOLN HOUSE
661 HIGH ROAD N12 0DZ

TEL: 081 445 7161

This consultancy was started in 1988 by the author in response to a need from the public for

1) advice on franchising before signing a contract
2) advice on what to do if problems arose.

Originally **FACTO - the Franchise Advice and Consultancy Trade Organisation** was formed to assist franchisees. However, it became apparent that unlike the BFA for franchisors, potential and existing franchisees did not want a club or association but simply excellent professional help. Once FACTO had resolved a case the franchisee did not need to continue as a member - indeed they wanted to forget what had happened and get on with their lives. Therefore FACTO aimed at giving only professional advice. Potential Franchisees were encouraged to have a report carried out on any franchise before they signed the contract.

A report consisted of a company search and a look at projections, a review of the franchise contract and interviews with at least three franchisees and the franchisor if necessary.

If potential franchisees were to go to an accountant and lawyer to have this type of detailed research carried out it would normally have set them back about £800 - £1,000. Nearly all franchisees that I came across were not prepared to lay out this sort of cash - even though they were going to be investing thousands.

There seemed to be a mental block against research. To encourage and educate franchisees to research I decided to set an affordable undaunting figure for a report - £250.00 + VAT which was later increased to £350-00 plus VAT. It was and still is a loss leader .

Reports have became very popular. Even more so when it got round that we could negotiate a better deal via side letters to the standard Franchise Contract. Reports were carried out on relatively unknown franchise operations to major PLC's like Servicemaster and Athena (Pentos Retailing).

The author made the discovery of a life time - "nothing was non-negotiable". While potential franchisees were green about the ways of "franchising" and could easily be fobbed off with "this is non-negotiable - take it or leave it", I had stumbled on quuite a different picture.

Negotiations for groups of franchisees had shown me that several different contracts may exist with the same franchisor. If you requested reasonable alterations then the franchisor's usually gave them. They needn't change the contract - changes could be agreed in side letters to the contract.

In one case the franchisor was clearly overtrading and technically insolvent and could go under at any moment. The set up was such that monies from customers went directly to the franchisor who then took his share and passed the rest to the franchisee. It took several weeks for payment to filter through to the franchisee. To my mind it was very feasible that if the franchisor went under my client the

franchisee could be left being owed several thousand pounds.
I put the above case to the franchisor who agreed he was overtrading and that the above scenario was possible. I suggested setting up an independent bank account where monies from customers were paid in and which the franchisor held on trust for the franchisee. The franchisor agreed that this was a reasonable request.

Existing Franchisees with problems

An amazing number of franchisees succussful and otherwise contacted FACTO to assist in negotiations with their franchisor. In many cases there was a breakdown in communications.

In some cases the franchisees had been trying to negotiate for up to a year. In many cases the franchisor did not bother to reply to correspondence. In others there was a bloody minded attitude - pretend the problems don't exist and they might go away. Some franchisors clearly knew they were in a strong position - the franchisees in most cases were totally broke and even if they had a case couldn't afford legal advice.

In most cases with problems there was no flexibility. Heavy handed tactics and even threats were common in the "lower cost service" franchises.

In a few cases I actually felt sorry for the franchisor who had done everything to help. Such cases were the exception rather than the rule.

One franchisor refused to deal with FACTO. It made little difference because we still assisted our clients in reaching settlements from behind the scenes.

Some cases went to litigation because the franchisor was totally unreasonable and unable to reach a settlement.

Most of the cases however were solved amicably via negotiations. FACTO'S motto **"negotiation is better than litigation"** appealed to most franchisors who firstly didn't want to wash their dirty linen in public and secondly didn't want to get involved in expensive and time consuming litigation.

Some franchisors contacted FACTO requesting that we undertake troubleshooting work for them. This was not taken on in 1989 because FACTO was set up to give franchisees advice.

However, from 1990 a complete franchise advisory service for franchisors and franchisees was made available and for administrative reasons provided by Streetwise Franchising Ltd.

Services Offered By Streetwise Franchising are:

- carrying out in depth reports on franchise opportunities for potential franchisees, lawyers and other professionals.

- handling negotiations and obtaining settlements for franchisees.

- advising on litigation and obtaining counsels opinion.

- advising would-be franchisor's how to set up their business as an ethical and successful franchisor.

- assisting franchisors and franchisees trouble-shoot.

Streetwise Franchising works closely with the media and other associations and has a magazine Streetwise Business Franchising, in which it aims to promote ethical franchising and expose sharp practice.

The consultancy handles reports and cases ranging from small franchises to major household names. Without playing such an active role in the franchise market place many experiences shared in this book would not have been possible.

One of the main aims of Streetwise Franchising is to obtain disclosure requirements in the U.K.

<u>The Franchise Shop</u>
ADDRESS
6 OLD HILLSIDE CLOSE
WINCHESTER
HAMPSHIRE
SO22 5LW

TEL. 0962 55530

The franchise shop run by Mr Ray Childs and described as a franchise estate agency operates to put prospective franchisees in contact with certain franchisors. The shop never meets potential franchisees but acts more as a contact. Franchisors on the shop's "books" pay a fee to the shop for promotions and pay a placement fee if a franchisee actually invests in the opportunity being offered.

At the time of writing The Franchise Shop is handling the promotions of eight franchises; Re nu, Goodebodies, Master Sharp, Colour Master, Master Thatchers, Name Machine and Open Fire Centres. The problem here is obvious - you may not be interested in these eight franchises. Then, the franchise shop can only give you details of the one you are interested in - which you could have obtained from a listing anyway.

Although the Franchise Shop claim to vet the franchises on their books you should remember that they obtain their fees from the franchisor and therefore cannot be entirely impartial .

There is no substitute for independent advice.

Other Consultants

Any consultant who works on a commisssion basis and tries to sell or recommend a particular franchise should be avoided like the plague.

Any consultant who claims that he can independently and effectively assess a franchise opportunity for say £60-00 should also be avoided. Good advice is worth what you pay for it.

A good advisor will be happy to give you details of their experience and background. Also remember that age does not necessarily mean a lot - they may just be dogmatic, set in their ways and closed to new business ideas. The saying that you can't teach an old dog new tricks is painfully true in the franchise profession. So choose someone who not only has experience but an honest and open approach.

4

The Franchising Revolution

Over the last few years, especially after the **La Mama** debacle, the public and franchise professionals suddenly seemed to have awakened from a long slumber to find that franchising doesn't entirely smell of roses - there is a pungency in the air, a smack of uncleanliness. Or could it just be incompetence on the part of advisors and those who hold themselves out as specialists in franchising? Probably, a bit of both.

Whatever, the result has been inevitable. It happened in the States. And now it is happening in the UK. **Harold Brown**, a pioneer of American franchise legislation, wrote one of the most enlightening books on franchise problems called very appropriately **'Trap For The Trusting**'. The title says it all.

In an address before the **American Bar Association Forum on franchising in October 1988, NASAA Franchise Committee Chairwoman Anne Nobles** gave a passionate and only too true view of franchising:

"...experience warns us that a darker, or fraudulent and abusive side of an industry usually grows up alongside a legitimate industry that is undergoing explosive growth and enjoying tremendous public interest. And the franchising industry is no different.....for every headline grabbing story about someone made a millionare by McDonald's or Wendy's or other franchisors there are quieter stories about the unknown people who have been made poor by unknown - and often nonexistent - franchise businesses".

She goes on to discuss another big problem which is rearing its ugly head in the UK as well:

"A related and growing concern is the increasing number of complaints about fraud, abuse and simple incompetence on the part of self acclaimed franchise consultants and lawyers....some of these so called consultants are no more than out-of-work executives armed only with a business card, and a resumé..But

these so called consultants are more apt to put together one sure-to-fail franchise after another..."

In the UK, there are franchise consultants who sell franchises to potential franchisees and take a commission from the franchisor. Their motive is the commission and not to ensure that the franchisee invests in a sound franchise. I know in one case where a franchisee invested on the advice of such a consultant and lost a large amount of money despite a settlement by the franchisor. The franchisee went back to the consultant and told him what had happened. The consultant quite shamelessly then tried to sell him another franchise on "his books" which was also having problems. While it is surprising that this particular consultant continues to promote franchise consultancy services, the problem is widespread. The DTI, while aware of the problems both with dodgy franchisors and consultants, seems content to sit on the fence and do precisely nothing but wait.

To prove to the DTI there is a problem research is necessary. To date it has not been in the interests of anybody to carry out research into franchise problems. Streetwise Franchising will be changing that. A campaign is being launched to identify the franchisees in the UK and log their franchise experiences.

What is worse is the fact that lawyers who know nothing or very little about franchising are quite willing to take on franchise clients and cock up their cases. Potential franchisees going to such lawyers who look at the franchise contract are usually fobbed off with "that's a standard contract", "its typically onerous" or "you have to take it or leave it". Rubbish. I've never said that to a client. There are many things in a contract that may need clarification and possibly modification and I have not failed to do just that.

Franchisees in the UK are becoming bolder and more are now prepared to speak out about their problems. And they want a solution. If not a solution, at least a fair bite at the chance of business success.

5

Which Franchise?

This is the question everybody asks. The answer is certainly not black or white. Information is the name of the game. After all, information, as communication specialists tell us, is "a source of power". And since Streetwise Franchising was set up I've been in the privileged position of being told about a wide range of franchise problems. At least there is recognition by professionals, albeit begrudgingly, that this information is vital for the promotion of ethical franchising.

After one franchise exhibition, when many exhibitors congregated in the Holiday Inn for drinks, one totally inebriated bank manager insisted at the bar that I write a list of franchisors that I knew had problems on the back of a cigarette packet. Needless to say, I did not take him up on the offer, and even if I had, regrettably a cigarette packet would not have been large enough.

Before the Olympia exhibition in March 1989, **Channel 4 Streetwise** phoned and asked if there were any franchises they shouldn't mention on their list - there most certainly were.

Generally speaking I never mention names. I like stating facts only. This is the only way to avoid one's own opinion colouring one's judgement. Besides, it is important to bear in mind that an opportunity may be good even though it is not as well known as McDonald's or the Body Shop. Let's face it, every franchise has to start somewhere. It can't be well known from day one. The important thing is to ensure that it is developing properly.

There is little point in taking a franchise that you're not interested in. Business is hard enough as it is. Why make it harder? **One leading franchisor** who has a large number of successful franchisees confided that even he had failures. He bemoaned the fact that he had done everything for one particular franchisee with no success. The franchisee had taken on the business to run together with family. The business involved constant contact with the public. When a customer walked in, no happy smiles, no polite chitchat. Family members looked at each other in awe and the silence was usually broken by an argument about ***"who's turn was it to serve this time ?***" Not surprisingly the customers didn't feel very welcome and usually didn't come back.

This is a classic case of people going into what they have heard is a good franchise but discounting their own abilities and interests. So, the question one should always ask is: ***" which franchise is good and suitable for me?"*** The following approach should be adopted:

1) Self analysis: list all your interests and fill in the forms set out on page....

2) How much money do you have?

3) Bearing in mind you can borrow 50 - 75% which franchise can you afford ?

4) What franchises are available which are within your budget and appeal to you ?

5) Send off for details of these.

6) Read details thoroughly and start your DIY research (specified in detail in Streetwise Franchising) and eliminate the ones that don't stand rigorous testing.

7) Have an independent report carried out before you sign on the dotted line.

The most important thing to realize in business is that you can't be brilliant at everything. You have to get professional advice because you can't be an expert overnight. I have met so many successful people who have taken a fall over franchising - sometimes it can't be helped simply because there is always a risk element. In many cases a bad investment could have been avoided if the correct homework had been done.

In your DIY research notice the obvious. I do in my reports. For example, ***one report was for a gentleman who had retired*** and this was the only bite of the apple he was going to get. He wanted to go into a car selling franchise. Apart from various problems with the contract and so forth (which the franchisor was prepared to negotiate - so we could have got an excellent deal for him) one thing became very obvious from interviews with other franchisees - it was a very cut-throat business and a lot of hard selling was necessary. I just couldn't see my client doing this. I stressed this in the report although otherwise giving the go-ahead subject to a few changes. He rang back: ***"I didn't realize so much selling was involved - I left a previous job because of the selling. I will not be going ahead".***

If he had carried out the initial DIY research more thoroughly he could have reached the above conclusion without the expense of advice.

In another case that **BBC TV's Watchdog** was investigating, I was invited to comment on the franchise contract. The contract was great. The franchisor promised a lot. There was just one problem. He didn't deliver. After looking through all the bumf, there was just one thing I didn't understand - it said he had 25 years expertise in the business. But he was only about 26 years old. His charm had taken in all those concerned.The programme couldn't go on the air because the police arrested him shortly beforehand. The people who lost money will probably never get it back. If they're lucky they'll see him go to jail.

By being over-enthusiastic and carrying out little or no research, most potential franchisees make it easy for the franchisor who is going to indulge in sharp practice or cons.

How Not To Be An Easy Touch

1) Never believe everything.

2) Check out facts via the research procedure.

3) Always get specialist advice before signing the contract.

4) Don't be over-enthusiastic.

5) Check that the franchise really suits your personality and family commitments.

6) Never be rushed into making a decision even if the franchisor pressurizes you by saying other people are queuing for the territory of your choice. It's better to be safe rather than sorry. Believe in fate -if you are meant to go into that business, it will wait until you have researched it.

Setting Up A Franchise File

Administration is something I particularly hate - partly because I'm so bad at it. But I realized a long time ago that to succeed in business your admin. has to be completely up to date. I used to go through a process of letting everything go to chaos and then having a blitz of organizational activity. It didn't really work. Mundane though it is I now accept that it is easier and more efficient to be organized from day one. You should have a file of material on the franchise of your choice and this should be handed over to your advisor. This should contain:

Part 1 Your self- assessment form.

Part 2 The franchisor's latest accounts. Company search if you have it.

Part 3 The projections given to you.

Part 4 The contract you are to sign.

Part 5 All the general franchise marketing literature.

Part 6 Any tit bits of information of interest, conversations with franchisees..etc.

In addition to the above I always carry out a company search and like to get a banker's reference although the latter isn't worth a lot because the banks are totally non-committal. Interviews with franchisees are the most important part of any report. At least 3 franchisees (preferably all) should be spoken to at random. Be very wary of a franchisor who only wants you to speak to certain ones. One franchisor I came across insisted that I don't phone anybody but instead write to them, the letters to go via him. There wasn't enough time to do this - especially as he was pressurizing the potential franchisee to sign. We had to recommend that our client think twice about proceeding. By being so evasive the franchisor didn't do himself any favours.

Objectivity is something very few people possess when looking for a franchised business. I always speak to at least 3 franchisees and am always amazed how I get answers different from those given to the potential franchisee. It's almost as if existing franchisees tell potential franchisees what they want to hear or potentials only hear what they want to.

Even what franchisees tell you must be treated with caution. I know of a number of cases where franchisees were very optimistic and later the franchise collapsed. New franchisees who had relied on what they were told asked why they had basically lied. Well, they hadn't. They genuinely believed that if they kept quiet about the problems and more franchisees joined, thereby making the franchise bigger and better, the problems would go away. Not so. If anything, they got worse because the franchisor didn't have the resources to support more franchisees. The cat's let out of the bag, usually too late - at receivership or just before. By then it's often too late to do anything because even if franchisees have a good case against the franchisor, there isn't any money to go after.

Looking for and researching a franchise is like piecing together a jigsaw puzzle. You have to solve it. The franchisor gives you a preview of the picture. You have to make sure that all the pieces fit. The careless, impatient or over-enthusiastic potential franchisee might as well take a pair of scissors and cut the pieces to fit. He will get a picture, but it won't be the right one.

The 4 P's of Franchising

The most important aspects of any franchise can be summed up in the following four words :

Product, Process, Profitability and People

In today's market, most people seem to have lost sight of what franchising is really all about. A franchise should be an investment in a proven concept with a well known trademark. And yet many opportunities are being offered which offer very little except perhaps the dubious privilege of handing over a large front-end fee. Checking the 4 P's is vital. If the franchise doesn't measure up to these you should forget it.

The Product must reflect everything in McDonald's **QSCV** formula - Quality, Success, Cleanliness, and Value. Look at the table on the next page and work out the score for the franchise of your choice .

Table 1 The Product Assessment

	Points 1 LOW	2 AVERAGE	3 GOOD	4 EXCELLENT
1) Does the product have a good reputation?				
2) How well known is the product?				
3) What is the customer need/desirability?				
4) How big is the market?				
5) What is the future market?				
6) Do you identify with the product?				

Score........

Score: Below 18. You need to find out more information.
Below 12. Forget it. You should not be franchising

The Process involves the type of training you will be given by the franchisor and whether there will be ongoing support. Some franchisors "mother" franchisees and others throw you in at the deep end and don't give a fig as long as they get their royalties.

What type of selling is involved in your franchise? Sooner or later, all business comes down to selling - the product, the service or you. I've known franchisees take on a franchise and realise only too late that door-to-door canvassing is a major part of the selling process - and they can't or aren't prepared to do it.

Before signing the contract you should ask to see the operations manual. Is it worth what you are paying. **One manual** I saw recently for a client contained absolutely nothing in it that could'nt have been gleaned from a few books in W.H. Smith. There was no secret method - which the franchisor admitted in a letter - and no well known trademark. If the trade name is not well known nationally, this might be cause for re-negotiating terms - after all, the established recognisable trade name should be one of the things you are paying for. If that can't be offered to assist your new business, you are in effect a pilot operation in your area and the franchise fee should reflect that.

You need to know exactly how many franchise and company units exist, how long they have been in operation and how well they are doing.

Table 2 The Process Assessment

Points	1 LOW	2 AVERAGE	3 GOOD	4 EXCELLENT
1) What is the management like?				
2) What is the training like?				
3) Advertising and Promotion?				
4) Company's financial position?				
5) Length of time Franchisor has been franchising - 1yr=av. 2-3yrs=Gd. 4 yrs or more=Ex.				

Score........
Score : 15 or over - it's OK to go ahead if everything else checks out.
10-15 - need more research.
Below 10 - forget it.

The Profitability - has to be gauged from the figures the franchisor provides in the financial projections. He should have based these figures on the performance of actual units. Most franchisors have a disclaimer on projections stating that they are illustrations only and not a guarantee that those figures will be achieved. Fair enough. There are no guarantees in business including franchising. However, the projections must be realistic.

In the United States the Federal Trade Commission requires that the franchisor state in the disclosure document the systems sales and the percentage of franchisees that earn above or below the stated figure. There is no such requirement in the UK. So, ask the question anyway. Get the answer in writing. Obviously, different units will have different turnover figures - but all should be reasonably close to the projections given to you.

To give you an idea of what can happen, **in one case** I dealt with recently, it came to light that after the franchisor had obtained "projected figures" from a specialist he had employed, he realised that on those figures one particular outlet was not viable. He simply doubled the figures and presented them to a prospective franchisee who took on the franchise based on the false figures. Not surprisingly, the business was an unmitigated disaster from day one. My client came to me on the verge of bankruptcy. By a stroke of luck we managed to get a copy of the original figures the expert had come up with and challenged the franchisor with doctoring the figures to make the business appear viable. A substantial out of court settlement for my client was the result.

Table 3 The Profitability Assessment

Points	1 LOW	2 AVERAGE	3 GOOD	4 EXCELLENT
1) Turnover				
2) Overheads - High OH=1 Low OH=4, Av OH=2, Reasonable OH=3.				
3) Start-up cost.Lower the better.				
4) Initial Franchise Fee.Lower the better.				
5) Royalty. Lower the better.				
6) Advertising Fee. Lower the better.				
7) Profits. Higher the better.				
8) Break-even point. Lower the better.				
9) Return on investment.				
10) Other fees eg.premium on lease. If payable = 1 Not payable=4.				

Score........

20 or above - OK to go ahead.
18-20 - do some more research.
Below 18 - forget it.

Franchising is a **people** business like any other business. The relationship between the franchisor (and staff) and the franchisee is like a marriage. When things are going well everything is great. But when there are problems or communications break down it is no better than an acrimonious divorce. In order for the system to work you must have a mutual respect (even if not a friendship).

Existing franchisees are the best people to ask about the franchisor. What do they think? Is the franchisor really helpful? Does he bend over backwards to really sort out any problems? Or is he heavy handed or more like "big brother"? Is the franchisor reasonable and can you communicate?

One franchisor I came across constantly hurled abuse and shouted at franchisees, even over the phone. At a meeting to try to resolve problems we all thought that my presence together with his solicitor might make him more reasonable. It was not to be. Old habits die hard. He paced about the room like a caged animal, shouted, and every time we tried to discuss something yelled **"are you calling me a liar?"**. This man should have no right to franchise because he hasn't even learnt to communicate. We decided the only way to communicate with him was to litigate.

It is a relief that most franchisors are not like this. In my experience most are very willing to discuss problems and cooperate to resolve them. Nevertheless, there are also those who give franchisees the run around by promising things will get better - but they don't. Eventually it's too late because either the franchisor or franchisee goes under.

Such problems can be avoided by finding out what the people involved are really like.

The people assessment of those involved in the franchise should take into account the questions in table 4.

Table 4 People/Franchisor Assessment

Points	1 LOW	2 AVERAGE	3 GOOD	4 EXCELLENT
Consider the following in relation to ability to communicate, reasonableness and efficiency.				
1) Franchise Chairman.				
2) MD.				
3) Franchise manager.				
4) Training staff.				
5) Field Support.				
6) Product Delivery.				
7) Accounts personnel.				
8) Promotions personnel.				

Score.......

The score should be 16 or over.

Franchise Shopping

Shopping for a franchise is no different from any other type of shopping. Buying a business is like buying a house or car. The big difference is that if you get it wrong you won't have an asset to dispose of. Just enormous debts you may end up paying off for the rest of your life. A franchise should not only give you value for money but an ability to make a lot more money. It has to be your livelihood. Don't be duped by hype and empty promises. You have to make sure the franchisor gives you what you're paying for. Its your money, your choice, and Caveat emptor (buyer beware) the rule.

If you treat a franchisor like a second hand car salesman you can't go wrong.

6

Franchise Essentials

Researching A Franchise

Over the last few years the most shocking discovery I made was to find how easily most people part with their money without adequate research.

It has constantly amazed me how individuals have phoned up saying ***"I've sent off the initial fee of £x. Is there something else I should do?"*** or ***"I'm having problems, I know I should have listened to my lawyer/accountant. They told me not to go ahead".***

Professional advisors pull their hair out as clients ignore advice. What can they do? Many potential franchisees seem to willingly sacrifice their money and become easy victims of sharp practice.

"Nobody would be so stupid as to part with thousands before researching" I hear you say. Not so. Fact. Some franchisees I've come across are the sort of people who would test the depth of a river by putting in both feet. Some advisors would argue that they get what they deserve. What's more disturbing is that franchisees with excellent professional backgrounds seem as gullible as ones with no business or professional background.

With hindsight many franchisees openly admit that they were completely taken in because of their own enthusiasm. Others admit to naivety and believing everything they are told. Some are victims of sharp practice. They are then anxious to ensure that the same does not befall other individuals.

As an **Oxford professor** said: **"If you work hard and intelligently, you should be able to detect when a man is talking rot, and that in my view is the main, if not the sole purpose of education".**

So educating potential franchisees as to what to look out for, the problems, the good points and how to research an opportunity, should in theory protect them from ***"smooth operators"*** out to earn a quick buck at their expense.

At the end of the day nothing beats common sense. The problem is that it's not so common.

It is not sufficient for you to carry out only your own research. It is vital that you take the advice of an expert before signing a contract.

The Franchise Contract

Franchise contracts vary enormously. They can be two pages or a hundred pages long.

As there are no restrictions or vetting procedures as to what they should contain it is worth remembering that they are drawn up by the franchisor - and therefore are bound to be biased in his favour. To be fair to yourself you need professional help.

One contract I saw surprised me so much because many important clauses were omitted that I asked the franchisor which solicitor had drawn it up. He replied *"firm x"*. When I expressed my amazement he sheepishly owned up ***"well OK we took out the bits we didn't like".***

A typical contract will deal with all aspects of your business - the financials, what fees are payable, the franchisor's obligations, your obligations, what happens on termination and so forth. At this stage please turn to the "Standard short form contract on page 219 which has been reproduced by kind permission of John Adams and K. Pritchard Jones.

Please also peruse the Burger King contract on page 233.

Good contracts usually cover all the issues in the short form - obviously varying slightly to suit different businesses.

While there are a number of standard clauses in contracts to cover secrecy, arbitration, inspection, indemnity, restraint of trade, protection of the franchisors trade-mark, choice of law, death or incapacity and life assurance there are others that need indepth analysis and possibly renegotiation.

" The Non-negotiable myth."

Technically all franchise contracts in a given chain should be exactly the same and non-negotiable. Indeed any franchisee should be on their guard if the franchisor readily accepts alterations.

It wasn't until I started handling negotiation/litigation for chains of franchisees that I found that contracts were different - and not because the contract had been modified over a period of time. Some franchisees had negotiated excellent deals while others accepted whatever was dished out.

Feeling bolder with this knowledge, Streetwise Franchising negotiated some good deals for its potential franchisees. It began with carrying out reports which recommended alterations. Potential franchisees felt happier if we negotiated changes because franchisors were more reluctant to try to fob us off.

Some franchisors quite rightly did not wish to change the agreement. However, every franchisor we dealt with was prepared to attach a letter to the agreement which clarified and if necessary changed certain clauses in the contract.

Clauses to look out for:

Distinctive Schedule

contracts invariably state that the franchisor has developed a specialised method and go on to say that you are paying for this expertise. You need to establish that this in in fact true.

Many unscrupulous franchisors have no such expertise and if you took the time and trouble to look you would find out.

Fees

In most cases these are divided into the Initial fee and then royalties/management service fees.

Initial Fees

This fee is supposed to be for the expertise which the franchisor gives you initially and covers such things as training. Be very wary of high initial fees. Unscrupulous operators survive by selling franchises. Once they have your money you will probably get little if any backup support.

You should not really have to pay more than a £10,000 initial fee.

Last year I came across a number of cases where a practically unknown franchisor was charging £20-25,000 initial fee. In another case the fee was stated as £70,000 which the franchisor kindly discounted at various times to £50,000 or £25,000 depending presumably on how desperate he became to take on new franchisees and improve his cash flow.

Another problem that came to light was whether or not the initial fee is refundable if you don't proceed. It should be - less reasonable expenses that the franchisor has incurred (for example assisting in finding a site). Again, some franchisors were taking advantage of the fact that there was nothing in writing stating the fee was refundable. In the **National Slimming Centre** franchise one franchisee paid a fee of £25,000. Over a period of a year premises were impossible to find and as a number of franchisees were experiencing problems and others had ceased trading due to heavy losses this franchisee decided not to proceed and requested back his initial fee less reasonable expenses. The franchisor refused.

Although counsel's opinion indicated that it would be worth pursuing through the courts the franchisee who was not entitled to legal aid did not have the financial means to pursue his claim. Streetwise Franchising have reason to believe that this was not an isolated case.

Such cases are not uncommon. Unscrupulous operators survive on initial fees. A number have taken on franchisees knowing that they themselves are in dire financial difficulties and may have to shut down; see Data Maid case study.

On-Going Fees

These are usually in the form of royalties or a management service fee calculated as a percentage of turnover. For example 10% of turnover. These ongoing fees are for the continuing back up and support that you should get. While good franchisors do give the required support many franchisors just haven't got their act together.

Be careful of a one-man support team. If you are having problems then probably other franchisees are as well - and that manager can't be everywhere at once. Many franchisees complained to Streetwise Franchising that either their complaints weren't taken seriously or they were fobbed off with a member of the Franchisor's staff, usually by someone who knew next to nothing about troubleshooting.

You need to ensure:

1) that the on-going royalty/management service fee is reasonable for the business and reasonable for the amount of support that you will be getting.

2) that the franchisor has an adequate support team and that if this deteriorates in the future, the fee will be reduced.

Advertising levy

In some cases this is included in the ongoing royalty/management service fee. For example a royalty of 8% of turnover may have 2% going into advertising. Some franchisors break down the two amounts and this is to be preferred. The advertising levy should be held in a separate account and the franchisor should be accountable to franchisees as to how that money has been spent.

Variations

Do exist quite successfully. For example Tie Rack has developed two systems of Franchising in the UK. While both methods utilise the company's expertise in areas such as site selection, lease negotiation and shop fitting, franchisees can either

1) pay for all initial and on-going property costs in turn paying 8% of gross takings (the continuing fee)

or

2) pay a proportion of the initial costs and **Tie Rack** pay for the on-going property costs (ie rent etc) and then charge 22.5% of gross takings.

Under the **22.5% system** Tie Rack partially funds the initial investment of property and shop fittings and the franchisee funding the remaining via a returnable deposit. Typical deposits or front-end fees are £30,000 and £55,000 for new units. This deposit is made against fixtures and fittings and is paid before the shop opening and is effectively used up as the shop operates. The rate of utilisation of this up-front payment is calculated on a straight-line basis over the 5 year contract period.

Of course the franchisee has to pay for stock (aproximately £20,000 + VAT), equipment (£5,000 + VAT) and a setting-up payment of £8,000 + VAT to cover franchise costs such as training.

The levy of 22.5% of gross takings (excluding VAT) ensures that Tie Rack pay all rent, rates and service charges.

Under the 8% royalty system the franchisee purchases outright all fixtures and fittings (unlike the above "deposit" system where ownership never passes to the franchisee).

Property Acquisition

The franchisor should have the expertise to assist with site selection - get this wrong and the business is doomed from day one. Some of the top franchisors have admitted to making mistakes and thinking on occasion that a secondary/tertiary site would suffice.

Good sites are expensive and landlords are often reluctant to give leases to individuals. Again, a good franchisor should be able to come to the rescue by negotiating special deals or even taking the lease and sub-letting to the franchisee.

While some franchisors do not mind the franchisee taking the lease others prefer or even have a policy that they will lease the premises and grant a sub-lease to the franchisee. Obviously this affords them even more control, as the franchisor also becomes the franchisee's landlord, if you can, take the lease yourself.

Premiums

May be payable and can be very large. As they vary they are not included in the start-up cost. However, a large premium could change your whole finance package from "acceptable" to "unviable".

Tie Rack always take the lease and sub-let to the franchisee via an "under-lease". If a premium on the lease is required the franchisee has to pay it. However, at the end of the franchise arrangement the lease premium is refunded to the franchisee by Tie Rack at either the original cost or market value whichever is the lower.

This method means that franchisees cannot profiteer in a rising property market - but they could lose if the market drops. So if the property is ever sold Tie Rack takes the benefit of its own acquisition expertise should the lease premium be worth more. Franchisee success is restricted to the operation of the business and not to speculation in the property market.

Further, Tie Rack franchisees are granted an under-lease outside the English Landlord and Tenant Act, thereby allowing Tie Rack to control the tenancy and continue to operate from the premises should the franchise terminate for any reason.

Minimum Turnover Clause

These should not be acceptable. Basically the clause states that you have to achieve a specified turnover over a given period, and a franchisee must pay a minimum royalty based on the minimum turnover figure regardless of whether actual sales are lower. If you don't the franchisor can terminate the agreement. The real problem lies in the fact that the turnover projected by the franchisor in the first place, may be (and probably is) ridiculously over-optimistic. Take that in conjunction with a downturn in the economy and perhaps poor support by the franchisor and you won't have a cat in hell's chance of achieving the required projections.

In one case I came across franchisees could not perform according to the minimum turnover clause. They all blamed the franchisor for lack of support in obtaining sales leads - but feared that their contracts would be terminated. At one stage at least one franchisee was desperately paying the minimum turnover royalty out of his own pocket (to avoid termination) and risking bankruptcy. The business simply was not viable.

Turnover and Profit

Many franchisees forget that these are two totally different things. Remember **"Turnover is vanity, profit is sanity".** While your business may have a very healthy turnover it may be in a severe loss situation. And as your turnover grows, your losses will probably increase.

Royalties/Management Service Fees will of course still have to be paid (and remember they are based on turnover). It is only at this stage (when they are making losses and especially if the losses are due to misrepresentations by poor support from the franchisor) that franchisees realize the unfairness of paying royalties .

In an ideal world I suppose royalties would be based on profits. Be that as it may it will provide the reader with some comfort to know that a good franchisor will always waive royalties and bend over backwards to help if things are going wrong. Verify that the franchisor will do this if necessary.

Some contracts will contain a clause that says you must do your best to always increase the turnover. From the discussion above, you will see that while this is in the interests of the franchisor (because his royalties increase) it probably is not in your interests.

Such a clause is unacceptable and should be modified so that you have the burden of increasing turnover BUT only if it does not affect the profit adversely.

Training

Details of training should be stated. You need to know how long the training period is, where it will take place and who bears the cost.

Training is one of the biggest "let downs" in franchising. Apart from a few excellent franchisors, training procedures are abysmal. **One franchisor** I dealt with seriously thought 2 hours training was sufficient to teach a franchisee how to run an entire retail business. After Streetwise Franchising started negotiations with them they upgraded their training programme and now have a training school.

Operating Manuals

The quality of these varies enormously. Good operating manuals are the exception rather than the rule. What exactly should an operating manual do? It should show you how to run the business and deal with problems. It should be a step by step guide to all aspects of that business. Technical franchises like printing retail businesses may have several manuals.

Many manuals in circulation today are far from desirable, primarily because of the following:

a) they contain no real information about running the business.

b) they contain only general information which could be gleaned from business books in W H Smith.

c) they contain little more than "photocopies" cribbed from similar operations.

d) they are not adapted to the English market. For example the franchise may be successful in the States. The same operating manuals are given to English franchisees with disastrous results. In one case Streetwise Franchising dealt with the franchisee depended on selling a service. Everything he had came from the States. The selling techniques worked well in America but were a complete non-starter when dealing with English companies. The franchisor had carried out no market research in the UK. The business was doomed from the outset.

A prospective franchisee should always request to see a specimen operating manual before they sign the contract.

Territory

You may or may not be given an exclusive territory. The relevance of this relates to the type of franchise you are interested in.

If you are given an exclusive territory it should be clearly delineated on a map annexed to your contract. Market research carried out by the franchisor should illustrate that the territory can provide you with a profitable living.
If you are not given an exclusive territory its not a problem providing the franchisor is reputable. For example a busy train/tube station may be able to support the same franchise at two different entrances simply because of the volume of people using each. Reputable franchisors will want all their operations to do well.

In one case Streetwise Franchising came across a major franchisor allowed a franchisee to start trading in a town centre. Parking was impossible for customers. The franchisee's contract gave him an "exclusive territory". The franchisor then decided to open a "drive thro" on the outskirts of the town (but still within the franchisees territory). The franchisee's sales dropped by at least one-third because customers preferred the drive-thro' because they had no parking problems. Naturally the franchisee complained. The franchisor seriously agreed that the franchisee had an exclusive franchise territory but that they had opened not another franchise but a company shop. Sharp? I think so. This big reputable franchisor had the good sense to realize they were being sharp and eventually compensated the franchisee in a deal to take over the drive-thru.

So, it is wise to establish exactly what "exclusive" means and under what circumstances if any the franchisor could open an outlet very close to you. You should also ensure that if the franchisor does this and you can prove that it has adversely effected your business, he will compensate you.

Advertising

Advertising is obviously more important to some businesses than others. The franchisor may state in the contract that a certain percentage of your royalty or management service fee will go towards national advertising. Or you may have to pay a separate advertising levy. In either case the advertising monies should be paid into a separate fund and the franchisor should be accountable for how that money is spent.

Many franchisors' idea of national advertising is not advertising the product/ service but advertising for more franchisees.

Breaches of advertising commitments by the franchisor are fairly common. It's a very wise franchisor and franchisee who know exactly what advertising is best for them.

Advertising is the life blood of most businesses. For example in the case of dry cleaning, Streetwise Franchising when acting for a number of **Euroclean franchisees,** found that the two crucial factors in running the business successfully were **1) site location and 2) advertising.** Competitors such as Johnstons or Bolloms who advertised nationally regularly actually got the customers. When a Euroclean franchisee advertised (irregularly) special promotions they coaxed customers for the duration of the promotions only. Obviously this did not benefit the franchisee because they had reduced margins considerably. Also they could not afford to compete with the advertising campaigns of their competitors. The franchisor undertook to spend a certain amount on advertising. According to an ex MD of Euroclean the franchisor was in breach of his obligations because the stipulated amount in the contract was not being spent.

Little consolation for franchisees facing bankruptcy.

Mark-ups

Can be made by the franchisor on various items;

1) stock supplied

2) equipment supplied eg computers, leased equipment, vehicles

3) shop fittings

Many franchisors see this as easy money. It is only the very reputable that seem to understand that the essence of franchising means giving the franchisee a fair deal, and competitive prices.

In relation to stock, obviously the franchisor is expected to make a mark-up. But it should be reasonable and not exorbitant. (The same goes for 2). However, in a number of cases Streetwise Franchising dealt with the franchisor was stating that there was no mark-up on certain equipment. It was only much later when the franchisees had been trading for some time that they realized they could get the equipment considerably cheaper outside the franchise. This happened in the case of **Microfilm Express**. Franchisees discovered the franchisor was making secret profits. Streetwise Franchising even uncovered a letter from the franchisor to a supplier saying words to the effect that Mr X (a franchisee) had discovered the equipment was being marked up and therefore was being difficult..........and that the equipment should be marked up even more. The franchisees have commenced legal proceedings against the franchisor.

In the **Euroclean cases** franchisees leased equipment from various leasing companies who were supplied the equipment in the first place by the franchisor EDS which is a 76% subsidiary of Black Arrow plc. The franchisor imported the equipment from Italy and made a large mark-up . The leasing company then made their mark-up.

The combined total mark-up made by the franchisor and leasing companies was exorbitant. Franchisees ended up having to make payments that the business could not support. In addition franchisees had paid a large franchise fee and mark-ups on shop fittings.

Many of the franchisees in England face horrendous problems and bankruptcy. A number are involved in litigation with the franchisor.

Shop fittings

are extremely expensive at the best of times. However a franchisor should not be making a mark-up on them.

A franchisor will not want to put the amount of mark-ups he's making in the contract. Nevertheless you should ask him to put it in a letter. Failing that ask the question and note the answer carefully in your franchise file.

Shop fittings may be leased. If you do lease them ensure that the business can support the payments. You should also ask the franchisor to guarantee the payment. This way if the franchisor's projections don't live up to expectation and you can't make the payment at least they are guaranteed by the franchisor.

Stock and Supplies

You should ensure that if you have any problems with the quality or delivery of stock you can buy from an alternative source. In such cases it is normal to allow the franchisor the right to "vet" the quality of the alternative source. However, if the franchisor will not give you the authority to buy elsewhere you should mitigate your losses by buying elsewhere and commencing an action against the franchisor for breach of contract.

In a number of cases Streetwise Franchising has dealt with the stock has been the major cause of problems. In some cases franchisees could show the product was inferior compared to competitors - for example a **Britool franchisee Mr Robert Baker** complained ***"I had so many returns of tools that had broken on the job.***

Some tools were twice the price of competitors and customers thought I was trying to rip them off - I was just following the franchisor's pricing guidelines. In the period of 12 months over 70% of new franchisees ceased trading *because* ***they couldn't make the business work - and yet the franchisor is still franchising and claiming there is nothing wrong with his concept. A number of us have got together and are suing the franchisor. But the real problem is trying to get justice when you have lost all your money. The franchisor is relying on the fact that those who can't get legal aid and haven't got any money have to go away quietly. But we are determined to inform the public of the true state of affairs".***

Pricing

Under the block exemption rules the franchisor can only recommend the price of goods. However you should be guided by his guidelines unless there is a very good reason for diverging. Above all you should ensure that goods are competitively priced.

Trading Hours

Ensure these are reasonable. If your business relies on Sunday Trading (eg convenience stores) then make sure your local borough does not object to it - see **Sperrings Case page117-9**

Sale or assignment by the franchisee

Most franchise contracts will allow you to sell the business as a going concern providing you have the franchisor's approval in writing - this should not be unreasonably withheld.

A franchisor may require a percentage of the sale price. This should be very small and should only cover reasonable administration and legal expenses the franchisor incurs in vetting the new franchisee and transferring the contract. Typically this should not be more than about £1,000.

If the new franchisee needs to be trained in the business then he should pay separately for that directly to the franchisor. Again you should verify that it is a reasonable amount.

A purchaser may want your business as a "going concern" but wish to operate it outside the franchise. Obviously he will have to change the trading name and "de-identify" the unit. Ensure that you can do this.

The franchisor may have an option of first refusal. If so this should be exercisable at market value (which should be defined) and over a short period of time.

Buy-Back clause

Ideally, a franchisee should request a "Buy Back" clause which stipulates that the franchisor guarantees to buy the business back at least at the cost to the franchisee, if the franchisee prefers to sell to the franchisor. The **Exchange Travel** franchise offers such a guarantee. At the time of this book going to print- September 1990, The Times newspaper has just reported the collapse of **Exchange Travel** which had become the seventh largest travel firm in this country. They applied to the High Court to continue trading in spite of being ' massively unsolvent'

The chain had 128 shops and an annual turnover of £110 million. A number of shops were franchised. Exactly what franchiees will do is unclear at the moment- they will probably be allowed to continue trading independently. However this is unlikely to help them because they will probably not get ABTA protection for the customers who will be reluctant to book holidays through them.

Gorden McNally, Exchange Travel Chairman said that ***"his mistake has been not to have sold office properties after developing them. According to him the group was property-rich but cash poor because of the high interest rates."***

Sale or assignment by the franchisor

Franchise contracts always contain a clause allowing the franchisor unlimited assignment. This simply means that the franchisor can sell or assign to anybody without the consent of its franchisees. This happens in many cases - (see La Mama, Entre Computers, Home Tune and Curtain Dream) with usually serious results.
The main problems arise because:

1) The new franchisor may be much smaller that the original franchisor and may not be able to provide the back up and support promised (Entre).

2) The new franchisor may not be dedicated to franchising and even decide not to continue franchising (La Mama).

3) The new franchisor may try to impose a new contract which franchisees find unacceptable (Home Tune).

Ideally franchisees should have the right to come out of the franchise and continue trading in the same business (albeit under a different name) if such a unilateral assignment takes place. Normally this is prevented by the restraint of trade clause.

The Restraint Of Trade Clause

This restrains you from trading in the same business for a given period of time over a certain area. While it is reasonable for a franchisor to insist on such a clause (because otherwise everybody would learn his trade secrets and then set up on their own) it does have to be reasonable. Thus, for example, a clause that says you can't operate that business anywhere in the world for five years will be construed as too wide and will be thrown out of court.

Usually a period of 1 year is deemed reasonable. A reasonable radius depends very much on the type of business.

If however you were already in the same type of business before taking the franchise you should have this clause taken out or modified because if the franchise doesn't work out you should be able to revert back to what you were doing before even if it is the same business. This was a problem experienced by some **Avis** franchisees. Some had previously owned garages and operated car rentals. Thinking that the "Avis" name would enhance their outlets they took an Avis franchise as well. When the Avis franchise failed to succeed in some of their cases they found that they could not continue as before because they were in breach of the restraint of trade clause. It cost them a considerable amount of money and time to negotiate/litigate out of this clause.

Termination of the contract

The contract should state exactly under what circumstances the franchisor can terminate, the notice period that he should give you and the consequences of termination. For example, details of de-identification of your unit. This simply means converting your unit into a "non-franchised" unit. Thus, you will have to immediately take down the franchise trademark and/or name and make your unit totally unlike franchised units. You may also have to hand back telephone lines and operating manuals. Just changing the name and de-identifying will not be sufficient if you are continuing to trade in the same business and there is a restraint of trade clause. The franchisor could slap an injunction to stop you trading and by the time you have it lifted your customers will probably have gone elsewhere. See injunctions page152-3.

Ceasing To Trade

Over the last couple of years Streetwise Franchising has been totally dumbfounded at the audacity that some franchisors have had when they have claimed loss of future royalties for the remainder of the contract in cases where franchisees have had to cease trading because the business is not performing. You should ensure that if the business is not making profits (or even if it is) you can stop trading at any time if you wish without incurring any penalties.

Arbitration

Streetwise Franchising has seen some contracts which state that you undertake to be bound by the decision of the British Franchise Arbitration Scheme in cases of dispute.

You should note that the British Franchise Association is an organisation with franchisor members who pay to join. Although British Franchise Association members are supposed to be ethical and vetted it is surprising how many have had problems and even gone into receivership over the last few years.

A number of franchisees who have tried to invoke the British Franchise Association arbitration scheme have complained that it does not work. One of the major complaints has been that documentation/letters setting out complaints and problems have been passed onto the franchisor who has then tried to sue the franchisee for defamation. Thus, instead of preventing litigation the scheme in some cases provoked it.

Arbitration is really only useful for the franchisor because it allows him to conduct proceedings privately.

In reality it is often the threat of public exposure (which will stop the franchisor recruiting more franchisees) that encourages the franchisors to settle out of court. Others are either too thick skinned to settle or simply don't have the money. They also rely on the fact that franchisees having problems can't afford good advice.

Franchisee Association

The contract should not prohibit you from forming a Franchisee Association.

Decisions In Writing clause

Stating that the franchisor is only bound by statements in writing and not oral statements is not acceptable. Franchisors always make oral statements to induce potential franchisees to sign up. Indeed, such comments are probably more persuasive than anything else.

A clause in the contract stating that you have not relied on oral statements will probably not stand up in court anyway.

Death or Incapacity

Ensure that the franchisor will undertake to buy back at market value or that he will manage the franchise (for a reasonable fee) until it can be sold profitably.

No Discrimination clause

Should be inserted to ensure that the franchisor treats all franchisee and company shops fairly in terms of quality of stock supplied. In many cases franchisees have complained that company shops are given superior stock. While it is inevitable that there might be some degree of favouritism, franchisees do need to protect their position and ensure that they are not the franchisor's meal ticket.

Miscellaneous Charges and Fees

Most franchisors really try it on when it comes to these.

Legal fees

Each party should be responsible for their own legal fees including taking over a lease.

Audits

If you operate as a company you will have to have audited accounts anyway which you can make available to the franchisor. **In one case** Streetwise Franchising handled franchisees already provided the franchisor with audited accounts. The franchisor then wanted them to sign a new contract which allowed the franchisor to have another audit carried out - which was also to be paid for by the franchisee.

Thus the franchisee could be faced with two audit bills - as if one wasn't bad enough!

If you're not operating as a company then you should allow the franchisor on to your premises in order to inspect your books and take copies thereof at his expense.

Renewal Of The Contract

You should not be charged for renewal of the contract. Obviously the franchisor will only renew your contract if you are not in breach of any of its terms.

The franchisor may require you to refurbish your premises before renewing. While refurbishment itself may be desirable it should not be a condition for renewal. See **Kentucky Fried Chicken** page132- 4.

The franchisor may also require that as a condition of renewal you sign his then current contract. The new contract could be much more onerous than the original contract. This was certainly the problem two franchisees of the **Seekers** estate agency franchise faced when their franchisor wanted to impose a more onerous contract when their old one had not yet run out. To avoid misunderstanding at a later stage it is wise to agree that you as a franchisee can elect to keep your original contract whatever the circumstances.

Assignment by the franchisor

Once a new franchisor takes over they seem to have an overwhelming egotistical desire

1) to show that the previous franchisor mismanaged the business (which is probably true) and

2) that they themselves are the best thing since sliced bread.

Equally predictably they always try to enforce a new contract - which is more onerous. In the case of one **Body and Face Place** franchisee the new franchisors **Alan Paul** wanted to replace an approx 3 page contract with a 90 page one. Not surprisingly the franchisees wanted "out".

Bearing in mind that assignment by the franchisor is a real possibility and that you will have no say in who takes over it is a good idea to put in a clause stating that your agreement is binding on any new franchisor.

Comment

At the end of the day you will have to live with the agreement that you sign. However it is not just the technical contractual terms that are important but the spirit of the agreement. Make sure you understand what both are.

If there are special circumstances you should re-negotiate clauses that cause concern by way of side letters. A contract can be one-sided and fair. It's when it is unreasonable and onerous that you should opt out.

7

Raising Funding

Are the banks clued up enough and honest enough to lend you money for a franchise reliably?

With slogans like *"Press for Action"* **(Nat West)** *"You're Better Off Talking to* ***Barclays****"* *"The Listening Bank"* **(Midland)** and so on, you, together with many other franchisees could be forgiven for thinking that the banks knew what they are talking about. Not so!

It's a very special bank that will want to turn away good business. The banks have come under much critisism from the author over the last few years - but not without cause. Indeed a number of bank managers have, off the record, expressed agreement with the author's sentiments and some are investigating opportunities more thoroughly.

The myth that the banker is God is on the decline. Until recently the bankers word was gospel. But would- be franchisees are realising that:

1) The bank always protects their own interests.

2) The bank lends on security - usually the home - and if things go wrong you could lose your home because the bank will have it sold to get back the money lent to you.

3) Your friendly neighbourhood bank manager may be prepared to lend up to 100% finance. Sounds tempting? Watch out!

4) A bank's reference on any particular franchise is always totally non-commital and tells you precisely nothing.

5) Most of the banks boast a 'specialised franchise unit' which carries out a detailed research on franchises but what they forget to tell you is that individual bank managers can make the decision to lend without reference to the specialised unit. This is the cause of most of the problems in relation to the banks.

One group of ex-franchisees of **Dampcure /Woodcure 30** who broke away from their franchisor and are now trading independently were given 100% finance by the franchisor's local banker - Barclays. All mentioned that they asked the manager many questions but were simply told the franchisor had a *"fine pedigree"* and was *"experiencing excellent growth"*.

Once it had been established that they were houseowners, the loan was given without further ado - secured on their property of course.

At the time these franchisees joined, other franchisees who also had accounts with Barclays were apparently on income support or re-mortgaging their homes to stave off bankruptcy.

One wonders - did the top franchise bods at Barclays know what was going on, what the real circumstances of these people were? Did they turn a blind eye? The manager concerned has since retired, and Barclays were threatening re-possession of at least one house.

Franchisees from other franchises we spoke to came up with similar stories about Friendly Neighbourhood Bank Managers taking little more than five or ten minutes to agree to loans for taking up a franchise. Such speed does not suggest conscience.

Perhaps what is needed is for the franchisees in the case cited to group together and bring a test case against the bank for negligence.

It is about time the banks realise they are not above the law - especially when they hold themselves out as having specialised franchise units researching franchise opportunities and prospects in detail.

In yet another case that Streetwise Franchising dealt with, a franchisee of **National Slimming Centres** had been lent £23K by the National Westminster Bank, secured again on their homes. They have decided not to proceed with the investment, but the so-called reputable franchisor checked out by the bank now refuses to return this initial fee less reasonable expenses.

How can any bank lend such large sums knowing the franchisor is so unethical? And if they don't know this, why not? Haven't they researched the franchise thoroughly enough before lending?

The Action Bank has lent and continues to lend money to potential franchisees knowing that over the past few years, a number of franchisees have ceased trading owing to heavy losses.

An ex-franchisee of **Crown Eyeglass** has given a major clearing bank notice that they will sue. In this case the franchisee owes the bank some £17K. His local bank manger referred to a report (from the bank's franchise unit) which was two years out of date. The report stated that there had been only one failure. Streetwise Franchising research showed that, in fact, at that time there had been about 24 failures. If the report had been up to date, the bank manager would not have recommended the franchisees to proceed. Indeed, no franchisee at that time would have gone ahead anyway - see case study Crown Eyeglass.

We get back to the issue of whether in such cases the bank owes franchisees a duty of care. In the above case the only defence the bank has put forward so far, is to say that the franchisee should not have seen, or been allowed to see, the date on the report. It will certainly be an interesting case if it ever goes to court.

HOW MUCH SHOULD YOU BORROW

Usually the banks lend up to 75% of the investment cost. As discussed above, they have been known to lend 100%. However, in practice, you should try not to borrow more than 50% so as not to over-gear your business.

SECURITY

If at all possible do not secure the borrowings with a charge over your house. If you do use your house as security REMEMBER if things go wrong you could lose your home. Even in franchising there is a business risk and this is a possibility you must be prepared for. How does your family feel about this?

If things go wrong, at best you may have to get a job and spend the rest of your life paying off the bank in instalments.

If you're lucky and the business doesn't work out but it is still viable, you may be able to sell it to a third party or your franchisor. Ideally it's good to have a "buy-back" clause in the contract - see page 42. Note that the franchisor saying he will assist in selling your business is not worth much because there are no guarantees and particularly no time limit. Because of financial pressures you may have to cease trading quickly and the franchisor may not find a buyer in time.

GOVERNMENT LOAN SCHEME

You can raise funds from the government in certain cases. If they are prepared to lend, then the government acts as guarantor to the bank for up to 75% of your total investment. The sting in the tail is that you have to pay a premium on the interest you will already be paying to the bank . You will be liable for the part of the monies not guaranteed by the government. The bank will probably require security for the monies you are responsible for.

The scheme is, of course, advantageous should your business fail. However, your business will be burdened by the extra interest charges which the franchisor will not have allowed for in the projections. If you do go via this route to raise funds, ensure that the business can sustain the high level of interest.

8

The Learning Curve To Success - Kall Kwik

The Kall Kwik franchise in the UK holds the master licence from the Kwik-Copy Corporation of America. It maintains close links with the States where the franchisees still go for a three week training course.

The Kwik-Copy philosophy

The founder of this system was **Bud Hadfield**. Bud's philosophy was simple; ***"Life is excellence and the pursuit of excellence is life".*** For him the pursuit of excellence was a continuing process; a constant drive towards another goal.

Moshe Gerstenhaber holder of the master licence in the UK has certainly not only accepted the challenge of "the pursuit for excellence" but seems very close to it although he will be the first to concede that he is continually striving to be bigger and better.

The Interview

My first interview with Moshe was at his home. He proudly showed off his blue "Kall Kwik company watch". This was a true company man. He seemed to live for the success of his company and for him his franchisees were like his family.

It was a strange experience. I had always advocated this type of relationship between franchisor and franchisee but had never experienced it first hand. In my experience of meeting many UK franchisors I had never until now come across this type of devotion to the franchise system.

And yet apparently this was not an "easy man to get on with", confided some of his staff. He has his high standards which he imposes on all around him. For example his management confided how he insisted they travel "economy class" even on very long journeys - it was a matter that could not be subject to negotiation.

Moshe regards franchising as ***"System Leasing"*** ie that the franchisee owners lease their business system for the period of the contract. He feels that his job is to give franchisees the training and back-up, namely the "tools" to succeed. It's then up to the franchisees to use the tools effectively.

One of the biggest problems in franchising according to Moshe, is selection of franchisees.

"Give me tigers and I can move the print industry" said Moshe. For him franchisees didn't always value what they had. For example, he discussed ***"the comfort level"*** when a franchisee was earning a satisfactory profit and was content to continue at the same pace. This was something he didn't want. As far as he was concerned it was much better if they sold out and someone new and *"hungry"* for more success took over.

With this in mind the Kall Kwik franchise operation is geared to helping franchisees sell if they want to get out.

Asked how he compared to the other print franchises he was quick to say that Kall Kwik has a better system. Asked why? - he put it down to a better management that was more committed to its franchisees and with a more long term approach regarding re-investment of profits together with more consideration for the customer.

What makes Kall Kwik so successful?

I decided to go to Kall Kwik headquarters in Ruislip to see exactly what made them tick. I worked my way through the company from the receptionist, typists, in house lawyer to the MD and even sat their franchisee selection test. The organisation of the company is impressive to say the least.

Everything is divided into several departments - each department bearing a vital function:

Franchise Sales
The Marketing Department
Property
Legal
Shopfitting
Training and
Franchise Services

The company lays a great emphasis on franchisee selection. To them its one of the most important ingredients of success. Consequently, the selection procedure consists of several steps with different people involved in assessing the same individual. Kall Kwik also uses psychometric testing which they claim gives them 85% accuracy. The particular test they used came from:

Thomas International
Management Systems (Europe) Ltd
Tel: 06284-75366.

I checked it out for myself. It only lasted about 8 minutes but worked on choosing words that most and least described your personality. It went off for specialist analysis and I actually got to see the results. It was spot on. The management confided that although they would take me as a franchisee they would keep a very careful eye on what I got up to because I was so independent !

Andrew Quail, Kall Kwik managing director, claimed that this test combined with their selection procedures actually gave them a **91% success rate** in choosing franchisees. He admitted that their procedures had become more stringent - to the point that some of their earlier (and successful) franchisees wouldn't now get through. The whole thing was a fine balancing act but was crucial to ultimate success.

Marketing

Surprisingly **95%** of Kall Kwik's business is with companies and small businesses rather than with the public. Therefore marketing is geared to going out and getting local business. Franchisees pay 40% of the 10% royalty to a national and local advertising fund. Half of this is rebated to them to spend locally.

Kall Kwik's marketing strategy for 1990 is **"Educate. Demonstrate. Bait"** with particular emphasis on increasing awareness of colour copying techniques.

The Kall Kwik management have taken marketing a step further and designed a range of corporate clothing for staff which include fun T-shirts and sweatshirts. Everything is geared towards happy customers and happy staff in bright surroundings.

Advertising is geared more locally rather than nationally . Andrew Quail believes local advertising is more labour intensive giving them more ***"bang for the buck".***

Franchisees are now encouraged and trained to go out and get local business. Its an aggressive strategy that appears to not only work but is vital for today's marketplace.

Property

The property department were only to ready to confess that even they had made a few mistakes in site selection. At the end of the day experience had taught them that prime sites were the ones to go for. Secondary sites in theory may suffice but they made it far more difficult to get good business.

They liaised closely with the market research department who produced a rather impressive "area report" before a franchisee committed himself to a particular site.

A typical Report - is compiled by contacting local Councils and other published sources of information and combining them with a personal visit to the area which also serves the purpose of evaluating the strength and location of the competition.

A typical report should contain the following:-

1) Assessment of prime marketing area

2) Facilities within area - access to motorways, railroad, airport.

3) Economic Activity - population, workforce, unemployment, local areas, industrial areas.

4) Market - post codes within the area under investigation. Statistics showing the number, nature and dispersion of businesses in the prime marketing area.

5) Competition - Photograph and details of competitors paying particular attention to:
- **visibility/accessibility/listing in Yellow Pages**
- **good/bad service or otherwise**
- **range of products**
- **prices**
- **average turnaround time**

Assessment: whether poor/average/strong competition.

6) Conclusions and Recommendations

And it goes without saying that up to date statistics are used. The depth of research is excellent. There are not many franchisors in the UK who take the time or trouble to do this. It is hardly surprising that many suffer from business failure due to poor site selection. Certainly site selection has been identified as another key area in the search for franchise success.

Training

Kall Kwik franchisees have a rigorous training procedure. They spend 3 weeks in the USA followed by an equally intensive week in the UK. Training is a full time job - a typical day starts at 8.30 am and ends at 6pm. It's a crash course on all aspects of the business. Kall Kwik has about 7 operating manuals.

In addition to the above, franchisees have one/two weeks on-site training in a shop where they can practise on someone else's customers.

The franchisor believes training is one of the most important ingredients of success, and continual training for franchisees and their staff is available in the form of short courses.

Kall Kwik has a special "technical support" system for new centres. **The Centre Support Programme** is for new franchisees over their first 6-12 months of trading.

Andrew Quail said originally they had opened units and let them get on with it on the basis that if they heard nothing everything was OK. Not so. Suddenly a cheque would bounce. Franchisees with problems didn't usually speak up - they kept quiet hoping everything would get better until it was too late. Now for the first 6 months they literally sit in the franchisee's pocket. If it isn't going well the alarm rings and something positive can be done.

The Legal Department

This not only serves to assist franchisees leasing shops, but ensures that all are complying with the contract. The management made it clear that while they were always ready to solve problems amicably sometimes in an extreme case even they resorted to legalities.

In one case a franchise shop was extremely dirty and the franchisee had "given up" and wanted to sell. After numerous friendly discussions the shop remained dirty and nobody was interested in buying it. In desperation the company solicitor wrote a letter to the franchisee saying that as he was damaging the image of the company he was in breach of contract and that unless he rectified the situation they would terminate the contract. It worked wonders. The shop was cleaned beyond recognition. More customers started coming in not only because of the improved appearance but because staff morale had also got better. The business picked up and the franchisee now confident went out to get more work. Without doubt success breeds success and in this case the franchisee decided to continue trading rather than sell.

Turnover and Profits

A Kall Kwik shop should achieve a turnover of about £1/4 million with a Profit of about 24% of turnover. A typical franchisee will make a profit of £60 k/pa while some centres make £150 k/pa. According to Philip Hanbury a good Kall Kwik shop should have a turnover of about £1/2 million with a profit of about 80k. The franchisor, however,very cautiously tells potential franchisees that they will be lucky to break-even in the 1st year with a work shedule of at least 14 hours a day. Contrast this with some franchisors who have projections in the realms of Disneyland, telling potential franchisees to expect profits of circa £17/20 K in the first year.

Some Kall Kwik franchisees own several shops in different areas. The company has shown flexibility to the extent that it has allowed multiple shops to have a seperate printing centre and even gone into partnership with a franchisee - see the success story of Philip Hanbury pages 57-9.

But this franchise has, like others, experienced problems and been on a learning curve since 1979. Indeed at that time franchisees were so dissatisfied with the franchisor that they formed IKKFOA - the Independent Kall-Kwik Franchise Owners Association. It was born out of anger, but accepted by the franchisor as a vital communication link between them and their franchisees - see pages 58-9, and pages 144-5. Franchisee Associations, see index.

So even successful franchises have their problems. The difference between a good and bad franchise is that the former can sort out problems while the latter collapses under the strain.

A good franchise system will be well structured with specific departments and managers experienced in the fields discussed above.

Success Story

Philip Hanbury -

Currently has 7 Kall Kwik printing centres. When he took his first franchise eleven years ago he was 31 years old.

His father was a furrier and although he enjoyed the trade he confided "I knew it wasn't for me - the fur got up my nose".

So, he went into partnership with **Alec Reed of Reed Employment** and opened a chain of drugstores called **Medicare.** The business built up and they had 10 units and he had been running them for 4 years. He then sold out his share to Reed Employment.

For a while he went into export and parallel trading but was interested in franchising because it was so big in the States. The first Kall Kwik franchisees **Joe Brim,** and **Danny Unger,** were friends of his. He was intrigued by the business and had his sister who lived in America check out Kwik Copy.

Everything checked out. He didn't fancy the food business and felt that printing was needed by everyone and not seasonal. He had lots of contacts and decided that Golders Green in London would be a good market with lots of cottage industry. He was right.

Philip Hanbury reminisces how he ***" worked 7 days a weeks from about 6 am to 2 or 3 next morning. The shops turnover grew rapidly and after three years I was able to open another unit in Edgware."***

After Edgware came Kings Road (in partnership with Gail Cedar), Marble Arch (in partnership with his father), Baker Street, London Bridge and (in partnership with the franchisor) Docklands.

The franchise concept was based on "printing on the premises". Now Philip has a printing centre on an industrial estate in Colindale which does the printing for all the shops. It was something that the franchisor didn't approve of but is working well. Its now been accepted. As Philip explains ***"it happened by accident. I had to sack the printers in Edgware and that units printing had to be moved to Golders Green temporarily. I noticed how clean, quieter and dust free Edgware became and decided to sell the printing equipment in Edgware. Kall Kwik weren't happy. Then, quite tragically my printer in Marble Arch died in an accident. He was a friend and I almost sold up the shop. Again the printing was passed onto Golders Green. I eventually got over the depression and decided to have a centralized production unit. It wasn't till 18 months later that we found something suitable in Colindale".***

Whatever reservations the franchisor had they seemed to have got over them and gone one step further - into partnership with Philip in two units.

I asked Philip what *skills a franchisee needed for success:*
According to him they need:

1) the will and hunger to succeed,

2) getting on with people and a face that fits,

3) a willingness to learn and work a system that exists rather than trying to invent the wheel when its already there,

4) initiative so they can cope with everyday problems,

5) confidence.

What did he look for in a unit? Philip had no doubts. To him the most important three things is **"position, position and position".** In his experience prime position is essential not only because you are more easily accessible but because its an insurance against competition.

Now that he was so successful what could the franchisor do for him? According to Philip the company still provided invaluable support and of course the Corporate image. If he had a problem they were there to assist.

"Franchisees are very lucky now" he said ***"because the company has really got their act together - it wasn't like that in the early days when IKKFOA (Independent Kall Kwik Franchise Owners Association) was formed. At that time the franchisor had no technical development and was at an embryonic stage. There was no American Know How and we knew more than the franchisor because we were running the business. The shop fittings were poor quality and the presses were "shute delivery" instead of "chain delivery" so that there were smudges on the paper. Within three months of opening I changed them to chain delivery. I and three others were really unhappy and we felt we were not getting***

the advice or products that we wanted, required, expected and were paying for. IKKFOA started to change that. At first Kall Kwik saw it as a threat and stranglehold. But in fact it gave them more strength. It has achieved a lot and no franchise should be without a franchise association".

Philip's immediate ambition is to increase to 10 shops all being serviced by the central production unit. He feels that although his role now is that of a manager he misses actually serving customers and hopes to become more involved in training people.

9

Franchise Insider

Now that we know what to expect from a franchise investment, theoretically the next step has to be what is available and what will you actually get? There is only one way to find out - look at real cases. I have referred to cases throughout the book but the following will open your eyes even more in relation to not only what to look out for but what a good franchisor should offer.

For easy reference the case studies are in alphabetical order.

Pardon the cliche but its true - good franchises don't grow on trees. They take years of hard work, continuing and on-going development and without exception a process of "learning from mistakes".

The most common cause of abuse is a well meaning franchisor who just hasn't got his act together. He starts off with the best of intentions and finds himself in financially dire straits.

So although he wants to give the franchisees support and back-up he struggles to survive by "selling franchises". It's either that or "shut down". Scruples fly out of the window for most franchisors when the bailiffs are about to knock on the door or a bank is about to pull the plug. **Sound familiar? Theres a lot of them about.**

The "problem" case studies explore not only what can go wrong but give an insight into how to see trouble coming.

The success stories show what franchising is really about - an exciting distribution option - something that works - something that is so good that it should be closely guarded against sharp practices. Good franchisors and franchisees talk about how they've done it, the problems they've had, how they've handled them and their ingredients for success.

After a review of all the case studies look at the league table in the next chapter so that you can recognise not only problems but how to solve them. It is very easy to get duped into choosing the wrong franchise. If you know what to look out for and what scams are operated you will reduce normal element of risk that is inevitable in going into any business.

Character of a "Down Beat" Franchisor

He's often undercapitalised, does not have a well known trademark and has carried out little or no market research. A favourite line is to tell you how brilliantly well the company is doing out in the States.

Cannot afford to be very choosy and takes on unsuitable franchises just to get the business going.

Relies heavily on up-front fees and royalties which are usually well over the top.

Probably makes undeclared secret profits on mark-ups on supplies

Is discouraged by a franchisee who asks too many questions and won't give you a list of all franchisees because he's paranoic that you'll find all the skeletons in the cupboard.

Rants and raves if you complain about anything.

Has little or no management experience

And he will usually hide behind the respectability of a glossy hype brochure and well known lawyer.

Alarms Direct

Fraud Or Not Fraud ?

Alarms Direct's prospectus gave potential franchisees

"an invitation to participate in an exciting, new, innovative and highly profitable business".

They claimed that by 1989 they would have in excess of 20 operations successfully trading.

They reckoned franchisees would between them in a year install over £5,000,000 worth of security systems and make a **profit in excess of £1,500,000.**

They claimed to be specialists with over 25 years experience. Their System-7 was marketed as the most advanced security system on the market. They even stated that the system was **supported by the Office of Fair Trading, built to British Standard BS 4737 and approved by the Home Office.**

Their research showed that in 1986 there were 8,492,000 household offences from 22 million homes. According to them less than 3% of homes have any security system.

They guaranteed franchisees a minimum of 250,000 homes in their territory. They promised a 5 day training period and a minimum of 5 installations per . They recommended recruiting on a "commission only basis" and said the business would attract "high flyers" because "of the unique product & sales package".

They claimed that on the minimum figures franchisees would make a **nett profit of £6,500 per month ie £78,000 per annum.**

The franchisor offered complete support and back up even to the extent of saying **"disputes settled amicably".**

The contract was extremely reasonable and listed a number of franchisor obligations.

It appeared to be a very nice business. Mr Fallon the Managing Director certainly had charm and marketing ability.

Several franchisees invested in the region of **£15k each.** They were sold on the idea.

But the method didn't work out. About the middle of 1989 they contacted **Watch Dog** on T V. Watch Dog in turn asked me to comment on the franchisees' contractual rights.

In a meeting with the franchisees they all complained of the same thing - no back-up or support. They had apparently all been duped by empty promises. Some claimed that they had not even received an operating manual. There was apparently no sales recruitment or advertising assistance.

It turned out that Mr Fallon couldn't have had the 25 years experience he claimed - he was only about 26 years old.

System-7 - the unique product was not what the franchisees got.

Most of the franchisees lost all their money. At least one couple stood to lose their home.

What could they do?

Not a lot. To start legal proceedings would have been fruitless. There was no money in the franchisor company. Besides, the franchisees could not afford legal advice. The fraud squad were called in to investigate the matter. On the day the programme was to go on the air Watch Dog were told that Mr Fallon had been arrested and therefore the programme had to be cancelled.

What happens to Mr Fallon remains to be seen. Just before the demise of Alarms Direct Mr Fallon had set up another company called InSat - to capitalise on the satellite installation business. This advertised as:

Needless to say a number of franchisees invested. The telephone number of the InSat H Q is now unavailable.

Everything now is in the hands of the Fraud Squad who are preparing a case for the Crown Presecution. Needless to say the franchisees are waiting with bated breath to hear what is going to happen. The Fraud Squad are not being very forthcoming but then the whole case is sub-judice. For the same reason the author cannot make further comment at this stage because if the case comes to trial, Mr Fallon's case may be prejudiced.

Comment

Most of the franchisees of Alarms Direct with the exception of a couple had no independent research carried out by a professional adviser. They simply believed what they were told.

Having said that one wonders whether a professional would have picked up that there was something wrong; the contract was reasonable and likely to be passed by most lawyers. The profit figures were however ridiculously optimistic and would have caused suspicion.

A bank manager who had lunch with Mr Fallon thought he was a very charming fellow and said he had suspected nothing.

Commonsense somehow seems to have been forgotten in this case. Nobody seems to have asked the obvious - how and where did Fallon get his experience, especially as he was so young?

It is highly likely that proper research would have avoided the tragedies faced by the franchisees who lost out in this franchise. It was all too good to be true.

Retailer Of The Year - January 1989 - The Body Shop

Anita Roddick nominated Retailer of the Year last year has more than one prize under her belt - Business Women Of The Year 1985, OBE-1988, Communicator of the Year 1988 and the United Nations Global Award in June 1989.

The Body Shop began in **1976 in Brighton** and went public in 1984. Today the business has **130 shops in the UK. Of these all except 23 are franchised.** There are several hundred shops throughout the world.

Body Shops annual Turnover for **1989 was £55.4 million with pre-tax profits of £11.2 million.**

The company's worldwide network is founded on common principles;
To sell using minimum hype and packaging, promote health rather than glamour, to use natural products, not to test ingredients on animals, and to respect the environment. Waste is recycled and recycled paper used wherever possible.

Today the Body Shop sells over **300** products. About 35% of these are manufactured by the company.

Franchising has always been the key to The Body Shops expansion policy. The first franchise was given in 1978 to **Michael Ross** in Aberdeen who said ***"it is an extremely rewarding and fullfilling partnership where the franchisees's personal enthusiasm, commitment and specific abilities can be utilised and harnessed...."***

In May 1989 the "the millionare franchisee" Peter Flynn took the franchise industry by surprise. Formerly head waiter on the QE2 he sold his store in Waverley, Princess Street, Scotland back to the franchisor for a figure in the region of £1.5 million. He had been asking for £2 million but said "he was delighted with the deal".

Mr Flynn decided to sell his business so that he could spend more time on charitable work and in advising new businesses. He is a sponsor of the Edinburgh Venture Enterprise Trust (EVENT). He had paid £35,000 only for the investment. In just four years he had become a millionaire.

Not surprisingly Body Shop have a very long waiting list for franchisees - a few years by anyones guess. However, they haven't yet reached saturation point the company told Today. The UK alone could support 200 more outlets and that a further 20 branches are scheduled to open in 1990.

Success Story
The Body Shop

Peter and Marcia Canter

- opened their first Body Shop in Bolton in June 1988 and their second one in Wigan in July of this year.

Peter worked in Marks & Spencers as an area administrator and Marcia was a teacher. While the thought of running their own retail outlet was attractive the risk factor was not. Peter in particular had the " ***small cog in the big wheel*** " syndrome.

A relative of theirs owned a Body Shop in London. The Canters' were impressed with the operation and wrote to the then franchise manager Peter Tyson . The waiting list was too long and they got a straight rejection.

Three months later they wrote again and got put onto the waiting list. They stated that they would like to meet the franchise manager and see how everything was run even if they had to wait a long time. They were also prepared to relocate. Filled with enthusiasm they took the initiative to travel to the Littlehampton Body Shop HQ. It wasn't until a year later that they were given the nod to open - in Bolton.

Apart from that the couple have no quarrels with the franchisor. If anything the franchisor has improved the services offered so that the Wigan shop was cheaper to set up. The Bolton shops legal expenses were a mega £22 K! - mainly because they had to use the franchisors solicitor, who didn't come cheap. The franchisor now has an inhouse lawyer so costs should be considerably reduced.

The franchisor also has their own shop fitting contract department (which franchisees do not have to use). A charge of 4% of the shop fitting cost is made. The Wigan shop has therefore cost less despite inflation over a two year period.

Franchisees meet about three times a year although there is no franchisee association as such.

The Canters' have a successful business. For the Bolton shop their **projected turnover for the first year was £620, 000** and they far exceeded this.

A well run shop with a good turnover could achieve a profit (before tax) of about **10 % of turnover.** However the Canters' feel that this trend may now be changing because only secondary areas are available for franchisees and even then they have to pay royalties. The rich pickings that were there for the first franchisees (many of whom did become very rich) are probably no longer available.

For these franchisees the business decision they made has come up trumps. But it hasn't been easy. As Peter states ***" We live and sleep the Body shop. During the day our paths don't cross. My wife is in the shop and I'm in the background dealing with the admin and stock. We spend the whole evening talking shop. We work extremely hard but the main reason for our success is that we are really interested in the product we are selling. "***

Like Mcdonald's, Body Shop donate part of the royalty (2%) to charity. This is ideal because it means that the public are actually getting something positive back.

"DoT investigation into Cookie Coach's affairs"

"Receiver moves in on Cookie Co"

"Cookie coachman say they are being priced out"

On BFA register of Qualified-Non-Member Companies Developing Franchises.

The Cookie Coach Company was formed in 1983 by Jack Liquonsh and Peter Grender, both former executives of the Smiths Food Group.

The franchisees wearing traditional baker's boy uniforms operated through red and gold production Edwardian delivery vans. The franchisees sold cookies and cakes. The franchise cost was £6,500. £7,000 working capital and £356 per month for the hire of the vehicle. By 1986 there were about 50 coachmen selling 70 lines with a projected 1986 turnover of £5 million.

However 1986 began on the wrong foot. A group of disgruntled franchisees got together complaining about the franchisors trading tactics. Their main objections being that the company's products were over-priced.

By December 1986 The Department of Trade and Industry had petitioned to have the Cookie Coach Co. compulsorily wound up. Peal Marwick, the accountancy firm was appointed receiver.

A Department of Trade directive resulted in a "Special manager" - Stephen James of K H G Thomas McLintock being bought in to run the affairs of the company while previous management had their powers taken away. He worked in conjunction with the DoT official receiver.

Two leading suppliers - Rod Bellamy (chairman of Carrs Foods) and his Managing Director Peter Canevale and Keith Suddaby manufacturing director of Argyll Foods, which owns Paterson Bronte called a meeting for franchisees. They came up with the idea that Carr's would co-ordinate the distribution of stock to franchisees. This way food that had been ordered could still be delivered. Franchisees felt that the offer gave them a life line.

Crown Eye Wash

Crown Eyewash - ***Mrs Thatcher has her eyes tested ....***

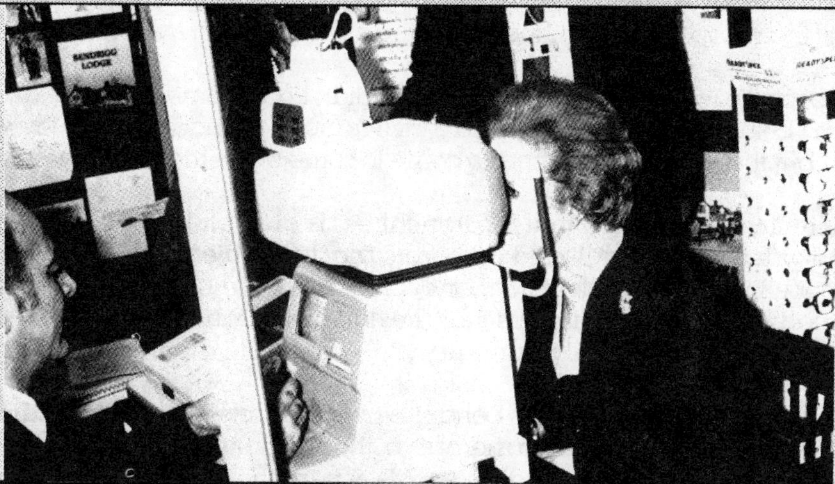

"Seeing is Believing" is one of the headings that Crown Eyeglass plc used in their brochure. They offered franchisees a chance to ***"make it with your own optical business" and spoke of the opportunity as "The jewel in the crown".***

Many franchisees however have ***"seen the light"*** in quite a different way. Crown Eyeglass began operating in 1983, shortly before the law was changed to allow people other than qualified opticians to sell retail spectacles, and shares were placed on **The Stock Exchange third market in May 1987.**

Franchise listings issued by the franchisor show that at one time there must have been about **132 shops (company and franchised)**. A listing dated 26/Sept/89 however l**eaves out about 46 shops** which presumably have shut down. Other shops have since shut down. Some franchisees have already been involved in litigation with the franchisor and others are contemplating litigation.

A large number of franchisees have just accepted big losses - of thousands. Some have had to shut down or face bankruptcy only to be faced with a threat from the franchisor for a claim for future profits. Catch 22. One franchisee said ***"I have already lost about £22k. I have to stop trading but have been told that I have to propose a settlement figure. I don't have any money".***

Another franchisee said ***"I will have to stop no matter what. He will probably sue but what can we do? He is not prepared to negotiate. I have lost about £13k".***

Streetwise Franchising Ltd approached Mr Joe Lee outlining the grievances and dire financial straits of two franchisees and in the first instant asked Mr Lee to take part in amicable negotiations to solve the problems. In particular we asked Mr Lee to let them stop trading without penalties as they had already lost large sums.

Mr Lee became rather abusive and said he didn't have time for negotiations as he wasn't being paid. He further said that if franchisees had a case they should sue him but that he was prepared to come to some agreement if they paid him.

When Streetwise explained that the franchisees had already lost a lot of money, he said it was their own fault and they were ***"nasty people"***. We stressed that we were concerned with the facts. Mr Lee declined to comment on all the units that had already shut but reassured us that ***"he had a reputation for being a Bastard and getting even"***. He finally hung up.

Rather concerned about Mr Lee's behaviour we contacted ***Mr Brian Smart of the BFA*** as Crown Eyeglass plc was a member of the BFA only to find that Crown have resigned membership. According to Mr Smart the BFA requested certain information which Crown declined to give. Apparently Crown also wanted to exhibit at the London exhibition but were not prepared to furnish the BFA with necessary information. Consequently they will not be exhibiting.

Mr Lee has always been keen to draw attention to his company and has successfully attracted ***Mrs Margaret Thatcher and the Duke of Kent*** to attend press conferences and visit the Blackburn factory. This has bought him a credibility that one wonders whether he should have had.

Royal Spectacle - The Duke Of Kent visits the Blackburn factory and is given a pair of glasses by Joe Lee

But this has not been the only publicity he has obtained:-

"Both the Advertising Standards Authority and The Trading Standards office are probing the company's nationwide "free-frame offer".

Complaints began after an Eyeglass customer was quoted £25.95 including frames at £9.95. He later saw the free frame offer but was told that the total price was the same.

Blackburn Mail 87/Home Truths On Crown
........By the DIGGER

"A few home truths need to be told about a grotty little company called Crown Eyeglass which came to fame by promising the short sighted public a good deal by providing them with free spectacle frames. What they do, in fact, is build the cost of a tatty pair of frames into an overpriced couple of lenses which do have to be paid for. "We challenge you to find a comparable pair of glasses at a lower price anywhere", says their ad. "If you do, we'll refund the difference on the spot. All you do is get the free NHS sight test you're entitled to from any opthalmic optician, then bring your prescription along to Crown". It goes on: "You'll end up with glasses identical in quality to those the optician would have supplied. But at a fraction of the price".

Unfortunately, Crown do not seem to offer any guarantees on their frames which are often of indifferent quality and have been known to almost immediately fall to pieces. So Crown's string of franchisees have to look after all the complaints at their own expense.

Already Blackburn-based Crown Eyeglass, which went public during the summer, have got themselves into a tangle with the Advertising Standards Authority which is investigating the ad quoted above.

Relations between Crown and its 60 or so franchise holders is also deteriorating fast. Crown boss, Joe Lee, seems obsessed with the notion that the shops will get cheaper spectacle frames from other suppliers, and there has been talk, obviously not true, of private detectives snooping on franchise holders. What is true, however, is that certain franchisees have found it impossible to make a profit on the way things are run and have incurred big debts and been forced to sue Crown.

One man made such a nuisance of himself that Crown slapped an injunction on him in an effort to shut him up at the sensitive time they were going public."

"Crown's free frames to stop"...........

The Advertising Standards Authority has asked Crown Eyeglass to stop advertising its frames as free..............

.... OPTICIAN Feb 88

Crown Eye Wash

"For a firm with a high advertising profile............Crown Eyeglass seem to spend a lot of time in court..............What particularly annoys the hapless franchisees involved is that Crown are backed by rate payers money via Lancashire Enterprises Ltd (according to their latest accounts LEL invested £55,000 to help Crown get "off the ground" and in 1985 £130,000 was made available to allow Crown to build a new factory to supply growing sales). Lancashire Enterprises is a publicly-funded company set up to promote industry in Lancashire..................

To sell these franchises Crown make extravagant promises - one franchisee in Oxfordshire was told: You're bound to do at least 25-30 jobs on this site. In fact the site which was a prime one, averaged seven jobs a week..................DIGGER 1988

Crown Eyeglass brushes with dissatisfied franchisees "According to Stuart Holford Crown Eyeglass terminated his contract and they parted company in September after 12 months. For him the arrangement was unsatisfactory. He was fed up with poor delivery, shoddy workmanship and general lack of interest. He had paid £6,750 for the franchise and "got nothing back" at the termination".....OPTICIAN DEC 86

Another Paper reported how Louise Chantal, 18, who paid £49.95 for a pair of red fashion specs, found them unwearable despite three return visits to the shop. When the glasses were taken to an independent optician he said the distance between Louises pupils had been incorrectly calculated.............

Last year Crown Eyeglass launched Readyspex reading glasses. Some franchisees have been angered that Crown Eyeglass is supplying outlets within their franchise areas with Readyspex when they thought they held the exclusive rights for the product in their area.............Joe Lee told Optician that each franchisee was given the opportunity to take on the agency for Readyspex.......and they were simply too lazy and stupid to take up the offer in the first place...........franchisees however believe the offer of a Readyspex agency was unfair and impractical to a person trying to run their existing franchise................

Optician July /89

Many franchisees have complained that their training has been inadequate, the glasses are of poor quality and faulty at times, and deliveries late. In addition a number have found that the PD (pupil distance) of the glasses does not conform to British Standards as stated in Optician. This is of course a criminal offence.

Mr Lee declined to comment about the PD's but has recently sent out a memo saying that the factory should ensure that future PD's are within British Standards.

Banks Negligence costs Crown franchisee £30 K......

...A major Clearing Bank's slapdash attitude has cost one Crown franchisee their life savings. The franchisee owes the Bank £17K and is currently in negotiations with the Bank through Streetwise Franchising. His local bank manager referred to a report (from the Bank's franchise unit) which was two years out of date.

The report stated that there had only been **one failure** and the manager therefore advised Mr and Mrs X to proceed with investing in a Crown franchise. Streetwise Research shows that at that time there had been in fact **about 24 failures**. If the report had been up to date and this information known no manager in his right mind would have advised a franchisee to proceed and no franchisee would have gone ahead with out a hell of a lot of advice.

Surely the banks' owe franchisee's a duty of care. Certainly in this particular case they have been negligent .

Streetwise Franchising has requested the bank to write off the amounts owing. If the bank does not agree the franchisee will be bringing an action against the bank for negligence.

Comment

While operations were shutting left right and centre, until recently this franchisor was a member of the BFA and obtained its credibility through this association and by using carefully planned publicity - **The Duke of Kent (November 1989) and Mrs Thatcher.** Surely these VIPs' advisors should have picked up some of the adverse publicity?

Because of a loop hole in the contract franchisees who are on the verge of bankruptcy are not permitted to cease trading and if they do, are threatened with litigation and asked for a cash settlement - when they have no money. In the meantime the VIPs don't do their homework and only help to lure more unsuspecting members of the public...

And the so called Pillars of the franchise community remain blissfully ignorant of what is really going on.

1) How can such cases be avoided?

2) Shouldn't the franchisor have to disclose vital information so that franchisees are aware of failures?

3) Shouldn't VIP's have more stringent vetting procedures before lending their credibility to someone unworthy of it?

4) What duty of care do the banks owe to franchisees?

5) What sanctions can be placed on the franchisor or the banks in such cases?

UPDATE:

Notwithstanding the above in August of 1990 Crown Eyeglass plc sent out a press release stating there intention to join the Unlisted Securities Market after the **"Group's record results"**.

They further refer to the **"excellent progress that the Group has made during the last 12 months......(that) would not have been possible without the tremendous efforts of our employees"**.

Comment

It is to be hoped that some gullible journalist doesn't give them free PR. At least not without mentioning the above problems.

It seems quite scandalous that in the UK such a positive press release can be sent out when there have been so many problems and that there is no real protection for potential franchisees.

Surely such a case as this is a prime example for the desperate need for disclosure and sanctions against any franchisor who omits to inform potential franchisee's of vital information that would influence their decision to invest.

Curtain Dream Nightmare

This retail curtain shop franchise may have started off as a dream but became a nightmare. It makes a fascinating study because signs of future problems reared there head several times during 1988 and 1989 but little notice was taken.

£350,000 was injected into Curtain Dream in October 1987 by a get-together of venture capitalist firms, **Quester Capital, CIN Venture Managers, Partech Associates, Paribras and Rothschild Venture.**

The scene was set and the hype got under way. No expense was spared as C D glamorised this otherwise traditional business with expensive, glossy brochures and lavish exhibition stands which certainly put every one else in the shade.

Hypnotised by the splendour, 60 franchisees were lured in. The **BFA** were duped again. Together with T**ouche Ross and Midland Bank**, they awarded franchisees of C D a £10,000 prize for the National Franchise Opportunities Award for excellent business planning. At the conference for the "prize giving" it was rumoured "how difficult" the decision had been - to ensure that who ever was chosen didn't then go down the pan.

In November 1988 C D secured a further £1.5 million from Quester Capital.

By early 1989 accountant **Stuart Pearson** was appointed chairman of C D. He had previously left Moss Trust after a re-audit by Coopers Lybrand indicated a £1 million plus loss.

At this time **Chris Whitehead was MD & Steve Sargent was co-opted as Finance Director** in the summer of 1989. Sargent found problems with several of the companies accounting policies.

In April & May of 1989 C D franchisees started complaining to journalists about the problems they were experiencing.

In April of 1989 one franchisee explained to me how poor the quality of goods and services from H O was.

Franchisees had got together to form a franchise association. M D Chris Whitehead, worried about my conversations with franchisees, phoned to reassure me that **"all was well"** and that "he had encouraged the franchise association". Shortly afterwards he resigned.

All the time that problems existed the National Newspapers turned a blind eye and continued to re-gurgitate the PR and hype C D was churning out.

In particular **Daily Express journalist Iain Murray** prolific writer of franchise eulogies highlighted C D as a *"retail dream that's paid off"* and ***"one of Britain's Fastest growing retail franchises"*** which was introducing a ***"low risk package"*** for new franchisees.

At about this time Pearson was desperately trying to raise a further £2 million funding. He failed. By early July he had to call in **Coopers & Lybrand**. By 11th July he was gone, Barclays Bank having been asked to summon **David Waterman & Michael Moore from Cork Gully as administrative receivers.** The end had come.

Cork Gully had an unenviable task ahead of them. They were only too aware of the anguish of franchisees and set up a special helpline to help them deal with the **"Curtain Dream Nightmare".** Their objective *"to look after franchisees deeply concerned by the uncertaintly surrounding their businesses in the light of events at their Head Office".*

Franchisees however seemed unimpressed by Cork Gully's Helpline. They complained that they had no idea what was going on. Their future was on the line and yet they weren't being told anything. Even stock wasn't coming through unless they paid up front - and they didn't have the money to do that.

One franchisee **Mr Colin Eastwood** who eventually decided to go it alone commented that the franchisees were treated as **"a necessary evil by Cork Gully"** He went on to say that he had seen the problems coming and had formed a Franchisee Association - ***"Most of the franchisees were so green. It was inevitable that anyone borrowing as much as CD would come to an untimely end. By the time of the crash I had already formed another company and was ready to trade independently as Howards Way".***

Cork Gullys main task was to find a buyer for C D with its 70 outlets and factory. The buyer was Mostyn Interiors. Mr Mostyn Levene said in an interview in January 1990 that ***"he was just now sorting out the can of worms left by CD. The major problem had been CD taking rents from franchisees but not handing them over to the landlords".***

What was wrong with CD?

According to the franchisees, the company had been guilty of no less than financial hooliganism. Most of them had seen problems coming long before the crash.

1)The company was expanding too quickly.

2)The factory where the curtains and blinds were produced was totally inadequate.

3)The quality of the goods produced was poor and did not fit the upmarket image that the company coveted. There were about 10% returns to the factory. Compare this with about 1% when Mostyns took over.

4)The overheads were horrendous. Franchisees complained of a management structure where there were ***"too many chiefs and not enough indians". Apparently, the big boss had a Rolls Royce, his direct underling sported a Ferrari and nearly everyone else had "the ordinary car - a BMW".***

CD no longer exists.

On the take-over, franchisees had a choice: Go it alone or join Mostyns. Some of course had already shut their doors unable to keep going without stock and support. They lost their entire investment of up to £100 K each.

The loners changed their names and were let off what they owed in stock. The ones that went with Mostyns - about thirty - signed new agreements and appear content at the time of interview. They will be paying a 5% royalty on the goods ordered.

Mostyn Levene said there would probably be changes. His main concern at the time of takeover was to close the factory - ***"you can't teach an old dog new tricks".*** 98% of the goods are produced by Mostyns. He considers Mostyns to be ***"a vertical company" and intends to make the business "more competitive and the goods of a superior quality".***

Mostyns have experienced retailing via a number of distribution options - Pure Franchising, Franchising by License, Shop within a Shop and a Stand Alone Shop. He says they have no problem operating these different concepts through the same management.

However, it's no fairy tale ending for the franchisees that have decided to go their own way. Despite all they suffered at the hands of CD management - which lets face it was the reasons for their troubles and why they could not afford to pay fees and stock bills - seems to have been quickly and conveniently forgotten by Mostyns who have issued writs against some franchisees for repayment of debts.

Franchisees are currently defending their cases.

A TOUCH OF SHOW BUSINESS

The Dampcure Darleys ham it up like seasoned troupers with Henry Cooper at the opening of the new head office at Watford for their Woodcure/Dampcure 30 and Electricure/30 franchises. The entertainment also included a marching band and a dance troupe. Living up to the reputation of their franchise, Carole and John allowed nothing to dampen the evening.

Dampcure/ Woodcure 30 Ltd a franchise for the treatment of damp dry rot and wood rot

was set up in 1982, by franchisors Corole and John Darley. Within four years they had more than thirty franchisees nationwide. They became full members of the BFA - and still are.

A number of franchisees claim they were having severe financial problems and in 1986 formed a franchisee association - it's aim to air problems and to encourage discussion between the franchisors and franchisees.

By July 1988 20 franchisees had broken away to form **Countrywide Properties**. 5 others had already had their contracts terminated by the franchisor.

Ann Longbone, ex-franchisee in Cumbria now trading as **Acorn Building Ltd**, claims: ***"even after the second year we were making no profit. The royalty of 15%***

was too high and the training no good. We had no training in dry rot whatsoever even though we were expected to take on the work". She added: ***"we were led to believe that we were members of the trade associations*** **- the British Wood Preserving Association (BWPA) and British Chemical Damp Course Association (BCDCA).** ***After complaints from competitors and an investigation by a local Trading Standards officer we discovered we had never been members and we had in effect been misleading the public".***

The author has seen literature provided by the franchisor to franchisees telling them what to say to enquiries from the public - Question 8 is "Are you members of BWPA and BCDCA". The suggested answer is......... ***"Yes".***

A number of ex-franchisees' claim that they were led to believe that a **profit of about £16,000 could be achieved in the first year.** They say they actually made no profit.

Another ex-franchisee maintains ***"the on-site training was tantamount to suicide. The Chemical used..... can cause cancer or at least burn a hole in one's lungs unless special chemical filters are used in the respirators supplied, ...we were only supplied with dust filters".***

The ex-franchisee's biggest bone of contention was the membership of the trading associations. **Mr Griffiths the Trading Standards Officer at Hull** stated in a phone interview: ***"D/W/30 Ltd state they are members of the associations and the impression is given that franchisees are also members. This is not the case. A report is being compiled and we are investigating the involvement of franchisees and the franchisor".***

Mr Jones, Director of the BCDCA commented ***"this is a messy business that has been going on for years. The franchisor's membership has been terminated although they can appeal. A final decision will be taken at the next extraordinary general meeting in December".***

Mr David Scobie Director of BWPA stated ***"the franchisor started franchising in 1982 and they were told of the difficulties and that franchisees were not covered by membership automatically although they could attain membership after three years if they could prove they were technically good. We are still investigating the case".***

D/W/30 Ltd were members of the **Guarantee Protection Trust (GPT)**, which is an administrator of insurances for the security of long term guarantees. In 1985 GPT withdrew the franchisor's membership.

David Freeman, Managing Director of GPT, stated that ***"they withdrew membership because the franchisor refused to provide the names and addresses of fran-***

chisees - we needed these for assessment of insurance. Without those details the insurance risk was intolerable. Membership cannot be conferred on franchisees per se and over an 18 month period the franchisees had credibility with the public that they should never have had. However GPT will honour guarantees given by franchisees over that period."

At least two ex-fanchisees approached the **BFA** for assistance in negotiations. They both claim that the BFA was unhelpful. One claims that the franchisor threatened him with defamation proceedings after he wrote a letter of complaint to the BFA.

It appears from a company search that the franchisor's have changed their name from J and C Darling to J and C Darley. The company name has also been changed about three times. They have also held directorships of several other companies - some of which never traded, others traded and then shut down (such as Electricure) and Crimecure traded and was sold to a franchisee. The author asked the franchisors to comment on the issues raised by franchisees, but they declined to do so.

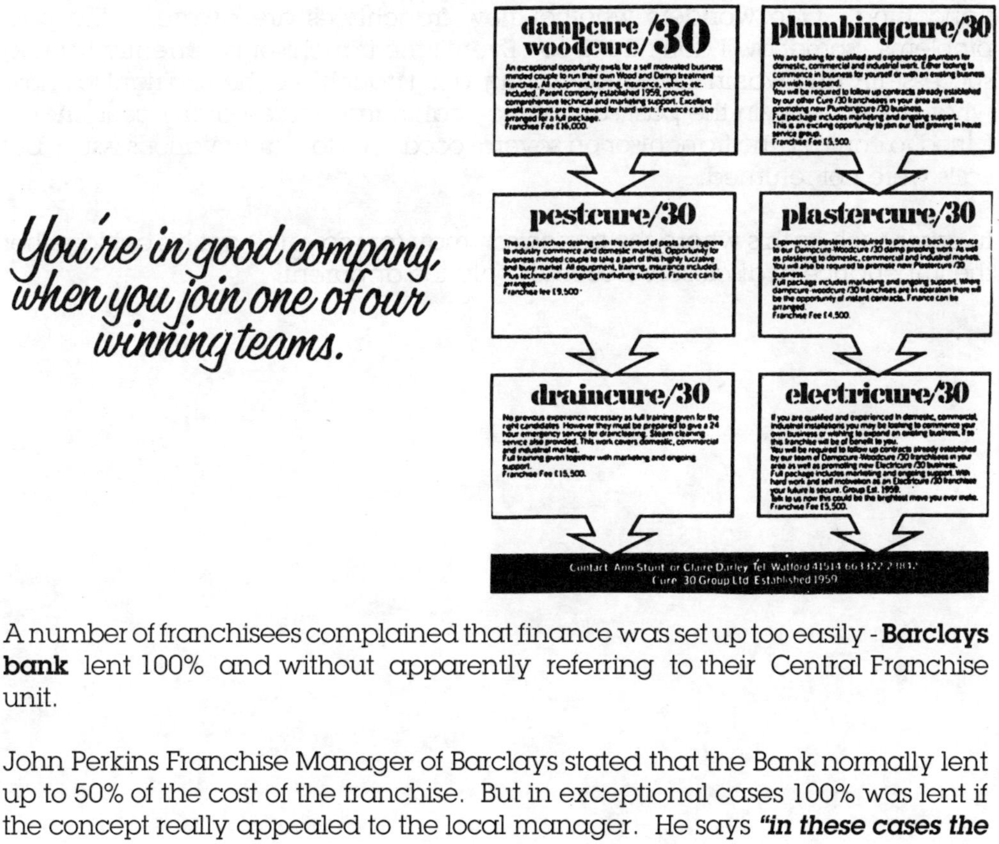

A number of franchisees complained that finance was set up too easily - **Barclays bank** lent 100% and without apparently referring to their Central Franchise unit.

John Perkins Franchise Manager of Barclays stated that the Bank normally lent up to 50% of the cost of the franchise. But in exceptional cases 100% was lent if the concept really appealed to the local manager. He says ***"in these cases the***

local manager was satisified and did not refer the cases to the centralised franchise unit. The manager in question has retired. If there is any suggestion that a manager has not been professional we will of course investigate the matter. We are treating the whole case with urgency".

The plight of many franchisees who owe many thousands to Barclays remains to be seen. Certainly it would seem that the bank bears some responsibility. Despite their privileged position in that they were also bankers to the franchisor, they seem to be totally unaware of the problems of these particular franchisees. What duty do the banks owe franchisees? If local branch managers can get away without referring to the specialised franchise unit what use are special units? If formalities can be forgotten so easily should franchisees not be warned?

Yet again the problems have arisen with a supposedly **"well established BFA member".** It is frightening to think what could go wrong with fringe operators. Franchisees would be well advised to rely on no one - but their own research. The advice given by the banks while useful does not guarantee success.

Despite these past problems D/W 30 are still members of the BFA and are still franchising. One wonders whether new franchisees are aware of the past problems - somehow I don't think so. Even if the franchisor is currently trading successfully and was in the right all along, don't franchisees have a right to know what has gone on in the past so that they can carry out research accordingly? I tried to contact the franchisor on several occasions to clarify various issues but calls were not returned.

In cases such as this where the franchisor may (or may not) get his act together the importance of disclosure becomes only too apparent.

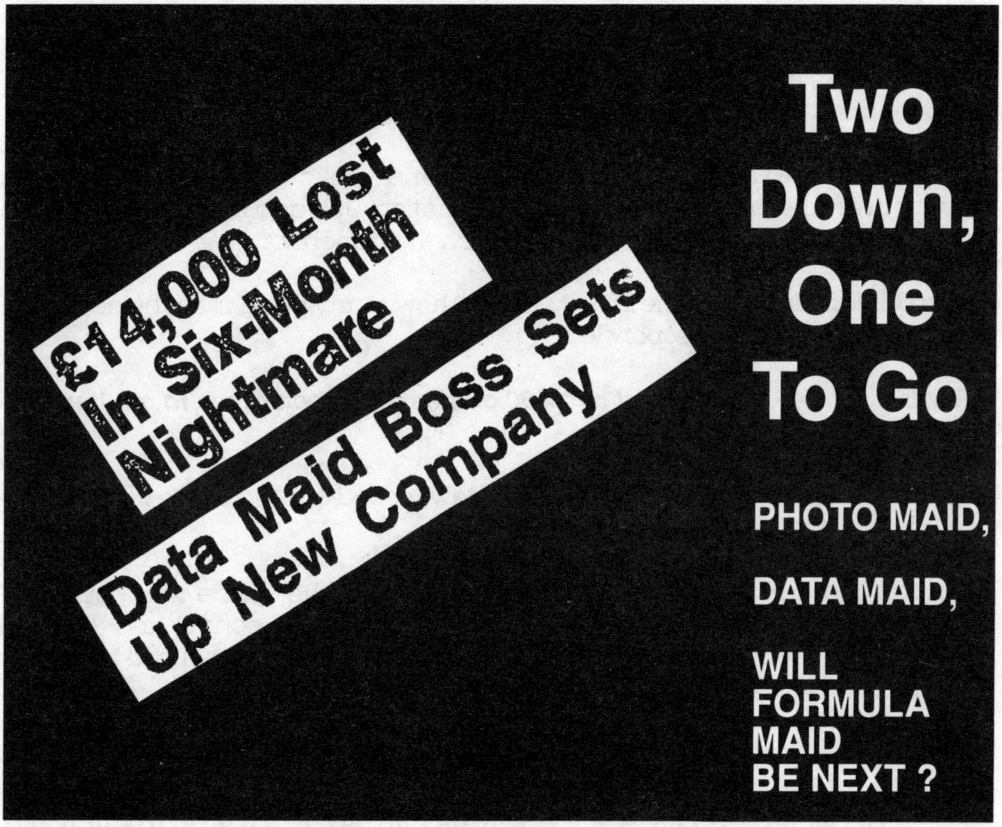

In **February 1989** I was contacted by a disgruntled **Data Maid** franchisee. He complained of no back-up and support and that the franchisor was witholding monies due to him. When monies were paid, the cheques usually bounced. Apparently the franchisor had promised that things would change. He stressed that it wasn't just him, but 100 odd franchisees were in this same predicament. He requested that we send details of FACTO (Franchise Advice and Consultancy Trading Organisation Ltd.) to all those franchisees. We did!

What could they do?

It was quite obvious to us at FACTO that the company was in big trouble. I recommended that the franchisees should get together and form an association and we would assist in negotiations with the franchisor to try to come up with a solution.

But there was a big problem. None of the franchisees could afford professional advice. My problem was that FACTO did not have the resources or the money to assist without charging what were already subsidised rates.

In informal talks with **Blenheim Exhibition Organisors** FACTO indicated the problems and suggested that Data Maid should not be allowed to exhibit until it had got its house in order. This was to no avail. I was told that the **BFA** made the decisions and had already vetted & approved Data Maid.

At the Glasgow exhibition the Data Maid stand was a bee-hive of activity as unwary investors clamoured for more information. It was a sickening sight and I could not repress the impulse to approach the franchisor.

I asked **Mr Ian McDougal** the Data Maid MD how many franchisees he had. ***"Oh, about 104,"*** he proudly responded.

"Why is it," I asked, ***"that a list of a 100 of them has been given to me because they're all having problems"?***

Mr McDougal, in a state of shock desperately looked around to see if any of the "would be's" had heard this.

He needn't have worried. They only wanted to know the upside of the business. He reassured me that everything was being done to gain control and that the problem had been their computer system but that was being rectified by giving franchisees new computers.

I had to leave it at that. Later we chased up some franchisees to see if things had improved. They expected matters to improve but weren't prepared to do anything positive to help themselves - but probably the real reason was that they couldn't afford to help themselves.

In **October 1989** the BFA and Blenheim Exhibition again allowed Data Maid to exhibit at the Birmingham National Franchise Exhibition.

Just one month later in an end of year meeting Ian McDougal admitted to franchisee's that the company was in financial difficulties. **Days later the company went into liquidation.**

The **Glasgow Sunday Post** stressed the fact (in relation to the October exhibition) ***"even at that time Data Maid were accepting new clients, investing between £12,000 and £14,000".***

Basically, Data Maid was using other people's money, knowing that the company was in a financial mess and that they would not be able to provide the services they had promised.

The BFA, on hearing of the liquidation, admitted it could do nothing to help. And yet as the Glasgow Sunday Post newspaper suggested, many of the Scots who had taken on the franchise did so, because Data Maid had BFA approval and had been accepted as an Early Development Category member. Franchisees of this chain as with some other chains in trouble all complained that letters to the BFA ***"brought no satisfaction".***

Franchisee, **Ron Duncan,** said ***"he received only two months pay between May and November despite having paid a £14,000 franchise fee".***

Former **BFA director (Tony Dutfield)** commented to the Post that franchisees should have had the franchise ***"thoroughly checked out by a bank".***

But this didn't help disabled franchisee **Jim Sharp** of Cumbernauld who says ***"he was assured by the Bank of Scotland that Data Maid were a reputable company".***

Sharp says that his Glasgow manager wrote to him saying they had received satisfactory responses to status enquiries. The **Bank of Scotland** explained to the Post that ***"when someone applies for a loan our bank would write to the banker of the company in question and ask for references. If that response is satisfactory the bank would rest on it. If not, other options are open which include checking with credit reference companies. But once the funds are advanced to a client he accepts full responsibility".***

Apparently, Sharp also claimed that ***"the Midland Bank had made investigations and recommended the investment".*** But Midland Bank franchise manager noted that a "***banks willingness to lend should not be construed as as endorsement....".***

It's quite clear that the public give too much credence to their bank manager's decision to lend them money. But whose fault is that? Don't the banks give the impression that they "vet" franchises? Definitely yes.

The real problem lies in the fact that the banks vet opportunities for their own benefits and in any event are covered by loans secured on usually the matrimonial home. So the banks can be in a "no lose" situation, unlike the franchisee - see page 47-50 re Raising Funding.

Most of the Data Maid franchisees have lost their entire investments and not surprisingly feel very bitter. The hardest hit were the new ones still undergoing training who might as well have torn up their £14,000 - because at the end of the day they got precisely nothing.

To cap it all - Mr McDougall certainly seems to have a nerve if not business acumen -

his next trick has been to set up another company called **Formula Maid** which seems to be operating from a London address.

Mr Macdougall's record leaves much to the imagination- he's been involved in at least three companies-**Data Maid** (in liquidation), **Photo Maid** (in liquidation) and now **Formula Maid.**

All have apparantly been at some stage in Wales but have undergone numerous changes of address and directors. Directors of these companies have been unavailable for comment.

Even more curious is the existence of a finance company, a South American Corporation called **The Rank Group** who hold the majority shares in Mr McDougall's latest venture, Formula Maid.

What could Mr McDougall be up to this time?

It is to be hoped that more innocent investors will not jump into this venture without adequate research.

A Thought.....

Too many franchisors who do go into liquidation leaving many with enormous financial losses find it only too easy to fold up and start again.

Surely there should be specific franchise legislation against this sort of thing? Surely there should be an investigation into why the business failed and whether the franchisor was responsible or whether they were trading fraudulently, and if so a ruling by law which prevents them from forming a company for a specified period of time and obtaining the advantages of limited liability.

In many such cases the franchisor often syphons off money before the actual liquidation knowing that the franchisees will be able to get nothing at the end of the day.

Certainly, any franchisor taking on franchisees when they know the company is in trouble should be made personally liable to those franchisees at least for the return of the franchise fee - or should face the prospect of imprisonment.

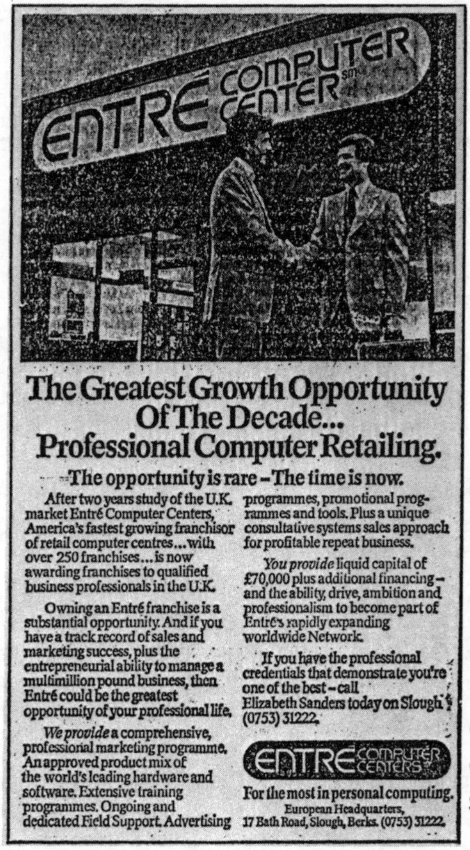

This franchise **Entre Computer Centres Inc** marketed under the slogan

"The Greatest Growth Opportunity of The Decade"

set up 15 high street franchises after it came into Britain in May 1984. By the time it had sold out to Combro a smaller British firm in 1986, 5 stores had already gone into liquidation and 3 more did so afterwards.

Potential franchisees needed **£70,000 liquid capital**, while the rest was available from the banks. The overall cost of the franchise was in the region of **£200,000** depending on the site location and size of premises.

The **franchisees in Croydon lost £310,000** and had to sell their houses and two of the three launderettes they owned.

The other franchisees **lost £1m** and at least three others more than **£200,000.**

Steven Evans whose two stores in Central London closed, **lost £1.2m**. In an interview with the Sunday Times he said ***"Entre promised to sell a quality system based on marketing expertise, and failed to deliver the goods".***

Franchisees paid an **initial fee of £40,000** and 8% of turnover as a management fee for back-up support and services.

Several franchisees said that Entre gave verbal assurances that it would always help if a store wasn't reaching targets. One franchisee commented ***"Entre's pull-out was the ultimate blow, they just pulled the plug and cleared out".***

Harold Sorsky, a receiver appointed to try to sell more than £100,000 of stock for one franchisee said ***" Entre gave these people the American hard sell and led them up the garden path".***

What went wrong?

According to the franchisees the problems lay not just in the change in the computer market but in the service provided by Entre head office - it was not the support promised before they signed the contracts. Many complained that the **cost of premises** was far greater than they were led to believe. Consequently from day one they were more heavily geared.

Further, most complained that the cost of obtaining special computer staff through **head hunting agencies was prohibitively expensive**, and an expense that had been grossly understated by the franchisor.

The ultimate blow for franchisees seems to be the exercise of the franchisor's right to **unilateral assignment - to Combro**. The new franchisor was much smaller than Entre and could not give the support the franchisees had been promised and desperately needed.

Many went into liquidation losing up to £1m each. Others reached settlements with the franchisor and tried trading independently.

"WHERE THERE'S TRASH THERE'S CASH"

Down Before It got Off The Ground ....

.....Flash Trash...

This is a classic example of something being flogged which the public did not want and at a price they weren't prepared to pay.

This franchise obtained a **£500,000** investment from **CIN Industrial Investments Ltd.** plus a **£200,000 facility from Nat. West Bank** and was launched in October 1986 at the height of the niche retail boom.

The funding indicated a faith the investors had which was unmatched by anyone else - except perhaps the promoters of the idea. The franchise retailed costume jewellery and accessories.

Flash Trash was reported as being the ***"brainchild"*** of **Karl and Sheila Gibbons.** It could more aptly have been described as a brain storm. The Gibbons combined retail experience included management positions with companies like **Miss Selfridge, Burtons, Dorothy Perkins, Wallis and Tie Rack.**

The first shop opened in Oxford Circus in October 1986 and was followed by a second in Kingston. The total initial investment was **£100,000.**

According to press reports there was an enthuastic response from the "public, trade and media". **CIN assistant Director Caroline Owen** apparently felt at once that ***"the business plan was excellent - clear, well thought-out, well presented - very impressive......[and that] the F T management was ideal - both had extensive experience in the fashion retail business......".***

According to Gibbons, ***"with the backing of one of the country's major financial institutions and one of the largest clearing banks, we will be able to go forth and multiply".*** Their general strategy was to have 30 retail outlets in 3 years, 20 of which were to be franchised.

Franchisee's outlay would of course be dependent on the size and location of premises. But on average a personal cash injection of £20k was necessary with the rest about £40k which could be borrowed. This included an initial franchise fee of £8,500.

Finding suitable retail sites was the biggest problem the franchisor faced and endeavoured to overcome this by finding the sites for franchisees and underleasing them.

So, what went wrong with this well thought out franchise?

In fact - it never got off the ground. Research indicates that not a single franchise was sold even though the franchisor had a stand at the franchise exhibitions.

Perhaps it was just as well - at least no franchisees lost money.

Clearly not enough **market research** had been carried out on the actual concept and whether there was a demand for it. Instead there seems to have been a "jump on the band wagon" attitude to yet another niche market. Most franchisors under estimate the importance of market research. Not only should this be carried out for the concept at the beginning but should be carried out for each area in which that franchise opens.

Choice of name also seems to have deterred potential franchisees and ultimately customers. While it may have become fashionable for women to wear costume jewellery, few like to think of themselves as wearing "Flash Trash ! "

....The Sweet Recipe That Left A Bitter Taste In Many Mouths...

The Fudge Kitchen concept was developed for franchising in South Africa by a South African based franchisor called **Barry Aitken** who was also chairman of the South African Franchise Association. He joined forces with **Roby Swan** to launch Fudge Kitchen in the UK.

Fudge Kitchen was launched in the summer of 1985 with plans to open 20 units within a year. An impressive management team consisted of **Ray Shuttleworth** (ex-Hepworths) and **Trevor Smith** who had 8 years experience with Prontaprint and had spent 18 months assisting the master franchisee establish Prontaprint in South Africa.

Edwin Thirlwell, acknowledged as being one of Britains' most financially successful franchisor's was regarded more as a franchisor rather than "quick-printer". He decided to apply the business experience he had gained in other areas to the

F K and Poppies concept.

At the time it was stated that:

"the variety of the two new franchises Prontaprint has taken under its wing in the past year illustrates the depth of its franchising experience and resources. Also they serve to indicate the virtually unlimited scope for Prontaprint under the entrepreneurial leadership of Edwin Thirlwell, to build itself into a multinational franchising conglomerate - a possibility that the USM investor is likely to find irresistable".

On **October 1985** the Holding Company was floated on the Unlisted Securities Market. Of the company's £3.1 million turnover to March 1985 Poppies and Fudge Kitchen contributed £164,000. Fudge Kitchen had 3 outlets trading and Barry Aitken, one of the founders of Fudge Kitchen, had a 28% interest in the company.

Fudge Kitchen became a part of Prontaprint in 1984. The first units were opened in the North East with Newcastle the primary test bed. The F K product range was extended to include a soft ice cream machine and the capital cost of the franchise reduced so that a franchisee needed £10k instead of £15k.

The total cost of the F K franchise was **£40k** and the franchisor's royalty 10% (6% service and 4% advertising).

By **5th June 1986** The **Financial Times** was reporting that Prontaprint's results had been adversely affected by the disappointing performance of F K. It had taken longer to develop than planned and only 9 units had been opened - substantially below budgeted figures. Management changes were made and outside consultants called in to re-appraise the operation's potential.

Reports stated that not only was F K a tremendous disappointment but that it was responsible for the group's profit performance being down by £100,000.

In **June 1986** the Investors Chronicle reported that F K's 9 shops had run into unexpected difficulties and had absorbed about £100,000 additional development costs that year.

Throughout this period F K was being marketed as a ***"highly profitable, easily learned and simple to control as an ideal franchise for an absentee owner"***. An added attraction was that the F K kiosks could easily be re-sited if a site proved disappointing.

F K marketed as ***"The sweet recipe for success"*** was soon to leave a bitter taste in many mouths. The headlines accordingly changed to ***"Fudge Sticky"*** and ***"F K pegs Prontaprint".***

Even in **June 1987** headlines such as ***"Harsh Lessons for Prontaprint"*** (Independent) were common. The newspaper wrote of Prontaprint learning two lessons; namely that ***"not only were most of the ideas nurtured by budding entrepreneurs decidedly naff but its own management was nowhere near strong enough to monitor them"***. Investment in Fudge Kitchen and Poppies, of course, hadn't helped matters.

In **1988** Prontaprint sold out to **Continuous Stationery**, manufacturer of business forms in a £10m deal. The price included a premium of about £2m. Prontaprint's pre-tax profits for the year to 25 March were predicted at £750,000, compared with the previous period's of £200,000.

In an interview, **Prontaprint MD Derek Mottershead** stressed how much the print industry had changed. Now franchisees do need to go out and get work and those who just sit in the shop thinking that the mountain will come to Mohammed will need to rethink or sink.

He was prepared to concede that their experience of trying to diversify had failed but was not prepared to comment further.

Sue Rorstad, founder of Poppies, stated in a phone interview, ***"that there was a lot of assistance that Prontaprint should have given to the Poppies venture, but didn"t". However, she then became extremely cagey and issued Streetwise Franchising with a statement stating that the parting of the two companies was amicable and that "in order to protect the investments of the various Franchisees and Shareholders in both companies, each party agreed to a press embargo on the subject of separation..."***

When questioned about Poppies and, in particular, about the complaints received from ex-franchisees, Ms Rorstad declined to comment. The author wrote an article in the Today newspaper, interviewing one particular ex-franchisee, **Ms. Nina Jenkins,** who was a local government officer before taking the franchise. She recounted how her dream of being her own boss turned into a nightmare:

Ten months after investing in a domestic cleaning franchise, she lost her home and her life savings.

Nina gave up her job as a sheltered housing officer to start up a Poppies franchise in West London.

The operation was a full member of the British Franchise Association which Nina saw as a protection, and she raised her initial outlay of £18,500 by remortgaging her home.

"I started experiencing problems almost immediately and within five months my situation was desparate", she says.

"My franchise did not live up to its financial targets and I had problems getting workers. In the end, I lost £30,000 and had to sell my home".

Nina is now living rent-free at a friend's home until she gets on her feet again.

"I feel very bitter, particularly because many other franchisees also had to shut down. However, the franchisor is still trading", she says.

"I still think franchising is a good concept because it gives people a head start".

"In my case I blame the franchisor's concept and the fact that I was influenced by BFA membership. That meant nothing. The BFA is useless as far as helping franchisees is concerned".

Poppies franchisor Sue Rorstad declined to comment on Nina's case.

As Poppies continues to franchise Streetwise Franchising was anxious to get answers to various questions. However Ms Rorstad was unavailable and declined to comment.

In particular, Streetwise Franchising wanted to question her about at least fourteen other franchisees who have also ceased trading. All have lost substantial sums of monies. One couple lost about £45,000. Ms. Jenkins lost her home as well as all her investment. The franchisor is still franchising.

Comment

In this case franchisees (mainly women) complained that even though they had a legal case, because their spouse worked, they did not qualify for legal aid and therefore could not afford to bring a legal action.

Where there are high failure rates, surely something should be done to warn prospective franchisees. No franchisor parts with a list of failures. Most will not even give lists of franchisees currently trading. Why not? Surely this is vital information which every potential franchisee should be aware of - how else can they make an informed decision as to whether or not to invest?

The Billion Dollar Network

That will give you a roof over your head you won't complain about, at a price your bank balance can live with....

Holiday Inns is the worlds largest hotel group with almost **1600 hotels in 50 countries.** It is the international hotel business of the Hotel and Restaurant Division of Bass plc.

The Holiday Inn hotel system worldwide is made up of about **83% Franchised hotels,** and **17% company owned** and managed.

The birth of this hotel chain began in **1952** because one man refused to compromise his standards. **Kemmons Wilson** had repeatedly encountered uncomfortable, inconsistent and overpriced accommodation on family holidays. Wilson joined forces with **Wallace Johnson** a home builder and the first Holiday Inn hotel was built on the outskirts of Wilson's Tennessee hometown, Memphis.

This first 120 room hotel with private bathroom, air conditioning and phone also boasted a number of extras; swimming pool, free ice, free parking and dog kennels. In addition children under 12 years old could stay free in their parents room. These amenities were quite revolutionary.

By the end of **1954** (just 2 years later) 11 Inns had been opened including the first franchised one in Clarksdale, Mississippi.

In **1957 the company went public**, with the entire offering being sold on the first day.

By **1959 the 100th Holiday Inn** was opened in Tallahassee, Florida and the Holiday Inn University started to educate newcomers into the system.

Holiday Inn has earned a reputation for **innovation**. Not only was it the first to introduce bedrooms en suite, colour TV's and swimming as standard features but in 1965 it introduced the **first computerised reservations system - Holidex**. This is now the world's largest privately owned computerised communication system. It connects all the Holiday Inn Hotels around the world by cable through the computer centre in Memphis.

International Expansion

Holiday Inns America Inc. changed to Holiday Inns Inc. in 1969 to reflect International expansion. By this time Holiday Inn had opened in Montreal Canada, and in Puerto Rico. The company was en route for worldwide expansion. With expansion came the need for staff who not only knew what they were doing but could keep the high standards set.

In 1**970 The Holiday Inn University** was opened and it became a requirement that all General Managers attend for intensive specialised training. The Holiday Inn hotel system also became the first **BILLION DOLLAR** hotel chain in history.

International expansion continued with Holiday Inn opening in **Avignon** (France), **Kyota (**Japan) and **Caracas** (Venezuela).

After Wilson retired in 1979, Harrahs was taken over by Holiday Inn Inc. to make them the largest gaming company in the USA. In **1988 Bass plc** a UK-based company purchased Holiday Inns International and gave exclusive rights to own, operate and licence Holiday Inn Hotels outside the USA, Canada and Mexico.

New Concepts

In **1983** Holiday Inns introduced **Holiday Inn Crowne Plaza** to the United States and by 1987 they had also been opened in Amsterdam, Manchester. Guests have a range of business services.

The latest concept from Holiday Inns is the **Garden Court Holiday Inn.** These are located in smaller cities and towns and offer a courteous but no frills service. The cost of a room is about 25% less than a Holiday Inn.

This "low cost operation" concept which offers another superb opportunity for franchisees and developers who have limited capital.

Franchises

With **nearly 90% of hotels operated through franchise agreements** Holiday Inn seems to have discovered the secret of successful franchising. Consistent and far reaching professional assistance is provided to all franchisees and experienced staff with local knowledge are at hand. Holiday Inn spends more than **$1M each year monitoring customer needs** and provides franchisees with continuing support in systems, technology, advertising, marketing and staff training.

Head office is geared to providing what the customer wants at a reasonable price with the aim of helping franchisees improve their market share and the value of their investment.

Holiday Inn makes a particular effort to fit individual hotels into the community so that the franchisees can get the best out of the concept. Hence, the hotel in **Malta** has been converted from a former army barracks; the **Crowne Plaza hotel at Lyon** has been ingeniously transformed from a pre-war garage; in the Crowne Plaza Rome Minerva the original marble staircase and stained glass canopy and frescoes are being restored.

Franchisees don't have to be a hotel operator. They are permitted to hire hotel management companies or lease the hotel to independent operators - subject to the approval of Holiday Inns. Holiday Inns also offers management contract services.

The cost of the various hotels differ vastly depending on size and location but a franchisee needs capital of 25/40% of the anticipated cost with land costs accounting for no more than 20%. Sites can be owned or leased.

Franchise fees can be paid in two ways - by an initial fee followed by a royalty based on a percentage of revenue or fixed payments into a common fund which cover marketing, advertising and system reservations services.

The Success Formula

The management of Holiday Inns don't deny that they have had their fair share of problems. But rather than sweep them under the carpet they look at them as a challenge. They see their ongoing challenge as ***"living up to their business philosophy".***

And what is this business philosophy?

Quite simply to be the best hotel group and to be considered the best by customers, franchisees, employees and shareholders.

How has Holiday Inns achieved the best and continue to do so? Its certainly not by wishful thinking. The whole network is designed for efficiency, quality, cleanliness and value. The same ingredients that have made McDonalds so successful. A single mindedness, if you like, to settle for nothing but the best.

Without doubt the greatest contributing factor to the Holiday Inns success formula is the vigorous training given to managers and franchisees. It is mandatory that all General Managers of a Holiday Inn hotel graduate from the General Manager Programme conducted by the Holiday Inn University.

They Voted With Their Feet....

Hometune - founded in **1968 by Duncan Whitfield** (a former chairman of the British Franchise Association) has become a household name in the field of mobile car tuning. In those days franchisees had none of the benefits of the "franchise concept" such as a well known name. Hometune was unknown, there was no special training and no operations manual.

By 1980 HT had over 200 units nationwide - but there were problems. Franchisees with the necessary expertise to cope with modern engines were difficult to find. Many franchisees faced financial difficulties and started to pressurize Mr Whitfield into improving training.

This resulted in the birth of a **Franchise Advisory Board** - which consisted of an elected representative body of franchisees. According to some franchisees it was the Board that organised the first training seminar for franchisees - sixteen years after the founding of the company! Disillusionment and unrest within the fleet continues.

In **February 1987** Whitfield wrote to franchisees saying he was arranging for an injection of capital into HT and asking them to co-operatee in signing a letter assigning the franchise agreement to a new company called Hometune (UK) Ltd. He wrote: ***"you will not be disadvantaged by signing this letter", and all franchisees bar one signed.***

Some ex-franchisees claim that Whitfield failed to tell them that Hometune (UK) Ltd. was a wholly owned subsidiary of MCL Ltd, the importers of Mazda Cars into the UK. They maintain that the new management reassured them that no changes would be made without consulting them and that the royalty fee would not be increased.

However in **September 1987** a new agreement was proposed which **purported to increase the royalty from 10% to 12.5% and charge another 5% for advertising. It also sought to impose regional booking centres, transfer franchisees telephone numbers to the company and carve up territories (which some franchisees had operated for 19 years) into smaller areas. According to Mr Bernard Skan, an ex-franchisee, the new management admitted in an internal document (which was leaked) that the contract was "draconian" and that "franchisees would vote with their feet".**

This is exactly what franchisees did. **80%** of the HT fleet signed a petition and formed a co-operative. Later they formed a company and issued shares, thereby raising £30,000, which was used in ensuing litigation. **TUNE-UP, the breakaway group, started trading on 1st May 1988** with 76 ex-HT franchisees operating 110 units.

Duncan Whitfield who at the time of interview is still a director within the new management company said ***"franchisees were not disadvantaged. They have been stupid and if anything have disadvantaged themselves. I did not know changes would be made - but the changes proposed were necessary. MCL could have been more tactful - and I am sad about the breakaway".***

The new management tried unsucessfully to enforce the non-competition and non-solicitation clauses in the franchise contracts. Eventually an out of court settlement was reached. The new management paying Tune-up's costs up to a thousand pounds and Tune-up agreeing never to use the Hometune name.

Tune-up under the leadership of four executive directors applied and was denied membership - full, associate or early development, of the BFA.

Bernard Skan the Managing Director of Tune-Up who has 19 years experience of mobile car tuning commented ***" that he finds the BFA's conduct difficult to comprehend since HT are still members of the BFA despite breaching some of the BFA guidelines. It is about time the BFA ceased behaving as a private club and instead became representative of those involved in franchising:.***

Derek Ayling of Saffrey Champness Consultancy Services Ltd and consultant to Tune-Up comments: ***"we tried the BFA arbitration scheme with little success. We were disappointed at the way the application for membership was handled. The BFA must stand back and act like a professional trade association and take off their blinkers. The Tune-Up fanchisees have done nothing unethical in breaking away and qualify for the BFA membership criteria in every way".***

Whitfield's reply - ***"the BFA would be crazy to allow them membership at this stage - before they have proved they can run a franchise as franchisors"***.

Tony Dutfield(Former Director of the BFA) commented at the time that he would be happy to entertain the possibility of associate membership when they had fulfilled the criteria.

Skan's complaints extended to HT adverts which stated that franchisees can earn up to £40,000 profit per annum. He maintains this is not possible - He says the maximum is about £30,000. **Rodney Deslandes,** general manager of HT, stated that even though they have no franchisees currently earning £40,000, profit at this level is possible. He admits however that most earn between £16-£18,000.

Comment

The breakaway franchisees who now form Europe's largest mobile tuning franchise can be applauded for showing great entrepreneurial spirit - but it remains to be seen whether they will make good franchisors.

Most franchises experiencing unilateral assignment have major problems which usually result in litigation. The reason is that the new franchisor will always want to introduce new changes.

As a franchisee the best thing to do is to ensure before you sign the contract that if the franchisor does sell out, your contract will not only not be changed but that the new franchisor cannot put undue and unfair pressure on you to change. In addition you should ensure that any debts you have outstanding to your franchisor will remain with the old franchisor despite the sell out.

This is particularly important because it may be the franchisors fault that your business operated badly and you ran up the debts.

Franchising Leading Light

and

City University Visiting Profes-sor

Taken In by ......

........Identicar???

Identicar was founded in 1978 by a Birmingham businessman **John Harris** and was run by Harris and **David Morcom.**

In **December 1982** Identicar attracted **£350,000 from the City through the Lovat Enterprise Fund,** an investment fund backed by five leading financial institutions. The money was used to build up the UK network and accelerate overseas licensing.

In early 1984 (prior to the appointment of receivers into Identicar) **Martin Mendlesohn and Graham Crawford became founder shareholders of Franchise Investors Ltd which attracted £1.3 million from the Lovat fund.** Graham was also appointed director.

Martin Mendlesohn is a leading light in UK franhcising and now visiting professor of franchising at City University. He is also the legal consultant to the BFA.

Mr Mendlesohn was also a **director and shareholder of Identicar (Holdings) Ltd. which went into receivership in February 1985.** According to the Department of

Trade and Industry the company through which Identicar (Holdings) Ltd actually sold franchises was compulsorily wound up with an estimated **deficiency of "over £1 million".** This company was the wholly owned subsidiary - Identicar Ltd which was a **full member of the BFA.**

Mr Mendlesohn was not only one of two founder directors, being appointed a director on October 25th 1982 shortly before a group of City Institutions put in £350,000, but was also the company's solicitor and held a small shareholding of 2,345 shares.

The Times newspaper reported that sources within the franchise industry say that the institutions insisted that Mr Mendlesohn became a director as a condition of making their investment. The funds were supposed to be used to expand the franchise activities of Identicar. Mr Mendlesohn gave the Times a limited comment because he said he was constrained by his professional code of ethics because the company was a client. He did however state that he was a non-executive director of Identicar (Holdings) Ltd. & had taken his shares at their par value.

Comment

Nobody in franchising, or indeed any business is above "getting it wrong". Many professional franchisees experienced in accountancy, law, retail and so forth have got it wrong and lost money .

Furthermore, those working in franchising who give advice can only be objective. At the end of the day they are only human and business risk cannot be eliminated.

Like most professionals in business, franchising is no different when it comes to the carrot dangling syndrome - it can be very tempting. I myself have been approached by companies wishing to franchise who feel that my name linked with their operation will give them the credibility I have worked for in relation to ethical franchising. So far I've had to turn down such work because the opportunities were less than desirable.

However at the end of the day it is worth remembering that "money talks" and an advisor, franchise specialist or consultant who is involved in a venture is not impartial or independent and can get it wrong. No matter who the big name is it is no substitute for independent franchise advice.

An *Oasis* *that franchisees didn't think was* *Paradise*

The first retail **Oasis shop was opened in 1974 in Oxford**. The company described itself as ***"leading wholesalers and retailers of an exclusive range of merchandise from around the world"***. The main emphasis was and still is on ladies fashion wear.

Oasis was launched at the **Kensington Franchise Exhibition in 1984** - and at that time boasted seven large retail shops and ten shops within shops.

Over the years the chain grew to about **15** shops many of which were franchises. Generally the set-up cost of a shop was between **£35-£85,000** depending on size and location. At the time of interview only three franchisees exist. The rest have had to close down. Some have reached out of court settlements with the franchisor, some are litigating, others have just resigned themselves to great financial loss and are trying to pick up their lives and start again.

Ex-franchisees maintain that the stock was over-priced and of poor quality. Deliveries usually arrived late and projections were unrealistic. They say mark-downs were necessary and a lower than expected gross profit margin was achieved. In addition they claim that an advertising levy of 2% had to be paid into the company's current account and there was no way of ensuring that the money was spent on advertising.

Some of the franchisees had to pay a hefty 10% extra levy on rent (where the headlease was held by the franchisor) despite the fact that many franchisees claim they were not making a profit.

In **1987 Oasis was granted full BFA membership** even though at least one franchisee expressed in writing to the BFA that problems existed and **"improvement"** was necessary.

Franchisees continued to suffer financially and called a meeting in June 1987 to discuss problems. Minutes were sent to **Graham Brown, director of Oasis.** Franchisees claim that little was done to rectify the problems and they found themselves in an intolerable position. One ex-franchisee commented:

"I have lost about £50,000. I am paying back £30,000 to the National Westminster Bank. The stock either had to be reduced or recalled by the franchisor".

Another stated: ***"I owed money for stock and could not pay because the business was not making any. The franchisor threatened me with bankruptcy unless I gave a charge over my house - I did. Now they say they will go into possession unless I hand over the keys to my shop or pay them back. We haven't agreed on a figure yet - but already I have lost about £100,000. My house is on the market - to raise the money".***

Ex-franchisee **Jackie Brierton**, heralded as a ***"model"*** franchisee by the franchisor, owned the Edinburgh and Glasgow shops. Now she faced four writs. She commented ***"the ultimate let down for me was the discovery of Oasis stock in a shop called Razzle Dazzle near to me. The stock was considerably cheaper and bore a "Zavior Ferrazio" label - designed by Oasis".***

In **March 1988** she wrote to the BFA airing her grievances. The BFA passed the letter on to the franchisor who is currently suing her for libel as a result. Her solicitor Guy Martin of Carter-Ruck (the leading solicitors in libel law) at the time stated that her defence is ***"qualified privilege"*** on the basis that any information she gave to Mr Tony Dutfield of the BFA, he had an interest in receiving and that she was under a duty to provide that information even if it was not true because she honestly believed it to be true, and therefore was compelled to disclose it.

In an interview with two Oasis directors **Graham Brown and Maurice Bennett** the author put the above claims of ex-franchisees to them. They described the comments as ***"a nonsense and that a number of franchisees had two shops - something they wouldn't have done if they were unhappy. Deliveries were sometimes late for example if the goods were coming from India".***

They added that the ***"Croydon shop did miss the projected figures by 50% but this was due to the new shopping centre not taking off - and many other blue chip companies also suffered. We have done everything to help franchisees. But since the company has taken over franchised shops the turnover has increased by 400%".***

Apparently supplying special stock to Razzle Dazzle was a salesman's ***"mistake"*** even though they note that as wholesalers they can supply anybody. In this case they say they felt morally obliged to franchisees and therefore apparently offered them compensation. Looking to the future they comment ***"we still have three franchisees that we are supporting. Ex-franchisees were not suited to the***

franchise concept and we made a mistake in choosing them. More research needs to be carried out to establish what exactly makes an ideal franchisee".

Miss Brierton in Scotland still maintains she was not offered compensation.

At the time of interview an existing franchisee said ***"my personal experience of Oasis has been disastrous. If they had supplied a commercial stock I would not be in this mess. I have lost £70,000 and am negotiating with the franchisor about the future".***

Mr and Mrs Hussain have two Oasis shops - in Harrow and Kingston. They have been trading for about a year and state:

"We have had many teething problems. The old management was very disorganised and as a company didn't get it right. The stock has been very average and has had no great impact on sales. All the franchisees including us were undercapitalised. Cash flow is our problem and the original projections we were given were optimistic. So far we have made no money, but have suffered a lot of hardship. We are waiting to see what the new management do. They seem very professional and we hope the business takes off".

Considerable litigation between some franchisees and the Oasis franchisor has taken place. The BFA as usual sat on the fence. Mr Dutfield former Director of the BFA, said at that time that Oasis would continue as a full BFA member at least until the allegations are resolved.

Comment

While there are always two sides to a story it would appear that where a number, if not most, of the franchisees in a chain are having problems something should be done to prevent new franchisees joining. In the above case this was not an issue because the franchisor had decided not to recruit more franchisees anyway.

There is no excuse for the BFA's behaviour in passing on confidential information and having no control over members who try to take advantage of franchisees trying to invoke the arbitration scheme. Hopefully this will not recur.

There should also be a system where if several franchisees are having problems potential franchisees should be notified and BFA membership suspended.

Postal Centres were announced as a new franchise in Franchise World magazine in 1983.

This American concept was introduced to Britain by **Ken Taylor**, "an advertising media specialist". His Taylor Harrison Group included companies offering advertising space on parking meters, phone boxes and multi story car parks. He previously ran a group of garages in the Manchester area. Later press articles stated that he was made redundant.

The strength of the franchise was claimed to be Taylor's ability to sell advertising space. The same press report stated that in fact he bought advertising space, to the tune of **£250,000 annually**, to attract advertisers themselves onto his media.

Taylor acquired world rights to Postal Centres outside the U.S. He went on to franchise the concept in Europe. The banks did not support his franchisees but he himself made *unsecured loans* available to franchisees. This is a practice strongly discouraged by the clearing banks and regarded as one indication that the product or service is not viable.

By **October 1985 Taylor had 50 franchisees who had sold 4,000 of the postal centres to small shopkeepers.**

Franchisees paid between **£10,000 and £24,000** for the franchise and obtained revenue from sales of advertising space on the boxes, and from sales of postage stamps. The shopkeeper, who paid for the postal centre, derived revenue from sales of advertising space and postage stamps.

The franchisor negotiated the advertising deals and discounts on postage stamps from the Post Office, both activities generating the income for both franchisee and shopkeeper.

Press reports indicated that the Taylor Harrison Group had grown dramatically since its launch in 1980, and Taylor was grooming the company for a public launch in 1987/ 88.

Turnover **rose from £20,000 in 1980/81 to £1.2 million in 1983/4.** In **1984/84 turnover leapt to £5 million, and 1985/86 forecasts were between £5 - £10 Million.**

Taylor expected the THG to have a market valuation at the time of its public launch of more that £20 million. Another report referred to Taylor as **"the world's postmaster".** He was also reported to have been selling territories in France and Germany for £250,000.

Then **suddenly in April 1986** the trade press announced that PCI had **ceased trading during March 1986**. There was no indication that franchisees had suffered financially but **many traders lost substantial sums (£10,000 - £15,000)** by way of useless investment, and had not been paid their share of advertising or stamp money.

The post office was inundated with complaints, but stressed that PCI had no commercial connection with the Post Office. The PO did not object to retailers continuing to sell supplies of stamps.

A publication called the ***"Independent Grocer" ran an Action Line*** advisory service to readers (mainly small shopkeepers) and was also inundated with complaints against PCI. The newspaper team mediated between PCI staff, including Ken Taylor and aggrieved shopkeepers.

The shopkeepers had received little or no income from advertising space or stamp commission from PCI. It was discovered that advertising space had been offered free of charge to advertisers to attract them to the medium. "Negotiations" were in progress with a number of companies at normal rates.

Clause 11 of the Franchise contract stated that advertising revenue (for distribution) *"shall be reduced by the charges to advertising agents"*.

Taylor claimed that payments were not guaranteed and that sums distributed to retailers were made "as goodwill payments strictly as a gesture of goodwill".

A **firm of accountants in Manchester** (believed to be PCI's accountants) confirmed that from January 1983 - March 1985 charges made to Thomson

Directories, Coca Cola and Cadbury's were for the production of advertising panels, and no charges were made for the letting of advertising space.
There was a letter from the Deputy MD Eleanor Bursk stating that advertising had been offered free of charge but that they were negotiating for normal rate and they wanted the shopkeeper to get his 20% revenue. Meanwhile, they were prepared to make goodwill payments which once banked would be considered as an acceptance of full payment and settlement of any claims against PCI for any advertising up to 31st March 1985. Orders from retailers for Postal Centres which were delayed and subsequently cancelled attracted a non-returnable deposit ranging from £100-£150.

Taylor stated in a letter that before he considered whether or not to make reimburse deposits the Independent Grocer had to give written confirmation that they would not publish what was going on.

On the 9th August 1985 at Lancaster Buildings, 124 Barton Square, Manchester a special resolution was passed. The Taylor Harrison Group was to acquire the issued share capitol of Meter Ads, Call Point Advertising, Point of Sale Advertising, Postal Centres International, Car Park Ads, and another previously unreported company Taylor Harrison Group Travel Services Ltd - by means of a share issue to the value of £160,000.

It's worth noting that the entire group of subsidiaries was valued at £160,000. Further, this was probably an over valuation. In any event it is extremely doubtful that the Inland Revenue would have granted the necessary tax clearances to them to acquire share holdings worth millions for this amount, and yet the press statements were at this time suggesting that the Taylor Harrison Group was achieving sales of £5 million.

There had been no accounts filed and no shareholders listed.

On 5th February 1986 a petition was presented to the High Court to wind up Postal Centres International. This was heard and granted on 19th May in the Chancery Court.

Postal Centres Int. Ltd was a subsidiary of the THG and during 1983 at least was a qualified non-member of the BFA. The company describes its activities as the sale and franchising of Postal Centres. The only accounts published are interesting. Neither PCI nor any subsidiaries list the directors remuneration. There are accounts for 1983, which do not show much.

The accounts for 1984 show that the company turned over just **under £1.4 million and made a loss of £36k +.** The balance sheet is interesting. The fixed assets are of £4,798 and the current assets include cash of £154,361. But the other current assets (stock) are £85k and there are debtors of over £500,000.

The creditors on the other hand are nearly £800,000. Realistically, it is doubtful if the company was solvent. Also there is a net decrease on flow of funds of over £20,000. Given the general level of trading, the fixed assets are nothing to speak of and what keeps the company solvent is the fact that part of the creditors' total is falling due after one year (£37,113). If this were not the case they would have been insolvent in 1984. Even with this deferred liability the company's finances are not very secure.

While holding £154,361 in cash PCI guaranteed bank overdrafts of associated companies to the tune of £122,962. **So even though one company had money the others were overdrawn by £122,962.**
And this was a company that had been vetted by the BFA. When was the company vetted and admitted? Was this financial performance considered adequate to justify provisional membership?

We will probably never know because the BFA has declined to comment.

The winding up of PCI preceded the receivership of the THG and no appearance was made by PCI personnel.

There is little evidence of profitable trading anywhere within the group. And yet this was a group which was reported as being prepared for flotation, and who placed 2 1/2 page ads in the FT to draw themselves to the attention of the City and who claimed that by 1987 they would have a market capitalisation of £20 million.

Nearly **3000 retailers had to write off sums averaging £1,400 when PCI went into liquidation.** Most complained that the stamp machines were useless and operated badly. As one franchisee said ***"Postal Centres were a good idea, badly conceived - the machines are no good".*** Many complained that they had never received any promised revenue from adverts. Another retailer commented; ***"we eventually got some money for the stamps but it was always a terrible job; they would always say that the cheque was in the post... the whole thing was a botch... it is a nuisance as it doesn't dispense the stamps successfully: they either get torn or one and a half come out".***

Many retailers complained that the machine was overpriced. The full extent of the franchisor's hidden mark-ups will now probably never be known.

Wait for It...

Ken Taylor "once bitten but not twice shy" not satisfied with his previous unenviable record with Postal Centres made a come back (and departure) in 1989 with the **West Coast Video** franchise.

Franchise magazines who had not forgotten the previous fiasco were reluctant to give Mr Taylor the front cover stories that he desired so much.

Mr Taylor told Franchise Magazine editor ***Dr. D. Chaplin*** *"that PCI was an unfortunate episode for which he had been singled out for attack by BBC's Face The Facts team but that West Coast Video was very different"* - we only had to look at the successful operation in the USA.

It was fortunate that Mr Taylors reputation preceded him. For on **1st November 1989 BBC's Face The Facts documented the crash of West Coast Video.** With the operation in the hands of the receiver it is estimated that there are debts of at least **£1 million**. Taylor attracted investors through a ***"champagne, cigar, overseas jaunt and Rolls Royce life style".***

Many franchisees and investors were lulled into a false sense of security by representations made by Taylor suggesting that **he himself had risked £350,000 on the venture.**

When the USA master franchisor got sound of this they sent Taylor a letter noting that he had no such financial arrangement. All he was supposed to be doing was marketing the concept on a results basis.

Face The Facts highlighted that ***receiver Philip Long*** took the view that claims that the non-existent master franchise should be included in assets was a *"gross misrepresentation"* based purely on a directors subjective valuation of a payment which had not taken place.

West Coast Video - U K was bought out of receivership by a subsidiary of Goodmans Plc. People who had paid non-refundable deposits still lost out - to the tune of £80,000.

"For people who know they can earn £100,000 p.a., this is the opportunity of a lifetime"

Principal Conservatories described itself as:

.."probably the fastest growing and most dynamic in the business".

The company offered among other things:

no franchise fee
.genuine gross earnings of: £150,000 pa
.full training - plus marketing support
.low admin
.30% commission on all orders
.no hidden cost

The real picture couldn't have been more different.

The company went into **liquidation on 19th November 1989** leaving **debts reported in the region of £200,000.** At that time there were around seven franchisees. A further ten franchisees had already fallen by the wayside.

Franchisees lost as much as **£100,000.**

One franchisee **Dean Sims** told me ***"I am £100,000 worse off than last year. I am now totally broke. It took me 6 months and all this money to find that I had been conned".*** He took up a bank reference which was ***"non-descript".*** Months after he started trading he realized the problems that existed and started writing to the franchisor.

Indeed up **until 2 weeks prior to the liquidation** the company had been advertising in the Business to Business section of the Sunday Times and was sending out dozens of franchise packs to interested applicants.

Weren't the franchisor directors aware that they were in financial straits?

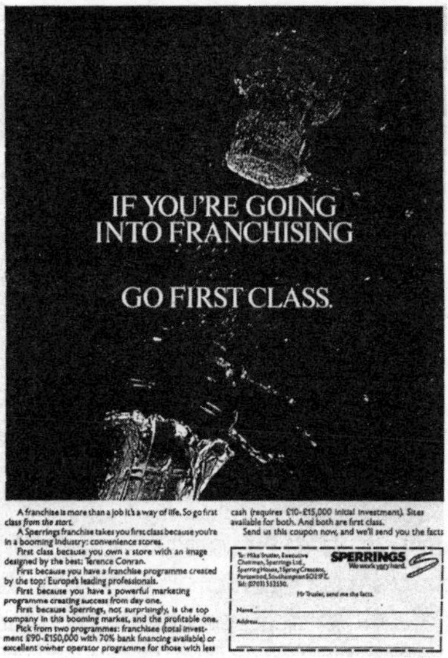

Sperrings

advertising read

"If you're going into Franchising GO FIRST CLASS".

But thats not what a number of franchisees felt in **October 1986** when they spoke to **"Super Marketing"** in an article headed "Sperrings takes a knock".

Sperrings is a convenience food store chain. The chain admitted in **October 1986** to The Times newspaper that it had lost 9 out of 18 franchisees and was in the process of losing another.

Apparently the first indication that not all was jolly was in an interview with a franchisee **Dave Rubins in January 1986 in Super Marketing** in which he said he had ***lost £7,000 in 12 months of running one of the first franchises in Portsmouth.*** The criticisms he raised were corroborated by a number of other franchisees who had followed a similar pattern to Mr Rubins.

The main complaints were:

1) That the initial **projections** were "too optimistic" or "disgraceful".

2) That the **net margin of 25%** stated by **David Saunders** (Sperrings MD) was misleading and that while stores might make this in the beginnng, the usual trend was for sales of high margin lines to tail off and sales of low margin lines (groceries, cigarettes and alcohol) to rise.

3) That there were **similar projections given for disimilar stores.**

4) The **5%** franchisee fee was too high for a business which often had a ***net margin of only about 20%.***

5) The **10% rent** charged as a management fee was unecessary and too high.

6) The cost of Sperrings **stationery** was too high.

7) The cost of a Sperrings franchise - **£90k - £100K** was too high compared to other convenience stores which only cost about £20k.

8) Sperrings **underplayed costs** and staff budgets were usually low and wastage allowances for a year could be used up within months.

9) Dave Rubins in particular complained that he had **little back-up support** and advice from the franchisor. This was backed by similar comments from other franchisees.

10) Another franchisee complained that the company tried to lift sales by adopting a policy of **cutting the price** of basic food like bread and milk. The problem was unresolved because all that happened was that sales of low margin products rose and this resulted in reducing the net margin further.

11) **The Shops Act 1950** didn't seem to help either. One franchisee- **Janice Davis** who had the franchise in Orpington Kent commented that ***"Sperrings advertises one of its merits as site selection. But they ommited to tell me that the local authority in Bromley strictly enforces the Shops Act".***

Charges were brought against her in **May 1985**. As Sperrings the franchisor was not the occupier of the premises they could not be held responsible. Mrs Davis **could have faced fines of £26,000** but an understanding magistrate let her off on the undertaking that no more illegal trading took place.

Consequently certain foods could not be sold. The whole thing was a disaster and yet Mrs Davis still had to continue paying the full franchise fee. In the financial year to June 1985 she made a **net loss of £20k** and in that same year **paid net franchise fees of over £28k.**

Sperrings was admitted to **full membership of the BFA in 1984 only 4 or 5 months after it took on its first franchisee. Tony Dutfield** director of the BFA told Super Marketing that the BFA can exercise ***"discretion"*** in this matter, and this happened in Sperrings case. It was awarded full membership ***"because of the nature of the company" he said, "But this is not likely to happen in the future".***
According to Mr Dutfield once accepted to full membership, companies could be expelled if there had been a **breach of the "code of ethics" and if such a breach had been substantiated in court.**

However, the cost of litigation is often too high for franchisees to take on.

Mrs Davis had to pay £12k in legal bills alone.

The BFA felt that blame for most failures should be laid at the door of franchisees. In a Times article on October 11th 1986 he said failure was ***"more often the franchisees fault. Often they do not research a franchise enough".***

In answer to the critisism of Sperrings, **Bob Sperring chairman of Sperrings,** said that the allegations from former franchisees were unrepresentative - ***"some are clearly wrong, and others just too broad generalisations, and others are out of date".***

Success Story

John Tonks, 39, previously in the air force, moved into retailing by joining **Marks and Spencers.** He spent 9 years there, five of which were as an assistant manager and then moved to Tie Rack in 1983 as an area manager.

John Tonks
Franchisee Tie Rack

Sophie Mirman (of Sock Shop fame) was just leaving Tie Rack when John joined. John felt that Tie Rack had enormous potential and over the next couple of years he together with three other area managers built up the chain from about 11 shops to 25 shops.

He was then raised to the position of **Tie Rack MD**, prestigious as it sounds, he confided ***"I was really MD only in name. If fact I was Roy Bishko's side-kick. Roy was demanding, tenacious and very exacting. I was responsible for anything and everything. It was very stimulating and I learnt a lot. It was difficult controlling smaller units and the company decided to franchise in order to get more motivated individuals running the business. I decided that I would prefer to run my own business and become a franchisee".***

John took over the Waterloo shop as a franchise. It had previously been a company shop. Within 6 months the takings went up by 45%. He then took over another company shop - Euston. At that time he paid £25,000 for each shop including the stock on a royalty structure of 22.5% of turnover which covered all his outgoings.

He expanded further by setting up mobiles at Euston (which later ceased trading because of redevelopment) and Waterloo. Each unit cost £10,000.

Karl Gibbons, another Tie Rack franchisee who had the Oxford Street and Regent Street units, decided to sell out and set up another franchise (see case study Flash Trash). John bought these two franchises for £100,000. At this stage he decided to take on a partner, Gareth Lloyd Jones, to assist him.

All the shops have a turnover of about **£2 million per annum.**

Asked about profit, John says ***"a well run shop performing according to plan should make a profit of about 10% of the turnover. Overheads for running a group of shops is higher and therefore the profit is reduced".***

Like any business, John admits to teething problems. Tie Rack, like any business, had problems in the beginning in terms of providing franchisees with support but these have now been ironed out. The most important ingredient of success is communication and support especially to a franchisee that is inexperienced.

He feels that the qualities of a good franchisee are firstly total commitment to the business and secondly an understanding and knowledge of the business.

Tie Rack does not have a **franchisee association** as yet, unlike a number of other franchisors like Prontaprint, Kall Kwik and McDonald's. However, in an interview with **Roy Bishko**, he said that he had no objections to franchisees setting one up and John feels that such an association would be good providing it was used to benefit both the franchisor and franchisee - ***"the parties in a franchised business must work hand in glove and although the contract is necessary legally it should be the spirit of the contract that is observed. If the franchisor is dictatorial without reference to the franchisee then he will achieve nothing."***

While John has had an ideal retailing background which has contributed to his success in Tie Rack - hard work - a seven day a week, twelve hours a day routine has been the price that he has had to pay for that success. Now, he is busier than ever seeing that each unit is run efficiently and in keeping with the National Tie Rack image of bright happy shops which are a pleasure for the customer to shop in.

ROY BISHKO'S GOLDEN RULES FOR CUSTOMER CARE AND ATTENTION

- Make eye contact in first 30 seconds - Smile with your eyes!

- Acknowledge customers warmly - like friends visiting your home.

- Help customers enjoy themselves. Everyone likes to have fun. Create a happy atmosphere! Demonstrate the products! Play the right music - rock is out, romance is in!

- Treat customers as you'd like to be treated yourself. Be polite, thank customers and invite them back.

- Always remember: The object is to sell <u>and</u> make people happy. Yourself included!!

"The most consistent fault I have seen in our shops is the haunting spectre of a Team Member, hypnotically tidying, restocking, folding hanks, fiddling with bows etc., blissfully unaware of customers, with eyes down, instead of being alert, aware and available to greet, smile and do business".

Roy Bishko 1989

"I always like these shops. They have such smashing cheerful colours".

Princess Diana at the Tie Rack shop in Harrow.

"When we create the right atmosphere in our shops with life, colour, music, a touch of excitement, an element of showbusiness - that's the magic of Tie Rack.

Roy Bishko 1989

TieRack

Franchisor experiments at franchisees expense....

On **Friday November 15th 1985** the **Young's Franchise Group** went into receivership. Ten days later it was bought out of receivership by **Cyril Spencer of the Burton Group for £1.5 million.**

Edward Young - ***The natural progression from bride to mother-to-be cost him his business and left franchising with a legacy of adverse publicity and a question mark over the ability of franchisors to diversify.***

The Young's Franchise Group consisted of **Pronuptia** (bridal wear), **Young's Formal Mens wear** and **La Mama** (maternity wear).

La Mama was a relatively new addition to the group. **23 La Mama franchisees** had taken on the investment over the previous couple of years reassured by the willingness of the banks to lend money, the fact that La Mama was a **full member of the BFA** and the apparently impeccable reputation of the franchisor management - **Mr Edward Young a founder of the BFA and Mr Lawrence Lewin** who had considerable retail experience in Canada.

Just months before the receivership a number of franchises were sold to the unsuspecting public. Existing franchisees that had problems with stock kept quiet - probably in the genuine hope that as more franchisees joined their overall situation would improve.

New franchisees could not have detected at that stage the financial difficulties the company was experiencing. Indeed, they could only be encouraged -

because 14 months earlier even the **British Rail Pension Fund had invested £750,000** of railwaymen's pension contributions in Youngs to acquire a 17% interest. This entire amount was also lost when Youngs went into receivership.

By March 1985 franchisees were complaining about poor stock, and inadequate quality control. Some had only been open for a few weeks, but were already realizing that they had been sold one thing and given another.

By November 1985 negotiations to rescue the Youngs Group broke down and **Barclays Bank** (the franchisor's bank) pulled out. Youngs then called in the receiver.

This was the first time franchisees were told of the severity of the company's financial problems.

Barclays Bank were heavily criticised by many including the British Rail Pension Fund and **Cyril Spencer who bought the group out from receivership**, as being "inflexible" especially as the livelihoods of many franchisees depended on the company. Once the franchise was bought out of receivership most of the £1.5 million realized went to Barclays.

After several months in action Mr Spencer the new owner of the Youngs Group declared the La Mama limb of the franchise unviable. Over this period several La Mama franchisees had already shut down because of losses. In any event only 3 of the 20 La Mama franchises had been viable.

Nearly all the La Mama fanchisees lost in the region of £10-£60k. But the price some paid was even higher that that. Homes had to be sold to pay off debts. A low risk business option turned out to be a nightmare.

And why?

1) Firstly, because the maternity clothes market was **not researched properly** in the UK, although Edward Young had personally represented that Young's had conducted detailed market research.

2) **Money was lent too easily** because most of the banks were star struck by the credentials of the likes of Edward Young and the BFA saw fit to apply their rules to others but not Mr Young. And ultimately, the franchisor's own bank got cold feet and pulled the plug. It saved their skin but sacrificed the franchisees who had had to rely on the professionalism and ethics of those involved.

3) The tragedy of the situation was overwhelming. The Times investigation revealed that La Mama should not even have been a **full member of the BFA**. It had been **let in through the back door** because Edward Young was a "friend" and a founder of the BFA. Nearly every La Mama franchisee had relied on the fact that La Mama had fulfilled the BFA criteria and thereby was a proven concept.

In an interview with a Times reporter in 1986 BFA director **Tony Dutfield** (retired 1989) stated that he was not sure what criteria for membership the BFA used in 1983 (when La Mama was admitted) but in any event no accounts for La Mama were sent to the BFA. Asked why La Mama leapfrogged registration into full membership he replied ***"Edward Yound had a very high exposure. He was an ex-chairman of the BFA. It may well be that his views held undue sway at that time, I don't know".***

4) By not checking their investments even The British Rail Pension Board inspired the public with confidence in the franchise. Certainly the franchisor made a big play on it with an attitude of ***"look here, invest in us, we're approved by everyone, the BFA, the BRB....." it all seemed to stack up.....***

5) There was a **poor management structure**. The franchisors motto appeared to be ***"Nepotism rules OK?"*** Alas, franchisees didn't have a choice.

6) It was rumoured Mr Edward Young was rather fond of his Roller. At any rate he liked expensive chaufffer driven cars . A luxury that the company could ill afford at the time.

After the receivership Mr Edward Young disappeared to Spain and Mr Lewin to Canada.

Franchisees were left with their enormous losses, and no means to pursue an action - especially when Young and Lewin were abroad.

One franchisee who had gone into the business so that she could earn enough money to put into a trust fund for a handicapped child ended up having to sell the very house that had been adapted for the handicapped child and working to pay off the bank loan ... Meanwhile rumours came back to London that Young was posing as a fashionable tax exile in Spain...

The morality of such goings on makes one wonder what conscience, if any, such franchisors have.

Howard, Henry and Peter Young went into a business called" Young Occasions" trading as Peter Shegara and importing wedding dresses from Asia. Surprise, surprise this went into liqudation too.

Comment

This case is a clear illustration that you should not believe anything you are told about anybody - no matter how good their credentials are.

Big institutions who invest in franchise operations also get their hands burnt so don't be impressed by them .

Food For Thought In Franchising

McDonald's "Big Mac"

Burger King's "whopper"

Just as **McDonald's "Big Mac"** has become a household name for a filling quick meal so has **Burger King's "whopper"**. Last year Burger King served up 670 million whoppers.

In **December 1988 the Pillsbury Company** including Burger King Corporation was acquired by **Grand Metropolitan PLC for $5.79 billion.**

Grandmet has many food interests and owns 5000 pubs and restaurants, including Berni Inns and Chef & Brewer. And on **October 2nd 1989** they acquired **UB Restaurants for £180 million** which included **Wimpy, Pizzaland and Perfect Pizza**.

Burger King decided that the 160 Wimpy Counter service units should be converted into Burger King units. The table service restaurants were to remain "Wimpy" and the company would continue to support them.

However, Max Wolfenden former Managing Director of Wimpy headed a management buy-out of the table service Wimpy franchised network consisting of a network of 216 units (190 franchisees) in the UK and 140 overseas in 18 countries. It is believed that £20 million was paid for the units to include the trade mark "Wimpy", the franchise contracts and head leases. Wimpy intend to continue franchising in the future. The start up cost of a typical outlet will be about £200,000.

Burger King

Burger King is part of Grand Metropolitan PLC. It was founded in 1954 in Miami, Florida, by James McLamore and David Edgerton.

Now, the second largest fast food hamburger chain Burger King has locations in 33 countries around the world.

Burger King employs approximately 250,000 people in nearly 6000 locations worldwide.

The Whopper

was an instant hit when introduced in 1957 and next to McDonalds Big Mac is one of the best known hamburgers in the world. 670 million whoppers are sold annually.

Franchising

There's no doubt that the chain has achieved quicker growth by the sale of franchised restaurants. By 1961 McLamore and Edgerton had acquired national franchise rights to the company which was then operating 45 restaurants throughout Florida and the Southeast of the United States.

Training

was recognised very early as a key ingredient to success and the "Whopper College" now known as Burger King University was established in 1964 in Miami.

Eating In

Burger King was the first fast food restaurant to introduce Dining rooms for customers so that they had a choice of eating inside.

In 1975 they extended services for customers "on-the-go" by providing a Drive Thru service.

Table service and Drive Thru are now a fairly common feature of large fast food restaurants

"Franchising Burgers"

While the burger chains have grown successfully via the franchising route no specific method has been employed.

The franchising "formula" for McDonalds and Burger King couldn't be more different.

Burger King - employ the more traditional formula where a franchise fee is payable together with a deposit of about 10% of the overall cost of the outlet. Once trading commences a Royalty of 4% of Gross Sales and a further 4% of Gross Sales for advertising is payable.

Compare this with **McDonald's** where the franchisee pays 40% of the purchase price in cash. Then, typically, a royalty of 24% on turnover which includes the service fee, advertising and major outgoings such as rental of the premises.

In 1989 McDonald's Corporation announced annual sales up to $16 billion. The Moscow Big Mac serves about 15,000 people a day.

McDonald's company owned stores tend to perform better that franchised units probably because the company retains better store locations. This is common in any franchise situation. While 'franchising" is the route to quick expansion it is inevitable that there will be some degree of competition between company and franchise units. The balance of competition is one of the keys to success. Unlike some franchises McDonald's can give franchisees a trademark second to none so that even secondary sites will achieve a good profitability level. Unfortunately not many franchises enjoy this privilege - site selection is crucial. Streetwise Franchising has negotiated in a number of cases where the sole cause for complaint was that the site just didn't bring in the customers.

The burger big boys, McDonald's and Burger King owe much of their success to successful advertising campaigns. While McDonald's has put particular stress in attracting children via the use of the **Ronald McDonald clown** and donating to children charities, Burger King has recently announced that it intends to **"break the rules"** and be unconventional in its marketing policy. Their new advertising campaign will be under the slogan **"Sometimes You've Gotta Break The Rules".**

Traditionally franchising has always been regarded as a distribution option designed to give the customer a reliable uniform product or service nationwide. Burger King, however are taking the view that they thrive on individuality. Another example of this can be seen with the Holiday Inn where each hotel is custom made to the surroundings. The uniformity aspect only comes in so far as quality of service.

Burger King are not alone in "Breaking the rules: - Big Mac have pre-empted this stance in the **New York McDonalds** outlet which comes complete with atrium, doorman, pianist, espresso and cappucino coffee and cakes.

The Wall Street Journal stated that during the Pillsbury days, a Burger King visit was unpredictable - sometimes it was sparkling clean - and sometimes not. Burger King have certainly taken any criticism to heart and now managers check sanitary facilities every 15 minutes. During very busy periods workers are supposed to wash their hands every hour in a steriliser.

Individuality is becoming a fashionable trend in franchising. And about time too. However, that is not to say it will always be right. A vital part of any franchise system should always be that the customer can expect a quality product or service. So while individuality might draw in customers a franchisor will have to ensure it is not at the expense of quality and a consistently good service.

At the end of the day it is McDonald's that have become famous for the **"QSCV" formula - (quality, service, cleanliness and value formula).** And fame has come not just from the hamburgers but from the considerable charity work carried out. McDonald's has established about 100 Ronald McDonald houses (a building near a hospital where parents and relatives of seriously ill children can stay) all around the world.

The Ronald McDonald Childrens Charity (RMCC) had been set up in the United States and the UK. Last year on McHappy Day (7th October) every McDonald's store in the UK donated 50% of the takings on Big Mac sales to RMCC, plus all contributions collected in special boxes. The Big Mac sales alone raised a quarter of a million pounds.

McDonald's encourages franchisee's and company shops to take the attitude that it is important to give something back to the community.

Without doubt this attitude is the most encouraging feature of franchising today. It's a pity that more franchises and businessmen cannot learn from this approach.

Kentucky Fried Chicken Wins

Finger Lick'n Fight

Colonel Sanders: built multi-million dollar empire

Kentucky Fried Chicken has become somewhat of a **"success legend"** so far as franchising is concerned - but even this franchising old hand has experienced and learnt from problems over the last few years.

Colonel Sanders started off selling his delectable quick cook chicken from his petrol station in Kentucky USA. The chicken recipe of 11 herbs and spices has become a familiar taste throughout the world.

In **1965 Kentucky Fried Chicken (G.B.) Limited** was formed. Marketed under the slogan ***"Finger lickin good"***. Colonel Sanders sold out in **1964 for about $2 million** and in **1986 Pepsi Cola** bought Kentucky Fried Chicken from a USA conglomerate for **£467 million.**

Some Kentucky Fried Chicken outlets in the UK had seats but most were take-aways located off the high street attracting a late night clientele. Most outlets were franchised and apparently because of the lack of supervision of purchasing policies there was a variation in quality of the product in the different units. At this time fast food operators in the UKsuch as McDonald's were not franchising and instead keeping a tight control over their product quality.

Mr Steven Fellingham president of Kentucky Fried Chicken's International operations, was quoted in the **Financial Times** as saying:

"the weaknesses in our system started to show with the entry of new competition which raised standards and increased consumer expectations".

Kentucky Fried Chicken started showing a **downward trend in their turnover in 1978.** The company tried to boost sales by launching an advertising campaign in 1983 and while this succeeded temporarily most new customers failed to make repeat purchases. The situation became more **critical by 1984**. The company blamed the imposition of VAT on hot take-away meals. But there was more to it than that. According to the Financial Times the company's own market research carried out two years before showed that Kentucky Fried Chicken UK was in trouble. Further, that compared to other fast food competitors such as McDonald's and Wimpy the public perceived it as ***"bottom"*** on issues of quality, service and value for money.

This poor image of Kentucky Fried Chicken existed in 50 countries in which it operated. Not surprisingly the company was shell shocked. As assessment panel was set up to identify weakness and to suggest solutions. Some franchisees disagreed with Kentucky Fried Chicken on quality control and deficiencies and two licences were cancelled after litigation.

By **1986 disputes** over closures of franchise units were common with the chain as were headlines such as ***"Finger-lickin-fight".***

The Kentucky Fried Chicken Franchise Association presidented by **Harry Latham** (who had bought the British rights from Kentucky Fried Chicken's founder Colonel Sanders in 1965) claimed that it represented more than 260 of the 320 British outlets and that a the personal investment of franchisees to the tune of £40 million was in serious jeopardy.

They claimed that at least **60 franchised outlets had been closed in six months** and that because the company had introduced a policy of making that franchise units into a restaurant-type chain there could be closures of another 200. The company denied this but did state that they were closing some units to improve standards. Others would be relocated to better sites.

Franchised units that had their contracts terminated continued trading under different names. Thus, Kentucky Fried Chicken shops in Scotland continued under the name ***"Mississippi Fried Chicken"***. Others started to operate as ***"Dixie Fried Chicken"*** or ***"Favourite Fried Chicken"***.

In **December 1986 Trusthouse Forte**, the hotel and catering group took a 50% stake in Kentucky Fried Chicken UK in order to get into the high street fast food market quickly.

Kentucky Fried Chicken has since altered its ***"poor value for money image"*** by offering larger chicken portions as well as special ***"family"*** and ***"lunch"*** promotions. They aimed at a cost of less than £1/head and introduced ***"bargain buckets"*** and a chicken sandwich.

The company also effected changes in the appearance of the shops and staff by introducing new shop livery and uniforms, menu cards for the windows and more efficient equipment so that the serving time was reduced to one minute per order. Additionally a big advertising campaign was launched to relate the changes to the public.

The author approached Kentucky Fried Chicken over the last several months in order to discuss the ***"problems"*** they had experienced and the lessons they had learnt. Kentucky Fried Chicken were very sensitive and declined to release any information about their past or present experiences.

However, there is little doubt that Kentucky Fried Chicken's problems lay in a neglect of quality and value control. Once those were rectified the image of the chain improved. It is to be hoped that the improvements are permanent.

"Franchise Opt outs"

Franchising has never been and never will be the easy option to quick business expansion. Its an option that can work spectacularly well but at the same time can be doomed to failure.

There are a number of big names in business that have tried the franchise route only to give up.

Holland & Barrett Health Food Stores

started franchising in 1982 when they already had about 150 company shops. They built up the franchised chain to 23 units and then decided to stop franchising. They adopted a policy of buying back the franchised shops at market value.

Why didn't franchising work for them?

Because the **"health products market"** became extremely competitive, with the big supermarkets moving in, the franchisor found that in order to keep up with the competitors decisions had to be made quickly. This was not possible in a franchised network where franchisee's had to be consulted and given time to make their own decisions.

Furthermore, stores needed refurbishment at least every five years and franchisees could not afford this. This resulted in the chain having stores of different standards and appearance which in itself did not favour a uniform quality franchised network.

The management also found that they had underestimated the cost of supporting a franchised network.

Franchisee selection was very difficult and despite close scrutiny franchisee's still resented paying a franchise fee once they had learned the tricks of the trade.

"Clean-up with Sketchley franchise wise"

Earlier this year the **Guardian** wrote **"it would be difficult to find a company which has had so many false dawns as Sketchley."**

Sketchley had not only decided not to continue franchising but has spent about 20 years trying to diversify into other businesses than dry cleaning without any success.

In 1975 they tried to diversify into jersey knitting only to **lose £244,000**. In **1981** their chairman, **Gerald Wightman**, admitted their investment in a greasing equipment distributor had been a mistake. The purchase had cost them £200,000 and they lost £2 million.

The early 80's saw expansion into the USA and Canada. By 1985 the company decided it would have to sell most of them.

Franchising

Sketchley decided to leap in and franchise. Their brochure stated ***"using our name, knowledge and experience gained from operating successfully in 500 of our own outlets you can now own and operate your own dry cleaning and shoe repair business". They further wrote of "the Sketchley success story (which) started in 1985 .....(and their).....100 years experience in the industry".***

The franchise cost was stated as being **£77,000** and the company suggested this should be financed by £25,000 cash and £52,000 medium term loan and overdraft facility.

The Proforma profit and loss account projections in 1987, stated that the figures had been prepared **"carefully, honestly and expertly"** and were based on average shops. The figures predicted in

	Year1	Year 2	Year 3
Sales	86,000	98,000	110,000
net profit before deducting interest and salary	17,020	21,755	27,065

Some franchisee's claim that they were told that in **eighteen months of starting to franchise there would be at least 200 franchised outlets.**

Indeed even **Derek Harris, commercial editor of the Times** wrote ***"with the cleaning chain contributing nearly half of Sketchley groups pretax profits - £10.8 million for the group last time - the chain stands to net in royalties from a likely 100 franchised outlets of about £1.2 milllion annually on today's prices. Of that 40% would be ploughed back into promotion leaving the chain with a clear £720,000".***

Needless to say things didn't work out as planned. Instead of the anticipated 200 franchised shops **only 11 were opened, 5 of which were later bought back** by the company, four franchisee's are still trading and one had three outlets. One franchisee complained that he was only achieving about 25% of his projections. After 4 years he was achieving his first year target.

He blamed the poor sales performance to lack of support from the franchisor and inadequate advertising compared to competitors like Johnstons who had a very powerful marketing strategy.

Mr Gudger, MD of Sketchley, took the decision **not to continue franchising in 1987**. He felt that franchising wasn't right for them because ***"it needed one hell of a lot of management. It took up a lot of time and effort especially in an area where the company was not well known".***

"We had successful and unsuccessful franchisees. Therefore on average it was the same as our company shops - of which we have 517 nationwide. Franchisee selection was difficult and we made some errors. However we are not anti-franchising and may revert to it in the future. In the cleaning industry service is all important and therefore franchising can be ideal. The problem lies in the fact that the layman thinks franchising is an easy option because the company doesn't need its own money. That is a fallacy. You do need to make an investment. The investment commitment was not a problem for Sketchley; the main issue was management time".

"MARLEY PAVING"

"There's no comparison"

Marley PLC is an International Group, the name being synonymous with Roofing and Flooring over several decades. Through subsidiary companies the group also manufactures Bricks, Paving and Concrete.

Paving products were introduced in 1978 and by 1986 Marley became one of the largest manufacturers of the product in the country.

On their **"Franchise Prospectus"** Marley wrote of franchising as a ***successful business expansion method and that their "development of franchising has been in accordance with the guidelines established by the British Franchise Association".***

The franchise prospectus further stated that Marley offered ***"Security...........Your contract with us gives you a licence for six years, with the option to continue for further periods of six years indefinitely, with the support of Marley Paving". Other hand-outs stated that the company policy was to "expand the domestic market to a network of franchisee's throughout the country".***

Franchisee's eager to start trading under the banner of a big name, which also led them to believe there would be a nationwide network of Marley Paving, franchisees paid an initial franchise fee of approximately up to £6,000 depending on when they joined.

At least one franchisee claimed that Marley Paving led him to believe that they would have 75 franchisee's by the end of 1989 and that if he had known at the time that this would not be the case he would not have taken the franchise.

In October 1989 Marley Paving decided that the franchise operation was not profitable and stopped recruitment at 17 franchisee's. In November 1989 they wrote to franchisee's stating **:**

"we have decided not to expand the existing franchise network in the foreseeable future...............Our experience in the first year of operation has shown that the franchise business units can be successfully launched and established but that the support level required in that first year is particularly high. By limiting the number of franchise areas since February of this year we have met that requirement during 1989 and a further expansion of the franchise network would affect our ability to continue this".

According to Marley the agreement between them and their franchisees had not altered by the fact that they had decided not to take on further licensees. But is this right? Surely representations that there would be a nationwide franchise network is a substantial inducement for any potential franchisee.

A number of franchisees have decided to continue trading in the paving business outside the franchise, and the franchisor has agreed to waive any breaches of the restraint of trade clause that this might cause. However, some franchisees have requested the return of their franchise fee. The franchisor has refused to return this. Some franchisee's are obtaining legal advice with a view to pursuing their cases in court.In an interview with the author Mike Roberts, MD of Marley, stated that the actual cost of the initial launch was much higher than they had originally anticipated and that the initial fee that was charged was not enough to cover costs. Consequently initially the company made losses: if they had charged much higher fees then the franchise concept may well have worked but then the business proposition would not have been so attractive. Three out of the seventeen franchisee's had decided to go their own way. Fourteen were still trading as franchisees and paying royalties.

Streetwise Franchising is aware that at least one of these franchisee's is not paying royalties and is considering legal action against Marley Paving.

Comment

If a company carries out adequate research and carefully plans a franchise strategy then costings should not be so way out that the business makes such horrendous losses that the whole concept is implausible from day one.

In any company expansion may not be as quick as anticipated. However, while franchisees can be expected to understand this, should they be expected to carry the cost of being little more than guinea pigs, especially when this results in their investment in an opportunity that turns out to be different from what they were led to believe. In such a situation shouldn't franchisee be compensated for the fact that they got it all wrong?

There are many franchisors who do think that franchising is an easy option that can be set up over night. They do exactly that and make money from the front end fees rather than franchising. Potential franchisees should be very wary of a franchisor who has not invested significantly in the business and who does not have enough staff to handle franchisee problems and administration. There should be separate staff for franchisees.

In order to set up a franchise system properly ie, have a proper contract, financial planning and market research pilots, of which there should be at least three in totally different areas could cost a few thousand pounds to hundreds of thousands depending on the type of franchise.

If the franchisor hasn't done his homework, you shouldn't take up the franchise.

As far as Sketchley are concerned it was not possible to talk to the people who had actually taken the decision to franchise but its quite clear from Mr Gudger's remarks that they were not aware how draining franchising would be on the time of their management. That leads to the inevitable conclusion that the company could not have carried out sufficient analysis of the franchising concept and its demands on them, or indeed the rigours of franchisee selection.

10

Insider Lessons

Most unsuccessful franchisors should never have franchised in the first place. They are undercapitalised and are trying to play the **"OPM" (other peoples money) game.** They are usually trying to flog an unproven system. Their trade name is more than likely unknown. Often high franchise fees are charged. In such cases a franchisee is just a guinea pig.

Setting up a franchise properly is an expensive business. In a typical case the immediate costs that could be incurred (excluding the costs of the pilot unit) are:-

Professional fees Solicitor/consultant.		**20,000**
Establishing a Corporate identity logos, prospectus		**10,000**
Preparation of Operating Manual Research Training facilities and Operations		**15,000**
Advertising for initial franchisees	**say**	**5,000**
TOTAL		**£50,000**

Obviously all these costs will vary dramatically depending on the type of business - setting up a restaurant is going to cost infinitely more than a car valeting franchise.

Potential franchisees should be wary of any franchisor who hasn't given this type of financial input into the system. Seriously ask can he provide the services he is supposed to?

Potential franchisors should think twice about franchising if they can't commit such funds or indeed if they can't dedicate enough man hours to assist franchisees.

There are many important lessons that can be learnt from the case studies :

Market Research

Extensive MR must be carried out not only before starting up the franchise - to ensure there is a market for it but to make sure franchisees will have enough business. As a potential franchisee you should see a MR Report which should include:-

1) Research from local government departments, population size, split into categories.
2) Research according to telephone areas.
3) Competition in the area - specified plus comments.

The Business set-up

Potential franchisees should look out for signs of overtrading and overgearing . **(Data Maid)**. Is the franchisor paying creditors on time (**Principal Conservatories**) Is the franchisor over extravagant - remember **Curtain Dream** where franchisees complained the ***"ordinary car was the BMW".***

Management Structure

The roles of management should be clear and franchisees should be provided with CV'S. Look out for too much "nepotism" - as in **La Mama**. Can they really do the job?

Franchise Selection

Every franchisor I met at some time or other complained about their franchisee selection procedures. Absolutely nobody had got it 100% right. Procedures varied from taking anyone who had the money to franchisees sitting a test.

Athena's Ken Beecroft, at a conference in Birmingham, stated how they had a ***"franchisees select themselves"*** procedure. So, providing franchisees met the financial criteria then it was up to them - could they be bothered to go to Birmingham for a meeting? How long did the meetings last? If it lasted less than an hour the potential franchisee stood little chance of success. If the meeting lasted nearer to 2 hours and the potential franchise was asking intelligent questions then he was half way there.

Grandmet Franchise & Development Manager Mike Cook said that ***"as a typical Burger King restaurant cost £600,000 +, most applying could raise that kind of money, they had to be pretty good businessmen in the first place".***

After that it was down to personality and committment to the work ethic.

One of the most vigorous vetting procedure is carried out by **Kall Kwik printing.** Applicants are invited in and firstly have to do an 8 minute "American personality assessment" test. A few of the KK managers have been trained to interpret the test. They claim that the test is 85% accurate. The test is used in conjunction with assessment by different recruitment managers - at the 1st and 2nd meeting. This brings in objectivity and allows managers to discuss borderline cases.

Andrew Quail MD of KK claimed that the test together with their own assessment gave them a success rate of about **91%.**

Training

This too came top on the complaints list. Franchisees in most cases had totally inadequate training.

Some franchisors provided a 2 hour training programme. Some didn't bother with providing an **operating manual**. Manuals have been a constant source of amusement - in one case the franchisors "secret method" consisted of information you could have gleaned from W H Smiths. In another case the franchisor actually told my client how to "drive the van" but forgot other pertinent details relating to running the business. Having said that excellent operating manuals do exist - Kall Kwik have about 7 which relate to all aspects of the business.

Good franchisors are increasingly spending more time on the initial and ongoing training and arranging special courses for staff.

Promotions

Good effective advertising is essential for any business. Many of the good franchisors now state a percentage of turnover that a franchisee pays specifically into an advertising fund.

Kall Kwik require 4%. 2% is used for national advertising, and the other 2% for local. So when the franchisee spends money on local ads he can claim back the 2% he has paid into the company.

Many unsuccessful franchise operators not only spend money on the wrong type of advertising but fail to carry out sufficient market research into which publications are the best. Furthermore their ads are hyped to extremes.

An advertising royalty should be paid into a separate fund and a franchisee should be given the accounts for the fund.

Watch out for franchisors who charge exorbitant advertising royalties and yet seem to be doing nothing for the money.In particular ensure that the money is being spent on advertising and not for recruiting more franchisees.

Site Selection

Choosing good sites is one of the most difficult tasks of the franchisor. Good franchisors usually have a full time person looking for sites and liaising with market researchers as to the sites potential.

Everyone makes mistakes. Some of the best franchisors are open to admit they have made a wrong choice - but they are in a position to assist and if necessary buy out a franchisee who has relied on their advice.

Poor and unscrupulous operators never admit their mistakes.

In one case I dealt with the franchisor had bought a site. Their consultant told them the site would not perform well. The franchisor nevertheless franchised it by making up ficticious performance figures. The business did fail as the consultant had predicted.

A primary position may well not be necessary. But at the end of the day it always helps. Again, market research is crucial to establish whether the business can operate effectively from a secondary or tertiary site. One franchisee of ***Service Master*** operating from home with a number of vans carrying out **"contract cleaning"** work makes a turnover of quarter of a million and a healthy profit.

Communication Between Franchisor and Franchisees:

Good communication is necessary if the business is going to succeed. This could be facilitated be newsletters and regular meetings. Franchisees should have access to a hot line whereby problems can be dealt with quickly.

Bad franchisors pursue a **"divide and rule"** policy. This is essential when a business is doing badly because they can tell each individual franchisee that its their own fault.

Most franchisees wise up to the situation quickly and do talk to each other - often to find they all have problems. Given half a chance all franchisees want to form franchisee associations. How do franchisors react?

- Some have reservations but are open minded enough to see the good they can do.

- Others applaud FA's and see them as no threat.

- Some see them as big threats and cannot even understand why franchisees want their own association. Often they do everything to prevent the association forming. Some franchisees have been threatened that supplies will be witheld if a FA is set up. Others are told that they will be prosecuted for incitement or that its a breach of their contract. Most franchisees in loss making franchises are very vulnerable and intimidated by such threats. Franchisors who take this view are very short sighted.

FA's should be the norm,rather than having to be formed out of necessity to discuss problems they ought to be initiated by the franchisor from day one.

Setting Up A Franchise Association.

Many variations of a FA exist. One thing is clear they all form an important function in the promotion of ethical franchising. In the case of **Home Tune/Tune Up it was FAB - the Franchisee Association Board** that was responsible for starting up training and then voting to opt out of Home Tune. There was strength in numbers. Tune Up has grown with the background that franchise communication and participation is essential. Tune Up franchisees are shareholders of the franchised business.

Kall Kwik franchisees set up **IKKFOA - Independent Kall Kwik Franchise Owners Association** in 1980 shortly after the franchise started trading. It was set up to deal with the problems franchisees were experiencing with stock, supplies, training and so forth. **Ian Swan Chairman of IKKFOA** fondly reminisced how the KK management dissapproved at the time - primarily because the master franchisor Kwik Copy didn't have such an association for franchisees in the States.

IKKFOA is now a well established part of the franchise and plays an invaluable role. Even the KK management are convinced of its virtues - particularly because new franchises take advice better from an old successful franchisee than even the franchisor.

The constitution of IKKFOA is reproduced by kind permission of its members in Appendix 2

The following variations should be borne in mind when setting up a FA.

Formation	**The FA can be formed by the franchisor, franchisees or jointly.**
Members	**All franchisees should be members or encouraged to be members. The franchisor may/may not be represented. His role can be to chair meetings or limited to a small advisory role.**
Discussion	**All areas of concern and importance should be discussed. For example:- support and backup finances training territories supplies research and future development.**
Meetings	**Several during the year, probably divided into an annual meeting and regional meetings.**
Cost	**Usually these are shared.**
Organisation	**A chairman, treasurer and secretary should be elected.**
Constitution	**Its a good idea to have a constitution - see IKKFOA constitution.**

Summary of Franchise Problems and their Resolution

1) Franchisor not advised properly before business franchised.	1) No business should be franchised without the aid of expert franchise advice.
2) None/Inadequate Initial Market Research	2) Extensive independent market research is vital.
3) Business set up badly. Poor financial Controls overgeared - overtrading	3) There should be tight controls on how money is spent - not on extravagent cars. The franchisor should ensure there is a strong cash flow.
4) Poor/Inadequate management structure.	4) CV's of staff should be excellent and there should be guards against nepotism.
5) Poor franchisee selection by the franchisor.	5) A specific procedure should be used - see eg page 53 Kall Kwik. Several managers should be involved to ensure objectivity.
6) Poor Training	6) Intensive training of at least 2 weeks is necessary. The longer the better. Should include theory and practical training on the job.
7) Inadequate operating manual	7) The operating manual should be more than a few photocopies - it should answer all the franchisees questions. A franchisee should see this before signing the contract
8) Poor advertising and promotions	8) Know exactly what you are getting for your money.
9) Inadequate market research of areas taken by franchisees.	9) Indepth research is necessary before allowing franchisees to trade in any area to ensure they will generate enough business to achieve the expected profits.
10) Poor Site selection	10) A report should be prepared on a site and the franchisee should be involved as he may know a local area better than the franchisor.
11) Inadequate equipment package	11) Ensure that mark ups are not exorbitant. The franchisor should get you a better deal than you could get by yourself
12) Inadequate communication and ongoing advice.	12) Set up a Franchisee Association/ Newsletter etc and have regular meetings.
13) Inadequate ongoing training.	13) Ensure training is comprehensive.

Half the battle in choosing a good franchise is to know what can go wrong and then simply to avoid it. Its not as easy as it sounds. However, if the franchisor provides the information you need to make your decision you should have no problems.

If the infrastructure of the operation is set up correctly then communication between the franchisor and franchisees should be very strong and problems can be dealt with in the early stages.

If the franchisor fails to provide information or is evasive in any way treat it as a big black mark against him.

The success case stories show you how good franchises operate and you should settle for nothing less.

Remember that franchising is a good method of operating a business and that the bad franchisors are not doing what they should. In order to succeed you must be able to recognise the difference between what is a good opportunity and what is over optimistic hype. Unfortunately many people don't have the knack to do this and end up losing a lot of money.

While the author has much sympathy for those who are conned, most who choose the wrong franchise do so because they have carried out inadequate research or just been gullible. At the end of the day they have only themselves to blame. Adequate research and awareness of problems will not guarantee success but will certainly help you find it.

11

Doing Deals & Handling Litigation

It's not unusual that things go wrong in business, even in a franchise. Like a marriage, the concept is a delicate balance between each party's obligations. When either, or both parties fail to carry out these obligations, then litigation is inevitable.

Streetwise Franchising has made a big breakthrough in promoting negotiations between franchisor and franchisee. However, it is clear that there will always be franchisors who hide behind the comfort of litigation knowing :

1) that the franchisee contemplating litigation is usually broke, facing bankruptcy and risks losing his house.

2) that time is on the franchisor's side.

3) even if the franchisee does qualify for legal aid, most solicitors who have excellent franchise experience, don't touch legal aid work.

4) they, the franchisor can afford a top notch solicitor.

Franchisees identifying with any of the above may take comfort in knowing that when I was once in a similar position, a franchisor stated ***"you haven't got any money and besides, for every lawyer you can get, I can afford two".*** He was (and probably still is) a millionaire. While he could afford the best advice that money could buy, I had to content myself with a small local solicitor who would carry out legal work. I knew I had a good case. For a couple of years my life was obsessed with proving my case. There was so much paperwork I had to delegate a room in the house for it. I spent a week listing defective products. I had so much concrete evidence in my favour that they never let the case go to court. They settled. But it took two years of hard work, anxiety and stress.

The number of times when I handle cases for franchisees and they say ***"but you don't understand what we're going through".*** I do.

Doing Deals

Litigation should always be the last resort. The best way to deal with problems is to have a meeting with the franchisor in the presence of a third pary and thrash out all the grievances you both have.

It is a good idea to take minutes of the meeting and to agree and sign them although it is not vital. Alternatively you can confirm what was said at the meeting in a follow up letter.

The third party can be anybody - but its good to have a professional advisor. So, while there is the formality of someone professional being present there is the informality of a meeting outside court.

Its no point negotiating if either party is not prepared to be reasonable and understanding and positively helpful.

I carry out many negotiations on behalf of clients and it is of constant amazement to me that people can be totally unreasonable and abusive. Some meetings are like acrimonious divorce proceedings. In many cases the franchisor is completely non communicative.Exhaust the negotiation process before resorting to litigation.

Litigation

Litigation is costly, tedious and very time consuming. Don't expect results overnight.

Many franchisees panic because they don't understand what is going on.

The first thing to remember is that **having a good case is one thing and proving it is another.** No matter how wronged or conned you feel, it all comes down to proof. In addition, the franchisor may have legitimate grievances against you.. Assuming you have a good case which can be proved, you then need to look at the whole thing commercially. Does the franchisor have the financial means to assist you, buy back your franchise or return your franchise fee. If the franchisor is a man of straw or he is likely to go into receivership, then it's not worth throwing good money after bad. Also, take into account how much you are claiming. If it's only a small claim, is it worth it, bearing in mind the legal costs?

If it is worth pursuing the action, you should always try to negotiate amicably first. Ideally this should be done through a mediator who can look at the case objectively. Only if negotiations breakdown or the franchisor is unco-operative should you contemplate litigation.

Clients are always terribly confused about the process of law and, for example, what is an injunction, and will it affect them and so forth. Therefore, there follows a brief description of the basic steps you may encounter. A detailed discussion is outside the scope of this book and the author would stress that you don't need a more detailed account because your solicitor will be handling the case. However, this will assist you to understand what he is doing.

Counsels Opinion

Should be obtained before commencing litigation. Counsel's opinions cost varying amounts depending on seniority. Queen's Counsel will cost the most. Opinions can be obtained in the form of just a conference (which will be cheaper) or a conference followed by a written opinion. The cost of an opinion will range from about £300 - £1,000+. If you are covered by legal aid the opinion will be paid for, but whether or not legal aid is continued will depend on the opinion.

You will have to obtain counsel's opinion whether you are defending the action as defendant or bringing the action as plaintiff. The action is given a reference number before sealing by the court.

The Writ of Summons

High Court proceedings are usually begun by a writ. This is a document addressed to the defendent by the Crown giving him notice that an action has been commenced against him. The writ is prepared by the plaintiff's solicitor. The writ has to be acknowledged by the defendant.

When your solicitor has drafted the writ, two copies are taken to the Central Office (or district registry). One copy is signed by the plaintiff or his solicitor and given an official court stamp (sealed) and stamped (to show the fee has been paid) and filed at court. The other copy is also sealed.

Specially Endorsed Writ

A plaintiff who believes that the defendant has no defence and intends in due course to apply for summary judgement (i.e. an order proving him judgement on the basis that the defendent could not show even a prima facie defence) may well wish to serve his statement of claim at the same time as serving the writ. In such a case, instead of serving the Statement of Claim separately, it is put on the back of the writ instead of the general endorsement. A writ can be served on individuals, companies or firms. Service is not effected by the court. Your solicitor will send it to the defendants solicitor (if he knows who they are) or serve it personally or through the post.

Acknowledgement of the Writ

Must be within 14 days of service. If it isn't, the plaintiff may enter judgement in default of appearance. However, if such a judgement is not entered you can still enter an appearance late, notwithstanding that the 14 day period has expired.

In franchising cases it is highly unlikely that a writ is not acknowledged.

The next step is for the parties to set out their cases in writing in the form of formal pleadings. The purpose of these pleadings is:

1) to clarify the matters in dispute so that the court can understand what the real issues are.

2) to let each side know the allegations in advance so that no one is taken by surprise at the trial.

The basic pleadings required are the Statement of Claim and Defence.

STATEMENT OF CLAIM is set out by the plaintiff. In the High Court this should be done within 14 days of the acknowledgement, although in practice parties usually agree to extend this time period.

DEFENCE sets out the grounds upon which the defendant resists the plaintiff's claims in the High Court. The defence should be served within 14 days of the statement of claim.

COUNTERCLAIM a defendant may not just want to defend but also wish to bring a cross action against the plaintiff. A counterclaim is then added to the defence. The plaintiff must then, within 14 days, serve a defence to the counter-claim. If the defence raises a good answer to the plaintiffs claim and in order to succeed, the latter has to raise another matter in answer he will have to file a reply.

REQUEST FOR FURTHER AND BETTER PARTICULARS If the party upon whom the pleading has been served feels that it gives him insufficient information to answer the case or prepare his case for trial he can request further and better particulars.

AMENDMENTS It is better to think carefully as to what goes into the court or pleadings rather than amend later - which can be expensive.

Each party can make one set of amendments without obtaining leave.

The writ can be amended once at any time, upon the close of pleadings. However, once the writ has been served, if amending means changing the capacity in which a party sues or is sued, or adds a party, or adds a new cause of action, leave is required.

The pleadings can be amended once at any time up to close of pleadings by just giving the amended pleading to the other side. The other side is then automatically given 14 days to answer.

INJUNCTIONS A number of franchisees panic over injunctions. A typical scenario is that either their contract is terminated by the franchisor or they themselves decide to repudiate the agreement but continue to trade in the same franchise business. Thereby they are usually in breach of the **"restraint of trade clause".** If the clause is reasonable it will almost certainly be upheld by the court. The franchisor may then threaten to restrain the franchisee defendant from continuing the wrongful conduct by an injunction;

1) it's grant is discretionary and will be refused if damages are an adequate remedy. In franchise cases usually the franchisor will have to show that he is suffering damage to such a large extent - for example revelation and use of his secret know-how that damages would not be sufficient to compensate him.

2) failure to carry out the order is generally an imprisonable offence on the basis of contempt of court. In the case of injunctions the court faces the problem that it has to make a decision affecting the rights of the parties, but without a full investigation of the disputed issues. In the **American Cyanamid Case the House of Lords** held that in order for relief to be granted the plaintiff had to show

a) there was a serious question to be tried

and

b) once that was decided whether the balance of convenience lay in favour of granting or refusing interlocutory relief.

The courts approach appears to be to ask the following questions:

1) Has the plaintiff shown a serious question to be tried?

2) If so, has he shown that if the injunction is not granted he will sustain more than direct financial loss.

3) If the above two are satisfied and damages would adequately compensate the defendant, the injunction should be granted.

4) If damages will not compensate the defendant the court has to look at the balance of convenience between the parties . If all else is equal, the court should preserve the status quo.

UNDERTAKING AS TO DAMAGES

Where an injunction is granted, the courts usually extract from the applicant an undertaking to compensate the other party if it emerges at trial that the injunction should not have been granted.

EX PARTE INJUNCTIONS

Where there is an urgent need for an injunction and the applicant will suffer irreparable harm if he has to wait while notice of the application is served on the other side, the court can grant temporary orders on an ex parte application. This basically means that an injunction is granted without giving notice to the defendent.

The plaintiff presents the court with an affidavit as to the merits of his case and if he is successful the court issues an injunction for a short period. Over this period the plaintiff has to serve notice on the defendant of his intention to apply for a continuation of the injunction for trial.

It should be stressed that ex parte injunctions are for real cases of urgency. They can be, and have been, granted in franchise cases, although the author would question the urgency.

The defendant can have an injunction set aside, but unfortunately it can take a long time - and by that time if the defendent is a franchisee he may have lost all his customers.

INJUNCTION TO ASSIST EXECUTION

If, for example, you are a franchisee or franchisor and you have reason to believe that the defendent in the case might try to defeat any award by disposing of the assets, then an injunction can be granted to restrain their disposal,

This type of injunction is very rare in franchise cases.

REPRESENTATIVE ACTIONS

In some cases where a number of people have an interest in the proceedings, they can be joined as co-plaintiffs or co-defendants. The main reason for doing this is that they have a common interest and the relief claimed benefits them all.

In franchise cases a large number of franchisees may all have the same grievances. The usual course of action is that they pay money into a common fund and use all the evidence collectively while still bringing independent claims. The reason for doing this is because often they require different remedies.

Most franchise cases are based on misrepresentation, negligent mis-statements and straightforward breaches of the contract which can range from non-payment of fees to breaches of the restraint of trade clause.

The contract is extremely important for the protection of both franchisor and franchisee and therefore both parties should ensure they are safeguarded.

If you are involved in litigation ensure you have a solicitor who knows what he's doing. Even then be prepared for a long battle. And remember, if the franchisor is or could go into liquidation, it is not worth litigating.

12

Insolvency

One of the biggest problems that may face a franchisee or franchisor is the prospect of insolvency. While the number of franchise failures is relatively less than traditional businesses there is no doubt that the poor economy in the UK at the present time is taking its toll and the obvious reason for the increase in business failures in 1988 and 1989 is the multiple increases in the interest rates. The business that is todays **"survivor"** not only has to be run efficiently but needs a competitive edge over rivals.

During 1st May 1986 to 31st December 1988 there were nearly 33,000 insolvencies and during the first 6 months of 1989 there were nearly 9,000. It looks like the rate of insolvencies is on the increase and therefore it is a prudent businessman that not only handles his business properly but know what insolvency is all about.

The law concerning insolvencies is complex. It is mainly governed by the **Insolvency Act 1986 and the Insolvency Rules 1986.**

Directors

The Insolvency Act 1986 and the Company Directors Disqualification Act 1986 has now extended director's responsibilities so that directors can be made liable for irresponsible actions.

What was happening?

Directors of limited companies were being eternally over-optimistic and ignoring cash flow problems with a philosophy that can only be described as **"out of sight, out of mind".** Needless to say it didn't work.

As far as franchising was concerned they were continuing to take on franchisees in an attempt to ease cash flow problems by the use of up-front fees. This was, and unfortunately, still is a common problem. Hence see **Data Maid case study** where franchisees were being taken on to the bitter end - some had not even started their training. In the case of **Transam** (parcel couriers which have recently gone into receivership) at least one franchisee paid an up-front fee only to be phoned up by another franchisee a couple of days/weeks later to be told ***"the franchisor owes the franchisees' money, and we are all having a meeting to discuss the situation. Would you like to attend?"***

Imagine the franchisee's shock. The franchisor had completely failed to mention to him that there were any problems let alone that they owed franchisees money and had failed in their own attempts to raise additional outside funding. If the franchisee had been told of the problems or there had been disclosure requirements he certainly would not have taken up the franchise. In this particular case there may well be an action against the franchisors personally.

Similarly see **Crown Eyeglass case study** where failures were not revealed. Previously over optimistic directors could not be made personally liable. Now they can. This is particularly important in order to control rogues and con-men, of which there is an abundance in franchising, who start up one company after another usually using the same assets and sometimes even the same name.

Let's face it, if a franchisor is having financial problems, the easy option is to cease trading. Then even if franchisees have a good claim they will be advised not to go ahead because there is no money to be had.

The aim of the legislation is to curb such sharp practice.

Now an insolvency practitioner has a duty to submit a report on the conduct of directors involved in an insolvent company over a period of 3 years preceding his appointment. The duty extends to cover non-executive and shadow directors.

Non-executive directors have to understand a company's financial position and if things go wrong could face personal liability unless they have acted properly.

Shadow Director is defined as a **"person in accordance with those directions or instructions the directors of the company are accustomed to act."**

This definition covers puppet directors or anyone else who can influence a company's decisions.

Can a Franchisor be a Shadow Director?

According to the definition, this will depend on the amount of control the franchisor has. If the franchisee has to take the advice then shadow directorship may well arise. However, if the franchisee has a choice whether or not to accept the advice it is unlikely that the franchisor will be held responsible.

Insolvency Procedures

The following procedures exist:

1) administration
2) receivership
3) administrative receivership
4) voluntary or compulsory liquidation

Administration
The directors or company or creditors can apply to the court for an administration order.

It is usually granted if the company can survive as a going concern or there is a better prospect of realising the assets than if the company went into liquidation.

Receivership
Anyone with a right to appoint a receiver can do so but in franchising it is usually the bank who have security over the company and a floating charge over the company's assets.

Administrative Receivership
When an administrative receiver is appointed he has powers of management over the company. The directors can no longer handle company affairs unless the administrative receiver approves. The task of this receiver is to review the company affairs and assess whether the company can continue trading. Most such receivers are appointed agents of the company as opposed to agent of the appointer.

In a franchise situation the receiver can be appointed either in respect of the franchisor or in respect of the franchisee. In each case the fundamental issues for the receiver is to establish :

- the financial status of the business and parties involved
- collection of debts
- payment of creditors

Liquidation
A liquidator is usually appointed by a creditor but can also be appointed by the court or shareholders.

Creditors Voluntary Liquidation
Here the shareholders put the company into liquidation. They usually also appoint a liquidator is. If the creditors, however, want a different liquidator their decision over-rules the shareholders.

A company in liquidation will eventually cease trading and the liquidator is involved in winding up the company.

The liquidator can investigate the company's affairs and bring legal proceedings against directors and other officers of the company. One of the most common areas investigated is something we touched on briefly previously - **"wrongful trading"**. This basically means that a director cannot hide behind limited liability protection if they knew or ought to have known that there was no reasonable prospect of avoiding liquidation and yet they continued to trade.

Now a director who realises that liquidation is inevitable should take **"every step"** to minimise loss to creditors.

How can a director protect himself if he is facing insolvency?

All the directors in the company should be made aware of the financial problems and a plan should be agreed. The issue of whether they should continue to trade must be discussed and really the advice of an insolvency practitioner should be obtained. The main issue the company will have to face is whether they can pay off all their debts.

Director's Disqualification

As stated earlier, a report on the directors is carried out by the Administrator, Administrative Receiver or Liquidator. The report is sent to the DTI. If he thinks that the directors conduct makes him unfit to manage a company then the Secretary of State can make an application to the court for a Disqualification Order.

A disqualification order can stop a director being involved in a company at management level for 2 - 15 years.

It is up to the DTI to make further enquiries if they want to. They can just shelve the matter and the practitioner who prepared the report has no say in the matter.

The Objective Test is applied by the courts. That is, did the director act with the reasonable skills that a director should have.

The DTI will particularly look at issues of wrongful trading, fraud and involvement with a number of insolvent companies as pointers as to whether or not a disqualification order should be granted.

Do you need to watch out?

If you are a director (franchisor or franchisee) then if things are going wrong you still only have to worry if you are doing something underhanded;

For a franchisor this usually means wrongful trading, taking on new franchisees when the business is doomed.

For a franchisee it usually involves wrongful trading but more in the sense of taking supplies and obtaining credit knowing that they cannot be paid for.

Providing the company acts competently and reasonably, there should be no problem if you do have to cease trading.

13

A Franchisee's Right To Know versus A Franchisor's Right To Protect

In the UK franchisees have no special franchise legislation to protect them. Of course, in the case of disputes the ordinary Common Law principles apply. Thus, while there may be remedies in contract law if things go wrong there is no protection for the potential franchisee.

The fact that there are remedies is little consolation for many franchisees whose businesses fail. The reasons are quite simple:

1) either they have lost all their money (and don't qualify for legal aid) and cannot afford to pursue litigation, or

2) the franchisor has already or probably will go into receivership and therefore although there is a good cause of action there's no point in throwing good money after bad.

The rule is **caveat emptor** - buyer beware. This onus is entirely on the franchisee to check everything out. At first sight this may appear reasonable; yes, a franchisee should have the contract vetted by his legal advisor (who should specialise in franchising) or a franchise expert. And if he doesn't he's obviously to blame up to an extent if it doesn't work out. But that doesn't mean he should be conned.

The real problem lies in the fact that a large number of franchisors lie about various facts. While the big names might only tell the occasional white lie which if things go wrong they assist with, the unscrupulous operators tell big black ones which they can never remedy because they do not have the resources to do so.

In the latter type of case even if the potential franchisee asks all the right questions (and gets all the lies) the business is doomed. There is no real way of checking the facts given by the franchisor. Talking to lots of other franchisees might help if they are experiencing problems already. However the business may not have developed to that stage.

If existing franchisees are at the "optimistic stage" they will state only good points in the hope that the situation will improve. Its amazing how many "model" franchisees eventually cotton on to the fact that everything is getting worse and their songs of praise suddenly turn to tales of woe. But too late. Many more have been induced to jump on the coffin wagon, only to witness the death of yet another business - theirs !

A franchisor's right to protect....................

There is no doubt that a franchisor has the right to protect his trade secrets. However this excuse should not be used to hide crucial information from a potential franchisee. All too often it is. For example potential franchisees may not be allowed to look at the operations manual. In many cases the operations manual hasn't been worth looking at. If the franchisee had seen this before signing the contract he may well have realised that the franchisor should not be franchising and more importantly has no trade secrets worth protecting. While such cases are the exception rather than the rule, exploitation of franchisees in this way is fairly common.

Another major problem is that a number of franchisors follow a divide and rule policy. Consequently they are loathe to give potential franchisees lists of all existing franchisees. Instead they give a selected list of "content" ones, omitting others experiencing problems or those that have left or are involved in litigation with the franchisor. Again, this type of information would be invaluable for a potential franchisee deciding to invest.

Disclosure as it exists.

The **USA**, **Alberta** and now **Franc**e have recognised that potential franchisees need protection and have disclosure requirements that the franchisor must comply with.

It is often argued by advocates that disclosure will hamper franchising growth. This has certainly not happened in the USA.

The USA

In the States franchising controls assert themselves at three levels;

A) Federal
B) State
C) Specific Industry Legislation

A) Federal

At this level regulation of franchising is governed by the Federal Trade Commissions trade regulation rule entitled **"Disclosure Requirements and Prohibitions Concerning Franchising and Business Opportunity Ventures" (The F T C Rule)**. This rule became effective on **October 21st 1979** and requires franchisors in all 50 States to give potential franchisees a detailed disclosure document.

The disclosure document contains about 20 categories of information that must be disclosed. This is divided into the following categories;

Information about the franchisor
Information about the directors and executives
Litigation history
Bankruptcy history
The Franchise - initial fee
The Franchise - recurring fee
Franchisee's initial investment
Obligations of Franchisee to purchase/lease from specified/approved suppliers
Financing arrangements
Obligations of the franchisor
Territorial rights
Trademarks, service marks, trade-names, patents and copyrights
Obligation of the franchisee to participate in the actual operation of the franchise business.
Restriction on goods and services offered by the franchisee
Renewal, Termination, Repurchase
Modification and Assignment
Financial audited statements
Actual, average projected of forecasted franchisee sales profits or earnings
Information regarding franchises of the franchisor
Contracts
Acknowledgement of receipt by prospective franchisee

The franchisor does have an alternative. Instead of disclosing the above he can disclose the 23 categories of the **Uniform Franchise Offering Circular (the UFOC).**

Whichever format is chosen the disclosure document must be provided at the earlier of the **"first personal meeting" or at least 10 days before signing of the contract** or payments by the franchisee.

In addition the Rule requires mandatory delivery of the standard franchise agreement and delivery of the ACTUAL agreement 5 days before execution if it differs materially from the standard agreement.
If the franchisor makes projections of earnings or income of the franchisee or discloses historical information about company owned or franchise operations then these "earnings claims" have to be given to a potential franchisee in a separate "Earnings Claim Document".

The UFOC requires disclosure of earnings claim information anyway.

The Earnings Claim Document must be given to potential franchisees at the earlier of the first personal meeting at which or after which the earnings claim is made or at the time for making disclosures.

B) State

The main form of State legislation in franchising is the registration and disclosure statutes.

A number of States have enacted legislation which requires franchisors to register with or ask for the approval of the State authorities before offering a franchise. Most of the information necessary in a franchise registration is contained in the offering circular.

Some States may request additional information for example copies of the Operating Manual and advertising proposed to be used. A fee is required for the registration.

The FTC Rule takes precedence over State Law where the latter is inconsistent with the Rule.

C) Specific Industry Legislation

Some specific industries which use franchising as a distribution method have special Franchise Acts - for example, **The Automobile Dealers Day in Court Act**. This imposes an obligation on automobile franchisors to act in good faith.

Thus while potential franchisees in the USA have had considerable protection since 1979 (The Rule) their counterparts in the UK still have no protection.

However there seems to be a general awareness in Europe that legislation and disclosure are necessary. Witness the **EEC block exemption** which came into force on **February 1st 1989 (See below) and the French franchise law - Loi Doubin which became law at the end of 1989.**

The EEC Block Exemption

The block exemption in the form of **regulations 4087/88** will be in force until December 31st 1999. Its a big step forward for Europe.
Currently franchising in the UK is governed by 2 sets of laws;

1) EEC law - Article 85 Treaty Of Rome
2) English Law and in particular the Restrictive Trade Practices Act 1976.

Article 85 of the Treaty Of Rome prohibits everything that prevents, restricts or distorts competition between member states. According to the Pronuptia Case this means exclusive territories, restriction upon sales between franchisees and price controls.

In the famous **Pronuptia case in 1986** it was decided by **The European Court** of Justice that various prima facie restrictions did not come within Article 85 in so far as they were necessary to protect the franchisors' know-how and the common identity and reputation of the franchise network. However it was held that in this particular case the combined effect of territorial exclusivity did infringe Article 85 and did require exemption. Since this decision there has been such an influx of agreements to be registered that the block exemption will be invaluable in terms of speed.

Now if an agreement is drafted in accordance with the block exemption the franchisor can for example grant exclusive territories. It is worth noting that many franchisors were not restrained by the Pronuptia decision because they could take advantage of the **"de minimis"** exemption which gives small franchisors exemption from Article 85 (1) as long as both parties goods/services do not represent more than 5% of the total market in the area of the Common Market affected by the agreement.

Larger franchises that can't take advantage of the de minimis exemption can still apply for individual exemption of their agreements under **Article 85 (3)** by notifying them to the EC Commission. This process can take a very long time.

The Restrictive Trade Practices Act 1976 provides that where there is an exchange of restrictions in an agreement between two individuals carrying on business in the UK the agreement is registrable with the Office of Fair Trading. Thus where exclusive territories are granted this means that the franchisor accepts the restriction not to appoint more franchisees in that territory and therefore the agreement should first be registered with the OFT.

The main advantage of the Block Exemption is that it removes much of the red tape that was previously necessary in applying to the Commission for individual exemption under Article 85 (3) of The Treaty Of Rome.

The Structure Of The Block Exemption

Article 1 - definition of terms
2 - exempted provisions
3 - provisions that can be imposed
4 - compulsory provisions
5 - prohibited provisions
6, 7, 8, 9 - Procedural matters

The block exemption is in effect a statement by the Commission that franchising is generally economically beneficial and is here to stay. That is not to say however that all problems will cease.

There are some areas of uncertainty in the interpretation of some of its terms. For example the franchisor cannot set a price for goods. This is black listed. He can only recommend a price. This means that a franchisee can sell goods or services at whatever price and thereby undercut other franchisees. This is bound to interfere with the uniformity image of a franchise operation.

A further difficulty which could arise from the black list is that a consumer may obtain goods or services from one franchise area and then if a guarantee or service is required, may go to a different area. The problem will arise that the first franchisee will be obtaining income from the transaction while the latter franchisee will be burdened by providing the service or guarantee.

In such cases, the franchisor may have to provide some sort of compensation service to franchisees affected in this way.

Under **Article 8 the Commission** can withdraw the benefit of the block exemption notwithstanding its applicability, if the agreement has certain effects which are incompatible with the conditions laid down in Article **85(3).**

Below are the basic provisions of the Block Exemption :

1)

Article 4 of the block exemption sets out preconditions intended to ensure that parallel imports of franchised products between Member States remain possible. In order to benefit from the exemption under the block exemption the franchise agreement must:-

- allow the franchisee to obtain goods from other franchisees.

- if the franchisor obliges the franchisee to honour guarantees for the franchisor's goods, that obligation must apply in respect of goods supplied by any member of the franchised network in the common market.

- the franchisee must be obliged to indicate its status as an independent undertaking as long as this does not interfere with the common identity of the franchise network.

2)

If the criteria in Box 1 are met then the Commission will accept certain restrictions in the franchise agreement by way of exemption under **Article 85(3).** These acceptable restrictions are:

-the grant of an exclusive territory the franchisor not to carry on the business itself in the exclusive territory.

-the franchisee only to operate from specified premises.

-the franchisee not to actively seek customers outside the territory.

-the franchisee not to deal in goods competing with the franchised goods (but restriction cannot apply to spare parts or accessories for goods in the course of a service franchise).

3)

The following restrictions are also acceptable to the Commission and therefore exempt from Article 85.

- not to disclose the franchisors know-how during or after the agreement.

- to communicate know-how acquired during the agreement to the franchisor and other franchisees to assist against intellectual property infringement.

- not to use licensed know-how for any purpose other than the agreement.

- to attend staff training courses to use the franchisor's business format.

- to allow the franchisor to check the franchisee's business.

- not to change the location of the franchise premises.

- not to assign its rights and obligations under the agreement without consent.

4)

The following restrictions in the franchise agreement can be exempt but only to the extent that it is necessary to protect the franchisor's intellectual property rights or to maintain the common identity and reputation of the franchise network:

- to meet quality control standards.

- to sell only the franchisor's goods (but only where the franchisor cannot set objective quality standards for goods to be supplied owing to their nature).

- not to engage in a competing business during the agreement and for a maximum of one year afterwards.

- not to acquire a financial interest in a competing business.

- only to sell franchise goods to end users, other franchisees or the manufacturer's other distributors.

- to use best endeavours to promote the franchise goods/services including stocking minimum ranges, placing orders in advance and achieving minimum performance targets to pay a contribution to advertising.

If a franchise agreement involves any of the following "BLACK LISTED' restrictions or situations it will NOT be automatically exempt. However an individual notification to the Commission applying for exemption can be made:

THE BLACK LIST;

- reciprocal franchise agreements are entered into between already competing businesses (this could amount to market sharing)

- the franchisee is prevented from obtaining goods of the same quality as the franchisor supplies.

- the franchisor refuses to designate as authorised, third party manufacturers proposed by the franchisee (except where intellectual property involved or there is a need to protect the common identity and reputation of the franchise network)

- the franchisee is prevented from using know-how after termination of the agreement which is in the public domain.

- the franchisee is required to charge certain prices.

- the franchisee is prevented from challenging the validity of the franchisor's intellectual property rights (but the franchisor can reserve the right to terminate in the case of such a challenge.

- the franchisee is restricted as to where goods and services may be provided by virtue of the end-user's place of residence.

Agreements should be scrutinized for black listed provisions. Franchisees should be wary of any contract which would prevent the block exemption applying and which the franchisor refuses to alter.

Franchisees who are already party to such agreements should notify the Commission so as to minimise their own exposure to fines.

If the franchisor is anxious to avoid notification the threat of it is a useful negotiating tactic.

The block exemption will strengthen the position of a franchisor who is properly advised and who abides by its provisions.

FRENCH DISCLOSURE REQUIREMENTS

Until the end of 1989 France had no franchise law. The **Three Two Rule** (Page 6) was applied in general practice but was not law.

The new law imposes a number of obligations on the franchisor. The franchisor must provide the franchisee with two dossiers. The contents of each dossier is regulated by Statute.

The First Dossier contains information about the franchisor's business. **The Second Dossier** contains financial information - for example the expected profits.

Both Dossiers must be given to the franchisee at least **10 days** before the contract is signed or before any part payment is given in exchange for a promise (which must be in writing) to contract.

If the franchisor does not comply with the time limits or doesn't provide the stipulated information then the contract may be declared null and void and the franchisor may even be held liable for losses incurred.

If the franchisor doesn't have the required information then this must be clearly stated. All information in the Dossier must be completely up-to-date and based on the last financial year. If there are material changes these must be brought to franchisees notice within 3 months of the change.

The Contents of the Dossiers are illustrated on page171.

The French disclosure requirements are a big step forward in protecting franchisees.

However, under section 1.11 (Disclosure Dossier) the author feels that it would be more beneficial to include names and addresses and phones of all outlets and not just ten.

We in the UK would be wise to follow the French example. Unfortunately, in this country there is incredible apathy. Franchisees who have suffered at the hands of sharp practice make a big song and dance about everything for a while but when it comes to doing something positive about it, they are nowhere to be found.

Most professionals spout forth about ethical practice but in many cases it's just talk to get more clients. Ask them to subsidise work for people having problems, carry out legal aid work or contribute to a fund for trying to get disclosure in the UK and they too disappear.

Last but not least those VIPs who encourage free enterprise and "getting into business" seem amazingly ignorant about franchising, its successes and failures alike. Or perhaps it's easier to remain ignorant? They happily promote undesirable opportunities without carrying out adequate homework oblivious to the fact that the public may assume that the opportunity is credible.

While franchisees in the UK have no real protection, they should ensure that not only do they seek professional advice but that they obtain "Disclosure Information" in at least the detail that is required in France, if not more.

FRENCH DISCLOSURE REQUIREMENTS

Disclosure Dossier

1.1 Identify, legal status, head office, trading name, nationality, company number and amount of authorised share capital must be revealed.

1.2 Trade marks - registration number of trade marks and logos must be stated. Where franchisor is the owner or licensed to use labels these must be stated together with the unexpired term of the licence.

1.3 Professional experience - a CV of the franchisor and the management team.

1.4 Legal History - of the franchisor and management over pre ceding 5 years.

1.5 Objectives - of franchisor and future growth plans.

1.6 Investment
- a) Assets required by franchise
- b) Initial Stock - value
- c) Initial Payments - any payments or fees

1.7 Regular payments must be declared - these include royalties management service fees, advertising fees, property rental and training.

1.8 Suppliers - list of principal suppliers must be provided.

1.9 Exclusivity agreements - if an exclusive area is given to the franchisee this must be clearly defined.

1.10 Involvement - the extent to which the franchisee is expected to become involved in order to be part of the operation must be stated.

1.11 Information about the Franchise Network
- a) Number of outlets owned by franchisor as company shops and held under licence.
- b) Number of outlets in operation during last financial year.
- c) Names, addresses and phones of 10 outlets closest to the franchisees location.
- d) Outlets repossessed over last financial year.
- e) Contracts repudiated during the past financial year and who repudiated them.
- f) Number of contracts not renewed at the request of franchisees.

1.12 Turnover
A full report on the rate of turnover during the year, and the percentage of contracts repudiated, terminated or renewed during that year.

1.13 Time Scales
Where the site has not been agreed or found, an indication is required of the average time between signing the contract, agreeing the location and starting to trade.

1.14 Training
Details to include type of training, duration and cost.

1.15 Accounts
Certified accounts for the last year must be revealed.

1.16 Financial Projections Enough information must be given so that the potential franchisee can draw up hypothetical plans and plan the financing of the operation. The information provided by the franchisor must be substantial and reason able and based on past experience and take into account the location of the outlet.

Financial Dossier

The information provided by the franchisor must be substantial and reasonable and based on past experience and take into account the location of the outlet.

This is required only if the franchisor provides accounting projections, or makes representation about turnover or profit.

2.1 WARNING
The dossier must contain a warning that there is a risk that the projections may not be achieved and that there is no guarantee of success.

2.2 Assumptions - upon which the accounts are based must be listed together with any factors which are capable of changing.

2.3 Accounts - these should be based upon the experience of other franchisees and they must state the percentage of franchisees in the franchisees area who have achieved them over the last year.

2.4 Calculations - the facts upon which the financial statements was based must be listed.

The financial dossier would reiterate the franchisor's experience with outlets in the same area or those that are similar.

The identity - of the person responsible for the financial projections must be given.

14

Reading Material

Prospective franchisees must subscribe to or read at least a couple of franchise magazines. These will highlight new opportunities and an insight into the franchise industry.

The Franchise Magazine
Castle House,
Norwich
T.0603-620301/667024
- available on subscription and in newsagents.

This glossy colour magazine carries many ads and free editorials for those who advertise and therefore you will need to differentiate between the "real" features and the paid for editorials.

Franchise World
James House
37 Nottingham Road
London
SW17 7EA
T.081-767-1371
F.081-767-2211

Mainly black and white magazine which is an affiliate BFA member and therefore has a strong tendency to report on BFA features and press releases. However it is available on subscription. Credit to the editor who does also occasionally refer to more controversial subjects. The magazine does include some interesting articles from lawyers on for example disclosure and EEC law.

Business Franchise
CGB Publishing
Newspaper House
Tannery Lane
Penketh
Cheshire
T.092572-4234
F.092572-2617

The magazine is available on subscription. It doesn't really offer anything different and mostly consists of ads and editorial which appear to be written by the franchisors.

Streetwise Business Franchising
Lincoln House
661 High Road
London
N12 0DZ
T.081-445-7161
F.081-446-5065

This is a mini-magazine/newsletter **published by the author** as a "balance" to the above magazines. It includes interesting articles for example what to look out for in contracts, what the banks are up to and how to form franchisee associations. The magazine concentrates on steering franchisees away from problem opportunities. Therefore it carries expose' stories on franchisors involved in unethical practice.

The magazine is a must and should be read in conjunction with one of the more conventional magazines discussed above.

General Business Books

Croners Reference Book for the Self Employed and Smaller Business
Croner Publications Ltd
Croner House
London Road
Kingston upon Thames
Surrey
KT2 6SR
T.081-547-3333

Is an excellent reference book for all the general issues that you will need to face when running your own business. It deals with everything from taxation, VAT to employment and company law.

UK Franchise Books

There are a number of franchise books on the market including **Streetwise Franchising** (written by the author, published by Century Hutchinson and available from bookshops, Streetwise Franchising Ltd and Franchise World) which aim at highlighting all the issues you should be aware of. Try to steer clear from those that are written just by financial journalists. Most of the time they haven't a clue about whats really going on and tend to regurgitate what they are told by the franchisor. Avoid also the ones that offer you a league table of the top 10 (or whatever) franchise opportunities or show you how to "make money". Making money in business just isn't that easy. Hard work is the only thing that will do it.

Books that contain ads from franchisor's obviously will not be able to be totally independent and therefore should be avoided or read with caution and objectivity.

You should ask yourself "what interests does the author have"? If the author also sells franchises again you will need to be cautious because there will obviously be a conflict between his desire to sell an opportunity and his desire to portray a true situation.

Whatever you read (and more the better) there is no substitute for obtaining specialised independent advice.

International Franchise Books:

How to Franchise Internationally By Martin Mendelsohn
Available from Franchise World Publication

A very short approximate 60 page book on the type of issues you should be aware of before franchising internationally. Good first read but if you decide to go ahead you will need not only a lot more reading material but expert advice.

The International Franchise Option By Mark Abell
Available from Waterlow Publishers

Detailed and interesting account of international franchising covering areas such as commercial preparation, financing and master licence agreements. The book also looks at franchising in different countries and a couple of case studies (Tie Rack and Fastframe in America). A must if you are thinking of international expansion.

Legal texts:

Franchising by Adams and Pritchard-Jones.
Published by Butterworths

Heavy reading for potential or existing franchisee's but a very good read for professionals going into franchising for the first time and franchisors.

Franchise Success Story:

McDonald's Behind The Arches. By John F Love
Bantam Press - also available from Franchise World.

Excellent book about what has made McDonald's so successful. Many useful philosophies come out of the book. Certainly all franchisors should read it so they know what to aim for. Potential and existing franchisee's would do well to read it so they know what to expect from their franchisor.

15
Conclusion

"[My] profit projections were so far into the realms of Disneyland that [I] ended up seriously over-reaching my-self".

"Franchising has made some millionaires and others bankrupt, but it gives everyone a chance of a life-time - a chance to run their own business".

"Buying a franchise was the best thing I ever did - but it's hard work!"

"Franchising is a successful business con-cept - but it has it's problems".

"Our franchisors a bit of a bastard when it comes to treating us like employees. He won't even let us have our own Franchisee Association and tries to resort to legal screws to prevent us".

"Franchisees complained they were going bankrupt because the franchisor was undercut-ting all the shop prices with mail order".

"We need a Franchisee Association to hep us with negotiations".

"Potential franchisees should question other franchisees - that's the best research".

"I get the feeling my franchisor has to continue selling franchises just to keep his head above water".

"A solicitor is quoted as drawing attention to the problem that the BFA is a Trade Association for franchisors and does not necessarily protect the interests of franchisees".

"A solicitor comments that franchi-sees can get so hooked on the idea of having found what they think is a great franchise that even if warned that the contract requires them to leap in the Thames wearing lead boots once a week as an initiative test - they'd just tell me they'll cross that bridge when they come to it".

Some franchisees com-plain their supply line is not efficient and they keep running out of stock".

"Streetwise Franchising author Danielle Baillieu refers in the Observer to the exploitation problem in some cases which usually takes the form of ficititious or unrealistic accounting projections, in-adequate market research, equally in-adequate pilot schemes and poor train-ing facilities... even blue chip franchises have failed to deliver all that was sup-posedly on offer".

"Professor John Adams, one of the UK's top academic franchise ex-perts has stated that misconduct in franchising does not confine itself to fringe operators - international names have been involved".

Statements like this and "Hype ads" are too common for comfort in UK franchise ads. Statements such as :

"Be a millionaire in 5 years" should be an immediate warning signal.

Promises that you will earn **£60 K in the first year** are unlikely to come true. I'm not saying it doesn't happen - its the exception rather than the rule. Watch out!

In the autumn 1989 edition of Franchise Magazine editor, **Dr Dennis Chaplin,** wrote an article headed Franchise Marketing - can you spot the hype? He began:

"We're going to be the McDonald's of sprockets. We'll do for satellite dishes what Anita Roddick did for defenceless animals - 'unique' - 'phenomenal' - 'be your own boss' - 'exciting' - 'fastest growing' - 'market leader' - 'dynamic' - 'on your own but not alone' - 'from little acorns' - 'entrepreneurial' - nationwide growth' - 'up and running' - 'opportunities' - 'our success is your success'...............and so on, pumping up the volume".

And pumping up the volume is all it is. But it works. The gullibles lap it up.

The most common place for abuse is of course the franchise exhibitions. Many of the big names in franchising do not exhibit - they have long waiting lists. The unknowns however don't miss a trick - and parasitically associate with the success of the winners. Vetting procedures for exhibitors need to be much more stringent. Walking round a typical exhibition I often know of the franchises having problems or those involved in litigation. What can one do ?

Franchise winners do exist and some of the case studies illustrate this. But having read this book you will be well versed with what can go wrong.

Poppies (see case study "Prontaprint ") is not alone in having a large number of franchisee's cease trading - **Britool** had a **failure rate of a least 70% last year** . **Crown Eyeglas**s franchisees dropped like flies - (see case study)

At the moment a franchisee is a blind man trying to cross a road without a white stick and a dog. Some failures are disguised by take-overs. However, many franchisees in financial dire straits don't sell - and feel guilty if they try to because they are aware that the business has failed.
The real problem is that if a franchisee does shut down the exclusive area reverts back to the franchisor who can and usually does franchise again - but omitting to tell the new franchisee of past failures. This happened to a franchisee in Britool who is now pursuing a legal claim against the company. Similarly with Crown Eyeglass.

In the **Chemical Express** franchise I recently interviewed a former army man **Ian**

Thompson stated that he was ***"forced to fold his business just six months after taking a franchise ".***

He had paid £2,500 cash and borrowed the rest of the £9,000 needed using his home as security. He claims that he was nowhere near making the sales of £30,000 per annum that he needed. He went on to say that then ***"to his horror he discovered that two other franchisees had already failed in his area. But that the franchisor had told him it was a new area and had not mentioned failures".***

Thompson claimed that bounderies had been changed although only very slightly in order to create a new area. He asked for the return of his fee. Eventually the company wrote off the £3000 he owed them. However he is still paying off the borrowings at £150 per month.

Richard Jackson MD of Chemical Express declined to comment on whether changes had been made to bounderies but did say that one of the previous failures in that area had problems with the Inland Revenue and that Thompson had been undercapitalised. He further stated that the company had 50 franchisees with over half earning between £12,000 and £16,000 a year.

Half the battle to successful franchising is knowing what the problems are and guarding against them. Anyone who has read and digested this book should know exactly what to look out for, and how to look after the downside so that the upside looks after itself.

Franchising : "no-risk way out of the rut" -

(apparently quoted by the press from a news release by the BFA) is simply not true. No business is risk free.

There will be many in the franchise industry who cringe at the thought of the real facts, frauds and fallacies as stated in this book. But who cares about the innocent members of the public who are the victims of sharp practice? Not the Government because there are still no franchise disclosure laws. Not many of the franchisors because they are perpetrating the problems and not addressing themselves to the solutions. Not potential franchisees because they don't know what the problems are.

The only people who seem to care are a handful of professionals, franchisees having problems and some successful franchisees because they want the world to know that this business method really does work.

As it is, the author has only written half of what really goes on and certainly has not revealed names of franchisor companies that she has had to sign secrecy agreements with because they have negotiated and "done deals" with clients.

But these franchisors are not the problem. Those that are the real cause for concern are the ones that cannot support franchisees and cannot afford to bail them out when things go wrong. Their usual solution is to opt out by putting the company into liquidation leaving franchisees high and dry. This is what needs to be guarded against.

Too many franchisors in the market place today are making their money by just selling franchises without the expertise or well known trade mark that should automatically go with the concept.

Hopefully this book will make some inroad into making inadequate franchisors pull up their socks, the public more streetwise and the Government more aware of the sharp practices and frauds that are being operated not just by fly by night franchisors but also by household names.

It is only by taking this approach - recognising the **FACTS**, not tolerating the **FRAUDS** and firing down the **FALLACIES** that business expansion by what can only be described as **"a unique distribution option that works"** will succeed and grow to the potential it should enjoy.

APPENDIX 1

Useful names and addresses

Streetwise Franchising Ltd
Lincoln House
661 High Road
London
N12 0DZ
Tel. 081-445-7161

(Complete franchise advisory service negotiation and litigation advice)

British Franchise Association
75a Bell Street
Henley-on-Thames
Oxon
RG9 2BD
Tel. 0491-578049/50

(Franchisor membership)

British Overseas Trade Board
Call: Department of Trade & Industry
Support for Business Information Service
Tel. 01-215-4021

Companies Registration Office
55 City Road
London
EC1
Tel. 01-253-9393

The Consumers Association
2 Marylebone Road
London
NW1 4DX
Tel. 01-486-5544

Department of Employment
Small Firms and Tourism Division
Steel House
123 Tothill Street
London
SW1
Tel. 01-213-300

Department of Trade & Industry
Ashdown House
123 Victoria Street
London
SW1E 6RB
Tel. 01-215-7877

Exhibition Organisers
Dresswell Ltd
Blenheim House
Blenheim Terrace
London
W11
Tel. 01-727-1929

HM Customs & Excise
Kings Beam House
Mark Lane
London
EC3
Tel. 01-283-8911

Institute of Certified Accountants
29 Lincolns Inn Fields
London
WC2
Tel. 01-242-6855

Institute of Chartered Accountants
PO Box 433
Chartered Accountants Hall
Moorgate Place
London
EC2
Tel. 01-628-7060

Institute of Cost and Management Accountants
63 Portland Place
London
W1 4AB
01-637-4716

Institute of Marketing
Moor Hall
Cookham
Berkshire
SL6 9QH
Tel. 06285-24922

The Law Society
113 Chancery Lane
WC2
Tel. 01-242-1222

Local Enterprise Agencies
(Information and counselling based on 250 local offices, covering all aspects of starting up and running a business). Use Yellow Pages or contact:
Business in the Community
227a City Road
London
EC1V 1JU
Tel. 01-253-3716

Manpower Services Commission
(for details of local small business courses and training programmes)
Moorfoot
Sheffield
SP1 4PQ
Tel. 0742-753275

Office of Fair Trading
Field House
15-25 Bream's Buildings
London
EC4
Tel. 01-242-2858

Scottish Development Agency
Small Business Division
Rosebury House
Haymarket Terrace
Edinburgh
EH12 5EZ
Tel. 031-337-9595

Small Firms Service of Department of Employment
(Information and direct counselling from 12 locations nationwide including details on government support for business)
Telephone: 100 - ask for Freefone Enterprise

The Welsh Development Agency
Pearl House
Greyfriars Road
Treforest Industrial Estate
Cardiff
CF1 3XX
Tel. 0222-32955

Solicitors for commercial enquiries

Adlers
22-26 Paul Street
London
EC2A 4JH
Tel. 01-481-9100

Alexander Tatham & Co.
30 St. Ann Street
Manchester
M2 3DB
Tel. 061-236-4444

Baker & McKenzie
Aldwych House
Aldwych
London
WC2B 4JP
Tel. 01-242-6531

Bird Semple & Crawford Herron
249 West George Street
Glasgow
G2 4RB
Tel. 041-221-7090

Boswell Bigmore
25 New Street Square
London
EC4A 3LN
Tel. 01-353-3344

Drummond & Co.
31-32 Moray Place
Edinburgh
EH3 6BZ
Tel. 031-226-5151

Edge & Ellison
Rutland House
148 Edmund Street
Birmingham
B3 2JR
Tel. 021-200-2001

Field Fisher & Martineau
Lincoln House
296-302 High Holborn
London
WC1V 7JL
Tel. 01-831-9161

Forsyte Kerman
79 New Cavendish Street
London
W1M 8AQ
Tel. 01-637-8566

Gately & Wareing
Post & Mail House
26 Colmore Circus
Birmingham
B4 6DD
Tel. 021-236-8585

Hopkins & Wood
2-3 Cursitor Street
London
EC4A 1NE
Tel. 071-404-0475

Kenton Brandman Solicitors
Property Centre House
828 High Road
North Finchley
London
N12
Tel. 081-445-5246
Tel. 081-446-5225

Ladas & Parry
52-54 High Holborn
London
WC1V 6RR
Tel. 01-242-5566

MacFarlanes
10 Norwich Street
London
EC4A 1BD
Tel. 01-831-9222

Martineau & Johnson
St Phillips House
St Phillips Place
Birmingham
B3 2PP
Tel. 021-200-3300

McKenna & Co.
inveresk House
1 Aldwych
London
WC2R 0HF
Tel. 071 836 2442

Mundays
Speer House
40 The Parade
Claygate
Esher
Surrey
Tel. 0372-67272

Needham & James
Windsor House
Temple Row
Birmingham
B2 5LF
Tel. 021-236-9701

Wm. F. Prior & Co.
Temple Bar House
23-28 Fleet Street
London
EC4Y 1AA
Tel. 01-353-3571

Owen White
Gavel House
90-92 High Street
Feltham
Middx
TW13 4ES
Tel. 01-890-2836

Peters & Peters
2 Harewood Place
Hanover Square
London
WLR 9HB
Tel. 01-629-7991

Paul Shrank & Co.
7 Bell Yard
Temple Bar
Strand
WC2
Tel. 01-404-0888

Silverman Sherliker & Co
New City House
71 Rivington Street
London
EC2
Tel. 071-739-3495
Tel. 071-739-2194

Wallace & Partners
9 Great James Street
London
WC1N 3DA
Tel. 071-404-4422

Chartered Accountants

Arthur Young
Rolls House
7 Rolls Buildings
Fetter Lane
London
EC4A 1NH
Tel. 01-831-7130

Binder Hamlyn
Ballantine House
168 West George Street
Glasgow
G2 2PT
Tel. 01-353-3020

Deloitte Haskins & Sells
PO Box 90
25 Abercromby Place
Edinburgh
EH3 6QS
Tel. 031-557-3333

KPMG Peat Marwick McLintock
1 Puddle Dock
Blackfriars
London
EC4V 3PD
Tel. 01-236-8000

Kidsons
Carlton House
31-34 Railway Street
Chelmsford
Essex
CM1 1NJ
Tel. 0245-269595

Levy Gee Consultants Ltd
100 Chalk Farm Road
London
NW1 8EH
Tel. 01-267-4477

Neville Russell
Franchising Unit
2 Dove Street
Norwich
NR2 1DE
Tel. 0603-617009

M Sorskey & Co
239 Regents Park Road
London
N3
Tel. 01-346-9361

Spicer & Pegler
Friary Court
65 Crutched Friars
London
EC3N 2NP
Tel. 01-480-7766

Stoy Hayward Associates
8 Baker Street
London
W1M 1DA
Tel. 01-486-5888

Sources of finance

Bank of Scotland plc
57-60 Haymarket
London
SW1Y 4QY
Tel.01-925-0499

Barclays Bank plc
Marketing Dept
54 Lombard Street
London
EC3P 3AH
Tel. 01-626-1567

Clydesdale Bank plc
PO Box 43
30 St Vincent Place
Glasgow
G1 2HL
Tel. 041-248-7070

Lloyds Bank plc
Monument Building
11-15 Monument Street
London
EC3R 8JU
Tel. 01-626-1500

Midland Bank plc
Small Business Unit
120 Cannon Street
London
EC4N 6AB
Tel. 01-260-6379
Tel. 01-260-6380

National Westminster Bank plc
Franchise Section
Small Business Sector
Commercial Banking Services
8th Floor
Finsbury Court
101-117 Finsbury Pavement
London
EC2A 1EH
Tel. 01-726-1875
Tel. 01-726-1920
Tel. 01-726-1986

The Royal Bank of Scotland plc
42 St Andrew Square
Edinburgh
EH2 2YE
Tel. 031-556-8555

TSB Scotland plc
Henry Duncan House
PO Box 177
120 George Street
Edinburgh
EH2 4TS
Tel. 031-225-4555

3I
91 Waterloo Road
London
SE1 8XP
Tel. 01-928-7822

Franchise information centres of the world

UK

Streetwise Franchising Ltd
Consultancy
Lincoln House
661 High Road
London
N12 0DZ
Tel. 081-445-7161
Fax. 081-446-5065

British Franchise Association
Franchise Chambers
Thames View
Newtown Road
Henley-on-Thames
Oxon
RG9 1HG
Tel. 0491-578049/578050
Fax. 0491-573517

Franchise Consultants Association
James House
37 Nottingham Road
London
SW17 7EA
Tel. 01-767-1371
Fax. 01-767-2211

AUSTRALIA

Franchisors Association of Australia
6a Post Office Street
Pymble 2073
NSW
Australia
Tel. 02-449-5311

BELGIUM

Association Belge du Franchising
60 rue St. Bernard
b. 1606 Bruxelles
Belgium
Tel. 322-537-30-60

CANADA

Association of Canadian Franchisors
595 Bay Street
1050 Toronto
Ontario
Canada
M5G 2C2
Tel. (416) 595-5005

DENMARK

Dansk Franchisegiver-Forening
Sjaelsmarkvej 1B
DK 2970 Hoersholm
Denmark
Tel. (45) 02765064

EIRE

Irish Franchise Association
13 Frankfield Terrace
Summerhill South
Cork
Eire
Tel. 021-270859/50

EEC

European Franchise Federation
5 Avenue de Broqueville
b. 1150 Bruxelles
Belgium
Tel. 322-736-64-64

FRANCE

Federation Francaise de la Franchise
9 Bd des Italiens
75002 Paris
France
Tel. (1) 42-60-00-22

HOLLAND

Nederlandse Franchise Vereniging
Arubalaan 4
1213 Vg Hilversum
Holland
Tel. 35-83-39-34

ITALY

Assiciazione Italiana del Franchising
Corso di Porta Nuova, 3
Milano 20121
Italy
Tel. 392-650-779

JAPAN

Japan Franchise Association
Elsa Building, 3-13-12
Roppongi
Minato-Ku
Tokyo
Japan
Tel. 408-17-76

NORWAY

Norwegian Franchise Association
Astveitskogen 41
Tertnes Bergen 5084
Norway

SOUTH AFRICA

South African Franchise Association
P.O. Box 18398
Hollbrow 2038
South Africa
Tel. (011) 642-2921

SWEDEN

Swedish Franchise Association
P.O. Box 26002
S-100 41 Stockholm
Sweden
Tel. 08-723-05-33
Fax. 08-20-64-67

SWITZERLAND

Swiss Franchise Association
Avenue du Mail 5
CH-1205 Geneve
Switzerland
Tel. 022-28-36-38

U.S.

International Franchise Association
Suite 900
1350 New York Avenue
N.W.
Washington D.C.
20005
U.S.A.
Tel. 202-628-8000
Fax. 202-628-0812

UK representative
Martin Mendelsohn
Adlers
22-26 Paul Street
London
EC2A 4JH
Tel. 01-481-9100
Fax. 01-247-4701

WEST GERMANY

Deutscher Franchise-Verband
St. Paul Strasse 9
8000 Munchen 2
West Germany
Tel. (0 89) 53-50-27
Fax. (0 89) 53-13-23

APPENDIX 2

Franchises by trade classification

Franchises are listed in this section by the standard franchise trade classification system adopted by Franchise World magazine.

New franchises introduced during the year will be listed bi-monthly in Franchise World under the same trade classification system to make it easier for readers to update their records.

The activities of a number of franchisors fall into more than one classification, but to avoid repetition they will be listed only in the category which the publisher believes to be their main source of business.

Further information can be obtained from:

Franchise World
James House, 37 Nottingham Road
London SW17 7EA
Tel. 081-767-1371 Fax. 081-767-2211

Building Services

A1 Dampproofing (UK) Ltd
New Side Mill
Charnley Fold Lane
Bamber Bridge
Preston PR5 6AA
Tel. 0772-35228 Fax. 0772-628076

Type of business: damp-proofing and timber treatments
Total investment cost (exc. working capital): £12,000
BFA membership: associate

British Damp Proofing
The School House
Fleetwood Road
Esprick
Preston PR4 3HJ
Tel. 039-136441
Type of business: damp proofing etc.
BFA membership: full

Building Preservation
Timberguard (UK) Ltd
40 Lune Street
Preston
Lancs
Tel. 0772-204007

Type of business: damp-proofing and timber preservation
Total Investment cost (exc. working capital): £9,850

Dampcure Woodcure/30 Ltd
Darley House
Cow Lane
Garston
Watford
Herts WD2 6PH
Tel. 0923-663322 Fax. 0923-662578

Type of business: damp-proofing and timber treatments
Total investment cost (exc. working capital): £12,500
BFA membership: full

Pass & Company Timber Preservation UK Ltd
Passco House
635 High Road
Leytonstone
London E11 4RD
Tel. 01-539-1105 Fax. 01-558-9822

Type of business: timber preservation and damp control
Total investment cost (exc. working capital): £11,400
BFA membership: full

Drain Cleaning

Dyno Rod Plc
143 Maple Road
Surbiton
Surrey KT6 4BJ
Tel. 01-549-9711 Fax. 01-549-3870
Type of business: drain and pipe cleaning
BFA membership: full

Jet-Rod Franchising Ltd
Irwell House
89 Barton Lane
Eccles
Manchester M30 0EY
Tel. 061-788-7672
Fax. 061-787-7045

Type of business: drain and pipe cleaning
Total investment cost (exc. working capital): £34,500

Metro Rod Services Ltd
Metro House
Churchill Way
Macclesfield
Cheshire SK11 6AY
Tel. 0625-34444 Fax. 0625-616687

Type of business: drain and pipe cleaning
Total investment cost (exc. working capital): £30,000
BFA membership: full

Property maintenance & improvements

Bathcare
207a Linketty Lane East
Crownhill
Plymouth PL6 5XJ
Tel. 0752-775603

Type of business: renovation of bathroom suites
Total investment cost (exc. working capital): £1,500

The Bath Doctor
Suite 5
Britannia House
Leagrove Road
Luton
Beds LU3 1RJ
Tel. 0582-459336

Type of Business: renovation of bathroom suites
BFA membership: full

The Bath Wizard Ltd
Victory House
Somers Road North
Portsmouth PO1 1PJ
Tel. 0705-753719

Type of business: renovation of bathroom suites

Brick-Tie Services Ltd
Yorkshire House
Easy Road
Leeds LS9 8SQ
Tel. 0532-480943

Type of business: wall-tie replacement
Total investment cost (exc. working capital): £11,500
BFA membership: early development

Cico Chimney Linings
Westleton
Saxmundham
Suffolk
Tel. 0728-73608

Type of business: re-lining of chimneys
BFA membership: associate

Complete Weed Control Ltd
Langston Priory Mews
Station Road
Kingham
Oxon OX7 6UW
Tel. 060-871-8851 Fax. 060-871-8019

Type of business: amenity and industrial weed control service
Total investment cost (exc. working capital): £12,250

Countrywide Garden Maintenance Services
Countrywide Garden Maintenance Services Ltd
164-200 Stockport Road
Cheadle
Cheshire SK8 2DP
Tel. 061-428-4444 Fax. 061-428-0637

Type of business: gardening services
Total investment cost (exc. working capital): £15,000
BFA membership: associate

Creteprint
Cobblestone Paving Co. (UK) Ltd
Auckland House
Perry Road
Witham
Essex CM8 3SX
Tel. 0376-517766 Fax. 0376-500044

Type of business: pattern-imprinted concrete paving
Total investment cost (exc. working capital): £17,500

Crimecure Ltd
Ivatt Way
Westwood Industrial Estate
Peterborough PE3 7PB
Tel. 0733-332322

Type of business: installation of alarm systems

Dyno Rod Developments
143 Maple Road
Surbiton
Surrey KT6 4BJ
Tel. 01-549-9711 Fax. 01-549-3870

Type of business: emergency electrical repairs and installations
Total investment cost (exc. working capital): £7,000
BFA membership: full

Dyno Rod Developments
143 Maple Road
Surbiton
Surrey KT6 4BJ
Tel. 01-549-9711 Fax. 01-549-3870

Type of business: emergency door opening and lock fitting
Total investment cost (exc. working capital): £16,000
BFA membership: full

Dyno Rod Developments
143 Maple Road
Surbiton
Surrey KT6 4BJ
Tel. 01-549-9711 Fax. 01-549-3870

Type of business: emergency plumbing repair and installations
Total investment cost (exc. working capital): £7,000
BFA membership: full

Evvacote Franchise Ltd
Brent House
24-26 Friern Park
Finchley
London N12 9DA
Tel. 081-446-8491

Type of business: exterior property renovations

Garage Door Company (The)
Unit 7
Russel Road Industrial Estate
Edinburgh EH11 2NN
Tel. 031-337-3332 Fax. 031-313-2778

Type of business: installation and repair of garage doors including electric doors
Total investment cost (exc. working capital): £19,500

GBC Buildings for Leisure
Garden Building Centres Ltd
Jardinerie Garden Centre
Kenilworth Road
Hampton-in-Arden
Warks
Tel. 06755-2961 Fax. 0676-34572
Type of business: retailers of conservatories, greenhouses and timber buildings
Total investment cost (exc. working capital): £40,000 - £60,000
BFA membership: full

Graffiti Management
5 The Hamiltons
Torquay Road
Shaldon
Devon TQ14 0AY
Tel. 062-687-2488

Type of business: anti-graffiti treatments

Gun-Point Ltd
Thavies Inn House
3/4 Holborn Circus
London EC1N 2PL
Tel. 01-353-1759
Fax. 01-583-7259

Type of business: mechanised repointing and brick cleaning service
Total investment cost (exc. working capital): £14,900
BFA membership: full

Leadstyle Ltd
2 Sparken Hill
Worksop
Notts S80 1AP
Tel. 0909-475599

Type of business: leaded windows

Lockmasters Mobile Ltd

Security House
The Windmills
Turk Street
Alton
Hampshire GU34 1EF
Tel. 0420-541155 Fax. 0420-85022

Type of business: mobile locksmiths
Total investment cost (exc. working capital): £13,600
BFA membership: early development

The Marley Paving Co Ltd
Lichfield Road
Branston
Burton-on-Trent
Staffs DE14 3HD
Tel. 0283-713877 Fax. 0283-716001

Type of business: concrete block paving for the domestic market
BFA membership: early development

Master Thatchers Ltd
Rose Tree Farm
29 Nine Mile Ride
Finchampstead
Wokingham
Berks RG11 4QD
Tel. 0734-734203 Fax. 0734-328054

Type of business: roof thatching
Total investment cost (exc. working capital): £12,000
BFA membership: full

Mixamate Concrete
Mixamate Holdings Ltd
Beddington Lane
Croydon
Surrey CR9 4QD
Tel. 01-689-5500 Fax. 01-689-7656

Type of business: concrete delivery service
Total investment cost (exc. working capital): £19,000
BFA membership: full

Mortar Mason Ltd
Westleton
Saxmundham
Suffolk IP17 3BS
Tel. 072-873-428

Type of business: mechanised re-pointing

Mr Fixit
Bay House
Bramham
Wetherby
Yorks LS23 9JS
Tel. 0937-844848

National Security
Britannia House
Leacombe Road
Luton LU3 1RJ
Tel. 0582-459336

Type of business: installation of burglar alarms

Newlook Bath Service Ltd
Oaklands
Dorstone
Hereford HR3 6AR
Tel. 09816-297

Type of business: bath renovation

Potholes Ltd
Prospect Road
Alresford
Hampshire SO24 9QF
Tel. 0962-733025 Fax. 0962-734045

Type of business: repair of potholes and related services (line-marking, speed ramps, etc.)
Total investment cost (exc. working capital): £7,500

Re-Nu Ltd
130 Stoneleigh Avenue
Worcester Park
Surrey KT4 8XZ
Tel. 01-330-6148 Fax. 01-330-5721

Type of business: renovation of kitchen units, etc.
Total investment cost (exc. working capital): £15,000
BFA membership: associate

Servowarm Ltd
199 The Vale
Acton
London W3 7RB
Tel. 01-743-1244

Type of business: central heating systems

Stained Glass Overlay UK Ltd
23 Hurricane Way
Norwich NR6 6EJ
Tel. 0603-485454 Fax. 0603-487102

Type of business: decorative glass
Total investment cost (exc. working capital): £25,000

BFA membership: associate

Window replacement/ weather sealing

Alpine Windows
Alpine House
Honeypot Lane
Kingsbury
London NW9 9RU
Tel. 01-204-3393

Type of business: replacement windows and doors
Total investment cost (exc. working capital): £50,000
BFA membership: associate

Curadraft (G.B.) Ltd
Delmae House
Unit 1
Home Farm
Ardington
Nr Wantage
Oxon
Tel. 0235 833022 Fax. 0235 833072

Type of business: window and door weather sealing
Total investment cost (exc. working capital): £11,500

Fersina Windows Ltd
Fersina House
Industry Road
Carlton Industrial Estate
Barnsley
South Yorks S70 3NH
Tel. 0226-728310 Fax. 0226-722090

Type of business: manufacture and installation of replacement windows and doors, and new conservatories
Total investment cost (exc. working capital): £45,000
BFA membership: full

Quattro Seal
Suite 1
New Mansion House
Wellington Road South
Stockport SK1 3UA
Tel. 061-480-4991

Type of business: window and door sealing

Trident Warehouse Co
Units 6 - 9
Venturebank
Claybank Road
Portsmouth
Hants PO3 5NH
Tel. 0705-673303 Fax. 0705-693895

Type of business: window replacement

Ventrolla Ltd
51 Tower Street
Harrogate
North Yorks HG1 1HS
Tel. 0423-67004

Type of business: draught proofing and renovation of windows and doors

Catering
Home delivery/take-away

Dial-A-Dino's
Empire House
Hanger Green
London W5 3BD
Tel. 01-991-9911

Type of business: pizza delivery and take-away

Domino's Pizza
Unit 10
Maryland Road
Tongwell
Milton Keynes MK15 8HF
Tel. 0908-618222 Fax. 0908-615434

Type of business: pizza delivery
Total investment cost (exc. working capital): £80,000 - £100,000

Gino's Dial-A-Pizza Ltd
4a Mill Street
Cannock
Staffordshire WS11 3DL
Tel. 0543-466032
Fax. 0543-53147

Type of business: pizza delivery and take-away
Total investment cost (exc. working capital): £63,000

Perfect Pizza
65 Staines Road
Hounslow
Middx TW3 3HW
Tel. 01-577-1711 Fax. 01-572-5112

Type of business: pizza delivery and take-away
Total investment cost (exc. working capital): £95,000
BFA membership: full

Snappy Tomato Pizza (U.K.) Ltd
17 Mercia Business Village
Torwood Close
Westwood Business Park
Coventry CV4 8HX
Tel. 0203-466647 Fax. 0203-466652

Type of business: pizza delivery and take-away
Total investment cost (exc. working capital): £50,000 - £60,000

Telephone Pizza Company (Franchise) Ltd
22 - 24 High Street
Crawley RH10 1BJ
Tel. 0293-548717

Type of business: pizza delivery and take-away
Total investment cost (exc. working capital): £59,000

Restaurants/take-away

Berni
Oxford House
97 Oxford Road
Uxbridge UB8 1HX
Tel. 0895-70955

Type of business: restaurants
BFA membership: associate

Burger King UK Ltd
20 Kew Road
Richmond
Surrey TW9 2NA
Tel. 01-940-6046 Fax. 01-948-1630

Type of business: hamburger restaurants
Total investment cost (exc. working capital): £700,000
BFA membership: full

Chantegrill
24 Kingly Street
London W1R
Tel. 01-439-0645

Type of business: restaurants

Chicken George Food Systems Ltd
Shirley Lodge
470 London Road
Slough SL3 8QY
Tel. 0753-584926 Fax. 0753-40990

Type of business: chicken restaurant and take-away
Total investment cost (exc. working capital): £85,000

Dixy Fried Chicken (G.B.) Ltd
123 Clapton Common
London E5 9AB
Tel. 01-800-3615 Fax. 01-802-9405

Type of business: fried chicken restaurants/take-aways
Total investment cost (exc. working capital): £56,000

Don Millers Hot Bread Kitchens Ltd
166 Bute Street Mall
Luton
Beds LU1 2TL
Tel. 0582-422781 Fax. 0582-455810

Type of business: bakeries
Total investment cost (exc. working capital): £48,000
BFA membership: full

Grandma Batty's
Wondercourt Ltd
Yorkshire House
Vulcan Street
Birds Royd Lane
Brighouse
West Yorks HD6 1LQ
Tel. 0484-714459 Fax. 0484-400019

Type of business: Yorkshire pudding restaurants and distribution
Total investment cost (exc. working capital): £30,000

Kansas Fried Chicken
130A Wilmslow Road
Handforth
Cheshire SK9 3LQ
Tel. 0625-531517 Fax. 0625-528691

Type of business: fried chicken restaurant and take-away
Total investment costs (exc. working capital): £150,000
BFA membership: associate

Kentucky Fried Chicken (Great Britain) Ltd
88-97 High Street
Brentford
Middx TW8 8BG
Tel. 01-569-7070 Fax. 01-569-8733

Type of business: fried chicken restaurant and take-away
Total investment cost (exc. working capital): £400,000 - £1.2m
BFA membership: full

McDonald's Hamburgers Ltd
11-59 High Road
East Finchley
London N2 8AW
Tel. 081-883-6400

Type of business: hamburger restaurant

Merryweathers
109 Hersham Road
Walton-on-Thames
Surrey KT12 1RN
Tel. 0932-247368 Fax. 0932-246205

Type of business: fish and chips

Mister Donut
353 North End Road
Fulham
London SW6 1NN
Tel. 01-386-9133

Type of business: doughnuts, muffins
BFA membership: early development

Morley's (Fast Foods) Ltd
162 Clapham High Street
Clapham
London SW4
Tel. 01-622-4821

Type of business: restaurants and take-aways

Mr Cod Ltd
6 - 7 High Street
Woking
Surrey GU21 1BG
Tel. 0483-755407

Type of business: fish and chip restaurants
Total investment cost (exc. working capital): £100,000

Olivers (UK) Ltd
Eagle Works
Harpur Street
Bedford MK40 1JZ
Tel. 0234-328181 Fax. 0234-325454

Type of business: coffee shop and bakery
Total investment cost (exc. working capital): £270,000
BFA membership: full

Pancake Place
Clydesdale Bank House
20 New Road
Milnathort
Kincross KY13 7XT
Tel. 0577-63969

Type of business: restaurants
BFA membership: full

PizzaExpress Ltd
29 Wardour Street
Soho
London W1V 3HB
Tel. 01-437-7215 Fax. 010-494-1653

Type of business: pizza restaurant and take away
Total investment cost (ecx. working capital): £230,000
BFA membership: full

Pizza Piazza
Little Dudley House Ltd
B30 Barwell Business Park
Leatherhead Road
Chessington
Surrey KT9 2NY
Tel. 01-391-0198 Fax. 01-974-1298

Type of business: pizza restaurants and take-aways

Poppins Restaurants
28 Sudley Road
Bognor Regis
West Sussex PO21 1ER
Tel. 0243-864647 Fax. 0243-821511

Type of business: family restaurants

Spud-U-Like
34-38 Standard Road
London NW10 6EU
Tel. 01-965-0182
Type of business: baked potato restaurants

Trading Post Restaurants
63 Carlton Place
Glasgow G5 9TW
Tel. 041-429-6308 Fax. 041-429-0167

Type of business: 'Wild West' theme barbecue restaurant and saloon bar
Total investment cost (exc. working capital): £240,000
BFA membership: early development

Wimpy International
10 Windmill Road
London W4 1SD
Tel. 01-994-6454 Fax. 01-994-0563

Type of business: hamburger restaurant, and take-away
Total investment cost (exc. working capital): £600,000
BFA membership: full

Winstons Pizza
10 Lune Street
Preston
Lancs PR1 2NL
Tel. 0772-210881 Fax. 0695 622433

Type of business: pizza restaurant
BFA membership: early development

Other

Baskin-Robbins
Glacier House
Old Field Lane
Greenford
Middx. UB6 0BA
Tel. 01-575-2004

Type of business: ice cream parlour

Dinkum Dog
Plumcourt Ltd
88 - 92 Wallis Road
London E9 5LN
Tel. 01-985-3633

Type of business: retailers of hot dogs

Toasty Kitchens
2 Castle Street
Salisbury SP1 1BB
Tel. 0722-27456/0722-339811
Fax. 0722-331313

Type of business: mobile catering
Total investment cost (exc. working capital): £9,870

Cleaning Services

Carpets, etc.

Chem-Dry Southern Services
The Weltech Centre
The Ridgeway
Welwyn Garden City
Herts AL7 2AA
Tel. 0707-375113/336969 Fax. 0707-375137

Type of business: carpet and upholstery cleaning
Total investment cost (exc. working capital): £7,000 - £11,000

Rainbow International
Mansfield Franchising Ltd
Phoenix House
Mansfield Road
Sutton-in-Ashfield
Notts NG17 4HR
Tel. 0623-440150 Fax. 0623-440265

Type of business: carpet dyeing and cleaning
Total investment cost (exc. working capital): £14,500

Safeclean
D.G. Cook Ltd
Delmae House
Unit 1
Home Farm
Ardington
Nr Wantage
Oxon
Tel. 0235-833022 Fax. 0235-833072

Type of business: on-site cleaning of carpets, upholstery, leather; and stain, flame, pest retardancy treatments
Total investment cost (exc. working capital): £8,750
BFA membership: full

ServiceMaster Ltd
308 Melton Road
Leicester LE4 7SL
Tel. 0533-610761 Fax. 0533-610517

Type of business: on-site carpet and upholstery cleaning
Total investment cost (exc. working capital): £15,000
BFA membership: full

Commercial

Coverall
Stanley House
Stanley Gardens
London W3 7SY
Tel. 01-749-8686

Type of business: commercial contract cleaning

Global Franchise Services Ltd
8 - 10 High Street
Sutton
Surrey
Tel. 01-642-0054
Type of business: building maintenance
Total investment cost (exc. working capital): £10,000
BFA membership: full

ServiceMaster Ltd
308 Melton Road
Leicester LE4 7SL
Tel. 0533-610761 Fax. 0533-610517

Type of business: contract cleaning
Total investment cost (exc. working capital): £15,000
BFA membership: full

VDU Services Franchising Ltd
VDU House
Old Kiln Lane
Churt
Farnham GU10 2JH
Tel. 0428-713713 Fax. 0428-713798

Type of business: hi-tech equipment valeting
Total investment cost (exc. working capital): £12,500
BFA membership: early development

Domestic

Country Cousins
26 High Street
Mertsham
Surrey RH1 3EA
Tel. 07374-4211

Type of business: domestic help service

Dial A Char
DAC Ltd
77 London Road
East Grinstead
West Sussex RH19 1EQ
Tel. 0342-328391 Fax. 0342-327242

Type of business: domestic cleaning
Total investment cost (exc. working capital): £8,500

The Maids Ltd
Venture House
7 Leicester Road
Lougthborough
Leics LE11 2AE
Tel. 0509-266535

Type of business: domestic cleaning

Merrymaids
ServiceMaster Ltd
308 Melton Road
Leicester LE4 7SL
Tel. 0533-610761 Fax. 0533-610517

Type of business: domestic cleaning services
Total investment cost (exc. working capital): £10,000
BFA membership: full

Molly Maid UK
Hamilton Road
Slough
Berks SL1 4QY
Tel. 0753-23388 Fax. 0753-511554

Type of business: domestic cleaning
Total investment cost (exc. working capital): £6,500
BFA membership: full

Odd-Jobs (UK) Ltd
5 Bridge Street
Macclesfield SK11 6EG
Tel. 0625-610765

Type of business: domestic and light commercial cleaning
Total investment cost (exc. working capital): £6,500
BFA membership: early development

Poppies (UK) Ltd
31 Houndgate
Darlington DL1 5RH
Tel. 0325-488699 Fax. 0325-381185

Type of business: domestic cleaning
Total investment cost (exc. working capital): £17,915
BFA membership: full

Square 1 Cleaning Services Ltd
221c South Coast Road
Peacehaven
East Sussex BN10 8LB
Tel. 0273-582335 Fax. 0273-583482

Type of business: domestic and commercial cleaning, including carpet and upholstery cleaning
Total investment cost (exc. working capital): £9,950

Commercial, domestic and personal services

Beverage services.

Catermat Fresh Drinks Ltd
13 Redhills Road
Eastern Industrial Area
South Woodham Ferrers
Chelmsford
Essex
CM3 5UJ
Tel. 0245-322465 Fax. 0245-329194

Type of business: coffee machines and supplies
Total investment cost (exc. working capital): £9,950
BFA membership: early development

Coffeeman Management Ltd
73 Woolsbridge Industrial Park
Wimborne
Dorset BH21 6SU
Tel. 0202-823501

Type of business: fresh-ground coffee delivery service
Total investment cost (exc. working capital): £6,420
BFA membership: associate

Krogab
Springleader Beverage Services Ltd
Chelford
Macclesfield
Cheshire SK11 9BD
Tel. 0625-21900 Fax. 0625-861994

Type of business: beverage systems and supplies
Total investment cost (exc. working capital): £10,000

Business Centres

Lambourn Court International Business Centre
1 Lambourn Court
Emerson Valley
Milton Keynes MK4 2DA
Tel. 0908-503300 Fax. 0908-504604

Type of business: business centre
Total investment cost (exc. working capital): £11.500
BFA membership: early development

OTSS Business Centres LTd
3 Spencer Parade
Northampton NN1 5AA
Tel. 0604-21051 Fax. 0604-230086

Type of business: business centre, serviced offices
Total investment cost (exc. working capital): £100,000
BFA membership: early development

Financial services mortgages, insurance etc.,

Allied Dunbar
Parliament House
North Row
London W1R 1DL
Tel. 01-734-7244

Type of business: financial services

The Commercial (Brokerage) House Ltd
261/269 Ecclesall Road
Sheffield S11 8NX
Tel. 0742-680476 Fax. 0742-589725

Type of business: commercial finance brokers
Total investment cost (exc. working capital): £20,000

Homebuyers Advice Centre Plc
Suite 401
India Buildings
Water Street
Liverpool L2 0RB
Tel. 051-236-2872 Fax. 051-255-1097

Type of business: mortgage advisory service
Total investment cost (exc. working capital): £15,000

Mortgage Advice Centre (Franchise) Ltd
Jacobs Wall
Ground Floor
20 Hook Road
Epsom
Surrey KT19 8TH
Tel. 03727-43111 Fax. 03727-43729

Type of business: mortgage services
Total investment cost (exc. working capital): £30,000

Swinton Group Ltd
Swinton House
6 Great Marlborough Street
Manchester M1 5SW
Tel. 061-236-1222 Fax. 061-236-9340

Type of business: insurance brokers
Total investment cost (exc. working capital): £24,950
BFA membership: full

William Green Financial Services Ltd
Ashton House
467 Silbury Boulevard
Central Milton Keynes MK9 2AH
Tel. 0908-665544 Fax. 0908-668822

Type of business: financial services
Total investment cost (exc. working capital): £15,000 - £30,000

Training

Future Training & Recruitment
Future Centres (Franchise)
Sandhurst Lane
Whydown
East Sussex TN39 4RH
Tel. 0732-740721

Type of business: secretarial training and recruitment
Total investment cost (exc. working capital): £20,000
BFA membership: early development

Priority Management Systems UK
Trend House
Dallow Road
Luton
Beds LU1 1LY
Tel. 0582-391608

Type of business: management training

RT Computer Training
15 Victoria Street
Wetherby
West Yorks LS22 4RE
Tel. 0937-63032 Fax. 0937-64067

Type of business: computer training centres
Total investment cost (exc. working capital):£12,000

Wetherby Office Training
Flockton House
Audby Lane
Wetherby
West Yorks LS22 4FD
Tel. 0937-63940 Fax. 0937-64067

Type of business: secretarial and computer training centres
Total investment cost (exc. working capital): £10,000
BFA membership: full

Other

The Accounting Centre
Elscot House
Arcadia Avenue
Finchley Central
London N3 2JE
Tel. 081-349-3191 Fax. 081-346-2038

Type of business: accounting services
Total investment cost (exc. working capital): £7,500 - £10,000
BFA membership: full

Anicare
23 Buckingham Road
Shoreham-by-Sea
West Sussex BN4 5UA
Tel. 0273-463022

Type of business: management services for vets
BFA membership: full

Cab Glazing Services Unit 6
Clifton Industrial Estate Cherryhinton Road
Cambridge CB1 4WG
Tel. 0223 212593

Culligan International , Blenheim Road
Cressex Industrial Estate, High Wycombe
Bucks HP12 3RS
Tel.0494 436484

Type of business: domestic and commercial water treatment

The Compleat Engraver and Colourist
TC Graphics Ltd
Valley House
Needham
Nr. Harleston
Norfolk IP20 9GL
Tel: 0379 852168. Fax 853598

Type of business: Glass engraving and decoration.
Total investment cost (exc. working capital): £17.575.

Countrywide Interior Landscapes Ltd
164-200 Stockport Road
Cheadle
Cheshire SK8 2DP
Tel: 061-428-4444. Fax 061-428 0637

Type of business: Interior plant display (rental and maintainance)
Total investment cost (exc. working capital) £9,750

First Impressions
1 Dover Street
Cambridge CB1 1DY
Tel: 0223-462700. Fax. 0223-464199

Type of business: Colour analysis and image consultancy
Total investment cost (exc. working capital) £2,500-£3,000

The Hall of Names Ltd
London House
Suite 323
26-40 Kensington High Street
London W8 4PF
Tel: 071-937-9996. Fax. 071-937-9992

Type of business: Computer-based surname history
Total investment cost (exc. working capital) £13,000
BFA Membership: Early development.

House of Colour
4 Dudrich House
Princes Lane
London N10 3LU
Tel: 081 444 3621

Type of business: Personalised colour and style consultancies
BFA membership: Associate

Infopoint
205 Cowley Load
Oxford OX4 1XH
Tel: 0865-791448

Type of business: Vending of information cards at tourist attractions.

Kwik Strip (UK) Ltd
P.O. Box 1087
Summerleaze
Church Road
Winscombe
Avon BS25 1BH
Tel: 0934-843100. Fax. 0934-844119

Type of business: Furniture stripping and restoration.
Total investment cost (exc. working capital) £10,500.
BFA membership: Full.

Marketing Methods Ltd
1 Buxton Road
West Disley
Stockport SK12 2AF
Tel: 066-365882. Fax. 066-364136

Type of business: Marketing agency
Total investment cost (exc. working capital) £20,000-£26,000

Mastersharp
P.A. Research Ltd
28 Glen Road
Boscombe
Bournemouth BH5 1HS
Tel: 0202-396002

Type of business: Mobile sharpening service for homes and trade
Total investment cost (exc. working capital) £9,000

National Vacuum Cleaner Services
Richmond House
1 Richmond Street
Herne Bay
Kent CT6 5LU
Tel: 0227-374656. Fax. 0227-740465.

Type of business: Repairs and servicing of electrical floor cleaning machines
Total investment cost (exc. working capital) £4,990

Nationwide Investigations
86 Southwark Bridge Road
London SE1 OEX
Tel: 071-928-1799

Type of business: Private investigation bureaux
BFA membership: Full

The Quill Group
Harbro House
Okell Street
Runcorn
Cheshire WA7 5AP
Tel: 0928-580007

Type of business: Writing of personal wills.

Recognition Express
Sketchley Recognition Express Ltd
P.O. Box 7
Rugby Road
Hinkley
Leics LE10 2NE.
Tel: 0455-38133. Fax. 0455-619056

Type of business: Manufacture and sale of name badges, signs, trophies, awards and vehicle signage
Total investment cost (exc. working capital) £27,000
BFA membership: Full.

Red Letters
2 Mews Court
Newton Avenue
East Grinstead
West Sussex RH19 4SW
Tel: 0342-315665. Fax. 0342-315665

Type of business: Text Agency
Total investment cost (exc. working capital) £7,500

Safeway Motoring School Ltd
P.O. Box 325
Bristol BS99 7XE
Tel: 0272-266466

Type of business: Driving schools
Total investment cost (exc, working capital) £3,500-£6,500
BFA membership: Early development

ServiceMaster Ltd
308 Melton Road
Leicester LE4 4SL
Tel: 0533-610761. Fax. 0533-610517

Type of business: Upholstery repair and re-upholstery of soft furnishings
Total investment cost (exc. working capital) £12,000
BFA membership: Full

Stockcheck
The Courtyard
Harewood Estate
Harewood
Leeds LS17 9LS
Tel: 0532-886565. Fax. 0532-886063

Type of business: Liquor, food and retailing stocktaking
Total investment cost (exc.working capital) £12,000

Time and Place Marketing Services
8 Beatrice Road
Worsley
Manchester M28 4TN
Tel: 061-728-1172

Type of business: Local advertising media

Tumble Tots (UK) Ltd
Cannons Sports Club
Cousin Lane
London EC4R 3TE
Tel. 01-621-0904

Type of business: Activity centres for pre-school children

The UK School of Motoring
39 Dee Street
Aberdeen
Scotland
Tel: 0224-572090

Type of business: Driving school

Uticolor
Acton Workshops
School Road
London NW10
Tel: 081-965-6869

Type of business: Repair of vinyl, etc.
BFA membership: Full

Val-U-Pak
Valuefuture Plc
Harpenden Hall
Southdown Road
Harpenden
Herts AL5 1PT
Tel: 0582-460977

Type of business: Co-operative direct mail
Total investment cost (exc. working capital)) £3,250

Vinyl Master (UK) Ltd
Unit 2a
Vulcan Works
205 Leckhampton Road
Cheltenham GL53 OAL
Tel: 0242-584511

Type of business: Repairing of vinyl

Distribution
Commercial markets inc. wholesaling

Autela Components Ltd
Regal House
Birmingham Road
Stratford-upon-Avon
Warks CV37 OBN
Tel: 0789-414545. Fax. 0789-414580

Type of business: Automotive parts distributor
Total investment cost (exc.working capital) £35,000
BFA membership: Full

Chemical Express
Ninian Way
Tame Valley Industrial Estate
Tamworth
Staffs B77 5DZ
Tel: 0827-251431

Type of business: Van sales of hygiene and maintenance chemicals

Codon Alloys (UK) Ltd
Codon House
Clifton Road
Marton
Blackpool
Lancs FY4 4QA
Tel: 0253-791872. Fax. 0253-692238

Type of business: Van sales of welding equipment and consumables
Total investment cost (exc. working capital) £16,000

The Cookie Coach Company
Division of Carrs Foods Ltd
Southside
Bredbury Industrial Park
Stockport
Cheshire SK6 2SP
Tel: 061-494-5171. Fax. 061-430-4973

Type of business. Van sales of cookies, cakes and confectionery
Total investment cost (exc. working capital) £5,000

Direct Salon Services
Newport Way
Cannon Park
Middlesbrough
Cleveland TS1 5JW
Tel: 0642-217978

Type of business: Distributors of hair care and beauty products to salons
BFA membership: Associate

G & T Video Services (Franchise) Ltd
35 Balena Close
Creekmoor Industrial Estate
Creekmore
Poole
Dorset BH17 7EB
Tel: 0202-601851

Type of business: Van-based supply of video films

Kendall Oil
C.A.N. Trading Ltd
2-3 Bacchus House
Calleva Park
Aldermaston
Reading RG7 4QW
Tel: 0734-811799. Fax. 0734-819024

Type of business: Oil supplier to the automotive, industrial and agricultural markets.
Working capital: £10,000-£15,000
Ready cash requirement: £6,000- £15,000
BFA membership: Early development

Motabitz
27-37 Craven Street
Northampton NN1 3EZ
Tel: 0604-231777

Scap-On-Tools Ltd
Palmer House
150-154 Cross Street
Sale
Cheshire M33 1AQ
Tel: 061-969-0126. Fax. 061-905-1175

Type of business: Automotive tools and equipment sales
Total investment cost (exc. working capital) : £35,000
BFA membership: Full

Spaceage Plastics Ltd
Spaceage House
85 Ringwood Road
Poole
Dorset BH14 ORH
Tel: 0202-732053. Fax. 0202-747037

Type of business: Distribution of uPVC plastic products.

Team Audio
The Diamond Stylus Co. Ltd
Mochdre Industrial Estate
Colwyn Bay
Clwyd LL28 5HD
Tel: 0492 49272

Type of business: Van-based sales of hi-fi and electrical products
BFA membership: Associate

Trafalgar Cleaning Chemicals
Unit 14 Fenlake Industrial Estate
Fenlake Road
Bedford MK42 OHB
Tel: 0234-64651. Fax. 0234-66807

Type of business: Van-based sales of cleaning chemicals to the motor and transport industries
Total investment cost (exc. working capital) £5,900

Trust Parts Ltd
Unit 7
Groundwell Industrial Estate
Crompton Road
Swindon SN2 5AY
Tel: 0793-723749. Fax 0793-724431

Type of business: Van sales of workshop and maintenance tools and consumables
Total investment cost (exc. working capital) £13,000
BFA membership: Associate

Domestic markets

Betterware Sales Ltd
Fairview Estate
Kingsbury Road
Curdworth
Sutton Coldfield
West Midlands B76 9EH
Tel: 0675-70094. Fax. 0675-70506

Type of business: Direct marketing of homecare and homeware products
Working capital: £10,000
Ready cash requirement: £6,000

Circles
Modernideas Ltd
786 London Road
Larkfield
Maidstone
Kent ME20 6BE
Tel: 0732 848966/843272

Type of business: Van-based hiring and retailing of videos, compact discs, etc.
Total investment cost: (exc. working capital) £17,500
BFA membership: Early development.

Roman Spa Home Hydrotherapy
Roman Spa Health and Leisure Products Ltd
30 Princess Victoria Street
Bristol BS8 4BZ
Tel: 0272-744960. Fax. 0272-237860

Type of business: Direct sales of hydromassage products
Total investment cost: (exc. working capital) £9,950

Employment and recruitment agencies

Alfred Marks
Adia House
84-86 Regent Street
London W1A 1AL
Tel: 071-437-7855

Type of business: Employment agency
BFA membership: Full

Ashfield Personnel (Franchising) Ltd
21 Bridge Street
Hemel Hempstead
Herts HP1 1EG
Tel: 0442-216618. Fax. 0442-49077

Type of business: Employment agency
Total investment cost (exc. working capital) £14,000-£16,000

EPC (European Personnel Counsellors) Ltd
Owl's Barn
Dorney Wood Road
Burham
Bucks SL1 8EH
Tel: 0628-604814. Fax. 0628-604816

Type of business: Recruitment agency
Total investment cost (exc. working capital) £30,000

KPR Recruitment Ltd
Crispin House
Maldon Road
Witham
Essex CM8 2UR
Tel: 0376-500594. Fax. 0376-500010

Type of business: Temporary and permanent staff recruitment agency
Total investment cost (exc. working capital): £15,000-£20,000
BFA membership: Early Development

Travail Employment Group
24 Southgate Street
Gloucester GL1 2DP
Tel: 0452-415676. Fax. 0452-303197

Type of business: Employment agency
Total investment cost (exc. working capital) £7,500
BFA membership: Full

Equipment and plant hire

Banson Tool Hire
Pellon Lane
Halifax HX1 5SB
Tel: 0422-331177
Type of business: retailing and hiring of tools
BFA membership: Associate

Hiretech Hire Centres
Hire Technicians Group Ltd
Chalk Hill House
8 Chalk Hill
Watford
Herts WD1 4BH
Tel: 0923-30337. Fax. 0923-38799
Type of business: In-store tool and equipment hire centres in Sainsbury's Homebase stores.
Total investment cost (exc. working capital): £34,000

M & B Marquees
Unit 16
Swinborne Court
Burnt Mills Industrial Estate
Basildon
Essex SS13 1QA
Tel: 0268-0728361. Fax. 0268-728361

Type of business: Marquee and function equipment hire
Total investment cost (exc. working capital) £25,000
BFA membership: Associate

Estate Agencies/Business Transfer Agencies

Balmforth Alliance & Leicester Property Services
10 Bank Street
Norwich NR2 4SE
Tel: 0603-666506. Fax. 0603-624193

Type of business: Estate Agents
Total investment cost (exc. working capital) £17,000
BFA membership: Full

Britannia Business Sales
Britannia Buildings
Park Gate
Bradford
West Yorkshire BD1 5BS
Tel: 0274-722977

Type of business: Licensed trade business transfer agents
BFA membership: Full

Century 21 Real Estate Agency Ltd
Station House
3 Darkes Lane
Potters Bar
Herts EN6 1AJ
Tel: 0707-46465

Type of business: Estate agency

Cornerstone
Abbey National Estate Ageency Ltd
Abbey House
Baker Street
London NW1 6XL
Tel: 081-486-5555

Type of business: Estate Agents

Country Business Sales Ltd
9a Churchgate Street
Soham
Ely
Cambs CB7 5DS
Tel: 0353-723350

Type of business: Business transfer agents, valuers, stocktakers
Total investment cost (exc. working capital) £13,950

Country Rose
Country Properties
41 High Street
Baldock
Herts SG7 5NP
Tel: 0462-896148
Type of business: Estate agencies
BFA membership: Full

Donald Storrie Estate Agency
40 Cadzow Street
Hamilton ML3 6DG
Tel: 0698-420621. Fax. 0698-428551

Type of business: Estate Agency
Total investment cost: (exc. working capital) £50,000
BFA membership: Early development

Everett Masson & Furby Ltd
18 Walsworth Road
Hitchin
Herts SG4 9SP
Tel: 0462-32377. Fax. 0462-420062

Type of business: Business transfer agents
Total investment cost (exc. working capital) £25,000
BFA membership: Full

The Flat Shop
119 The Promenade
Cheltenham
Glos GL50 1NW
Tel: 0242-222489

Type of business: Estate Agents specialising solely in flat sales and residential property management
Total investment cost (exc. working capital) £27,000
BFA membership: Early development

Link & Company (Franchise) Plc
The Estate House
High Road
Chigwell IG7 5BJ
Tel: 081-501-5500. Fax. 081-501-4763

Type of business Estateagency
Total investment cost (exc. working capital) £12,500
BFA membership: Early development

Quest Estates International
15 Saint Thomas Street
Lymington
Hants SO4 9NB
Tel: 0590-679983. Fax. 0590-72720

Type of business: Business transfer agency (specialising in hospitality market), overseas property sales (business and domestic), finance agency
Working capital: £12,500
Ready cash requirement: £15,500

Saunders of Kensington Ltd
40 Gloucester Road
South Kensington
London SW7 4QU
Tel: 071-581-3623. Fax. 071-584-4230

Type of business: Chartered surveyors
Total investment cost (exc. working capital) £5,00

Seekers
Thornganby Ltd
234-236 The Broadway
London NW9 6AG
Tel: 081-202-7882. Fax. 081-202-6739

Type of business: No commission estate agency
Total investment cost: £35,000-£40,000

Swinton The Estate Agents
24-26 Park Green
Macclesfield
Cheshire SK11 7NA
Tel: 0625-613664

Type of business: Estate agents

Your Move
Deanpeak Enterprises Ltd
51 New Bedford Road
Luton
Beds LU1 1HR
Tel: 0582-424616

Type of business: Fixed-fee estate agents
Total investment cost (exc.working capital) £36,000

Fitted Kitchens/Bedrooms

H-Plan Manufacturing Co. Ltd
Dallow Road
Luton
Beds LU1 1SP
Tel: 0582-424 222

Type of business: Fitted bedroom furniture

In-toto Ltd
Wakefield Road
Gildersome
Leeds LS27 OQW
Tel: 0532-524131. Fax. 0532-520154

Type of business: Fitted kitchen retailers
Total investment cost (exc. working capital) £45,000
BFA membership: Full

Texas Homecare Installation Services Ltd
Home Charm House
Park Farm
Wellingborough
Northants NN8 3XA
Tel: 0933-679679. Fax. 0933-674352

Type of business: Kitchen, bedroom and bathroom installation
Total investment cost (exc. working capital) according to number of stores in the franchise area
BFA membership: Early development

Strachan Studio
George Strachan & Son Ltd
Cross Green Way
Leeds
West Yorks LS9 ORS
Tel: 0532-4995694

Type of business: Fitted bedroom
Total investment cost (exc. working capital) £75,000
BFA membership: Full

Food and Drink Distribution

Alpine Soft Drinks (UK) Ltd
Richmond Way
Chelmsley Wood
Birmingham B37 7TT
Tel: 021-770-6816 Fax. 021-788-8413

Type of business: Door-to-door
Total investment cost (exc. working capital) £4,000
BFA membership: Full

The Bread Roll Co.
Unit 6
Veniam Industrial Estate
224 London Road
St,Albans
Herts AL1 1JF
Tel: 0727-35291. Fax. 0727-67247

Type of business: Bread roll marketing and distribution
Total investment cost: (exc. working capital) £25,000-£40,000

Coca-Cola Export Corporation
Pemberton House
Wrights Lane
London W8 5SN
Tel: 071-938-2131

Type of business: Soft drinks
BFA membership: Full

Northern Dairies
3 Balne Lane
Wakefield
Yorks WF2 ODL

Type of business: Distribution of dairy products
BFA membership: Full

Unigate Dairies Ltd
14/40 Victoria Road
Aldershot
Hants GU11 1TH
Tel: 0252-24522

Type of business: Milk distribution
Total investment cost (exc. working capital) £40,000-£80,000
BFA membership: Full

Hair and Beauty Salons

Alan Paul Hairdressing
164 New Chester Road
Birkenhead
Merseyside
Tel: 051-666-1060

Type of business: Hair salons
BFA membership: Full

Blinkers Franshising Ltd
Consort Court
High Street
Fareham
Hampshire PO16 7AL
Tel: 0329-230580. Fax. 0329-238555

Type of business: Hair salons
Total investment cost (exc. working capital) £30,000-£90,000
BFA membership: Associate

Command Performance
256 High Street
Slough
Berks SL1 1JU
Tel: 0753-822645

Type of business: Hair salons
BFA membership: Full

Das Haar (Franchsises) Ltd
Dundas House
166 Buchanan Street
Glasgow G1
Tel: 041-332-8822. Fax. 041-333-0074

Type of business: Hair salons
Total investment cost (exc. working capital) £25,000-£40,000
BFA membership: Associate

Essanelle Ltd
27-37 Georges Road
London SW19 4DS
Tel: 081-879-7111. Fax. 081-879-0379

Type of business: Hair and beauty salons

Francesco Group (Holdings) Ltd
Woodlings Yard
Bailey Street
Stafford ST17 4BG.
Tel: 0785-47175. Fax. 0785-57127

Type of business: Hair salons
Total investment cost (exc. working capital) £40,000-£50,000
BFA membership: Full

Keith Hall Franchising Ltd
119-121 Derby Road
Long Eaton
Nottingham NG10 4LA
Tel: 0602-729914

Type of business: Hair salons
BFA membership: Full

Saks Hair (Holdings) Ltd
57 Coniscliffe Road
Darlington
Co. Durham DL3 7EH
Tel: 0325-380333. Fax. 0325-381369

Type of business: Hair and beauty salons
Total investment cost (exc. working capital) £30,000-£40,000
BFA membership: Full

Votre Beaute (Franchise) Ltd
Cattespool Mill
Tardebigge
Nr. Bromsgrove
Worcs B60 1LZ
Tel: 021-445-5550. Fax. 021-445-6174

Type of business: Hair and beauty salons
Total investment cost (exc. working capital) £25,000
BFA membership: Early development

Hotels

Holiday Inns International
Rue Neerveld
101-103,1200 Brussels
Belgium
Tel: (2) 772-0058. Fax. (2) 772-0272

Type of business: Hotels
Total investment cost (exc. working capital) from £3m (100 Garden Court Holiday Inn)
BFA membership: Full

Quality International
2 Valentine Place
London SE1 8QH
Tel: 081-928-3333. Fax. 081-928-4762

Type of business: Hotels

Leisure

Great Adventure Game (The)
Unit 16
Smith's Yard
Summerley Street
London SW18 5HR
Tel: 081-944-1911. Fax. 081-878-4712

Type of business: Adult adventure games
Total investment cost (exc. working capital) £6,970
BFA membership: Full

Laser Sporting Leisure Ltd
South Thames Studios
5-11 Lavington Street
London SE1 ONZ
Tel: 081-929-8060. Fax. 081-620-0883

Type of business: Simulated Clay pigeon shooting systems
Total investment cost (exc. working capital) £16,000-£30,000
BFA membership: Early development

Skirmish (Europe) Ltd
The Warehouse
Sandy Lane
Oxted
Surrey
Tel: 0883-723590. Fax. 0883-712369

Type of business: Adulty outdoor adventure games (paintball)
Total investment cost (exc. working capital) £25,000

Spice-The Adventure Group
Spice (UK) Ltd
18 Henrietta Street
Old Trafford
Manchester M16 9GA
Tel: 061-872-2213

Type of business: Activity, travel and event organisers
Total investment cost (exc. working capital) £10,000

Splatoon
Licensed to Thrill (UK) Ltd
The Hunting Lodge
Stanbridge Lane
Kettlethorpe
Sandal
Wakefield WF2 7NT
Tel: 0226-383737

Type of business: Outdoor adult adventure games

Motor Services Cleaning

Autosheen Car Valeting Services (UK) Ltd
Everitt Close
Denington Industrial Estate
Wellingborough
Northants NN8 2QE
Tel: 0933-72347. Fax. 0933-72448

Type of business: Mobile car valeting
Total investment cost (exc. working capital) £8,950
BFA membership: Associate

National Car Care Club
Wilmslow House
Southend Road
Woodford Green
Essex IG8 8HJ.
Tel: 081-551-4911

Type of business: Mobile car valeting

PAS Clean
Professional Appearance Services Ltd
3 Avon Reach
Chippenham SN15 1EE
Tel: 0249-444182. Fax. 0249-444185

Type of business: Car valeting and contract cleaning
Total investment cost (exc. working capital) £9,850
BFA membership: Associate

Suds Ltd
Hine House
Randlesdown Road
Bellingham
London SE6 3BT
Tel: 081-695-5128

Type of business: Mobile car valeting
Total investment cost (exc. working capital) £5,995

Wash 'N' Wax Ltd
11 Randolph Place
Edinburgh EH3 7TA
Tel: 031-226-2823

Type of business: Mobile car valeting
Total investment cost (exc. working capital) £7,500
BFA membership: Early development

Rental/Leasing

ai Fullers International Rent a Car
240 Burlington Road
New Malden
Surrey KT3 4NN
Tel: 081-949-5421. Fax. 081-949-3966

Type of business: Car and van rental
Total investment cost (exc. working capital) £20,880
BFA membership: Early development

Arrow Car, Van and Truck Rental Ltd
Unit 3
26 Maybole Road
Ayr KA7 2QA
Tel: 0292-268188

Type of business: Vehicle rental

Avis Rent-A-Car Ltd
Trident House
Station Road
Hayes
Middx UB3 4DJ
Tel: 081-848-8765. Fax. 081-561-7571

Type of business: Car rental
Total investment cost (exc. working capital) £25,000
BFA membership: Full

Budget Rent A Car International Inc
41 Marlowes
Hemel Hempstead
Herts HP1 1LD
Tel: 0442-232555. Fax. 0442-230757

Type of business: Car, van and truck rental
Total investment cost (exc. working capital) £20,000
BFA membership: Full

Hertz Rent A Car
Radnor House
1272 London Road
Norbury
London SW16 4XW
Tel: 081-679-1777

Type of business: Vehicle rental

Med-Ped S.A.
Plaza Med-Ped
Palma Nova
Majorca
Spain
Tel: 010-3471-68-16-32

Type of business: Moped rental in Spanish resorts

Multilink Leeasing Ltd
1 St.John's Road
Hove
East Sussex BN3 2FB
Tel: 0273-821515. Fax. 0273-821523

Type of business: Vehicle leasing

Practical Used Car Rental
137-145 High Street
Bordesley
Birmingham B12 OJU
Tel: 021-771-4524

Type of business: Used-car rental
BFA membership: Full

Thrifty Car Rental
City Rentals Ltd
City House
14/16 Temple End
High Wycombe
Bucks HP13 5DR
Tel: 0494-464964. Fax. 0494-465404

Type of business: Car and van rental
Total investment cost (exc. working capital) £25,000
BFA membership: Early development

Venture Hire Ltd
Wincanton House
333 Western Avenue
London W3 OTS
Tel: 071-993-7611. Fax. 071-993-3194

Type of business: Vehicle leasing

Tuning

Computa Tune
9 Petra Road
Clayton Park
Clayton-le-Moors
Accrington
Lancs BB5 5JB
Tel: 0254-391792

Type of business: Mobile car tuning

Hometune (UK)
77 Mount Ephraim
Tunbridge Wells
Kent TN4 8BS
Tel: 0892-510532. Fax. 0892-548617

Type of business: Mobile engine tuning
Total investment cost (exc. working capital) £8,000
BFA membership: Full

Mobiletuning Ltd
The Gate House
Lympne Industrial Park
Lympne
Kent CT21 4LR.
Tel: 0303-64210. Fax. 0303-269555

Type of business: Mobile engine tuning
Total investment cost (exc. working capital) £11,000
BFA membership: Full

Tune-Up Ltd
23 High Street
Bagshot
Surrey GU19 5AF
Tel: 0276-51199. Fax. 0276-51198

Type of business: Mobile engine tuning
Total investment cost (exc. working capital) £12,500
BFA membership: Associate

Other

Auto Armour
P.A. Research Ltd
28 Glen Road
Boscombe
Bournemouth
Dorset BH5 1HS
Tel: 0202-396002

Type of business: Car paint protection system
Total investment cost (exc. working capital) £6,500

Colormatch
P.A. Research Ltd
28 Glen Road
Boscombe
Bournemouth
Dorset BH5 1HS
Tel: 0202-396002

Type of business: Van-based car paint repair service
Total investment cost (exc. working capital) £10,500

Highway Windscreens (UK) Ltd
Arodene House
41-55 Perth Road
Gants Hill
Ilford
Essex IG2 6BX
Tel: 081-518-5500

Type of business: Mobile vehicle windscreen replacement

Magic Windshields UK
12 Beehive Lane
Ilford
Essex IG1 3RG
Tel: 081-554-5008 or 081-518-6430

Type of business: Windscreen repairs
Total investment cost (exc. working capital) £5,000

Mr. Clutch
20 Lower Coombe Street
Croydon
Surrey CRO 1AA
Tel: 081-686-9330. Fax. 081-760-0287

Type of business: Clutch and gearbox replacement
Total investment cost (exc. working capital) £30,000-£40,000

Novus Windscreen Repair
The Glass Doctor Ltd
11 Darwin House
Dudley Innovation Centre
Dudley Road
Kingswinford
West Midlands DY6 8XZ
Tel: 0384-4 1860

Type of business: Repair (not replacement) of laminated glass and removal of scratches.
Total investment cost (exc. working capital) £4,950

Silver Shield Screens Ltd
Wheler Road
Off Humber Road
Whitley
Coventry CV3 4LA
Tel: 0203-307755. Fax. 0203-639188

Type of business: Windscreen and body glass replacement
Total investment cost (exc. working capital) £25,000-£50,000

Stop Thief (UK) Ltd
Unit 9
Avenue 1
Business Park
Letchworth
Herts SG6 2BB
Tel: 0462-670555. Fax. 0462-480044

Type of business: Vehicle security systems
Total investment cost (exc. working capital) £12,000

Truseal Car Care
After Market Specialists AMS (UK) Ltd
Panalpina House
1a Knoll Rise
Orpington
Kent BR6 OLR
Tel: 0689-36966. Fax. 0689-73155

Type of business: Car care systems
Total investment cost (exc. working capital) £40,000
BFA membership: Early development

Parcel/Courier/Taxi/Chaffeur/Removals Services

Amtrak
Company House
Tower Hill
Bristol BS2 OEQ
Tel: 0272-272002

Type of business: Delivery services
BFA membership: Associate

Brewer & Turnbull Removals
Holme Road
Bamber Bridge
Preston
Lancs PR5 6BP
Tel: 0772-626555

Type of business: Removals and storage facilities
BFA membership: Full

Business Post Ltd
Express House
8 Galleymead Road
Colnbrook SL3 OER
Tel: 0753-682042

Type of business: Delivery services

Captain Cargo Ltd
Wetherby Road
Ascot Drive Industrial Estate
Derby DE2 8HL
Tel: 0332-290810. Fax. 0332-295471

Type of business: Delivery services
Total investment cost (exc. working capital) £9,000

City Link Transport Holdings Ltd
Batavia Road
Sunbury-on-Thames
Middx TW16 5LR
Tel: 0932-788799. Fax. 0932-785560

Type of business: National express parceels/courier collection and delivery service
BFA membership: Full

Classic Carriages Limousines Ltd
Desborough Street
High Wycombe
Bucks HP11 2NF
Tel: 0844-292-420

Type of business: Chauffeured private hire limousines
Total investment cost (exc. working capital) £25,000

Duty Driver Ltd
42a Station Road
Twyford
Berks RG10 9NT
Tel: 0734-320200

Type of business: Chauffeur services

G-Force Couriers Ltd
Old Smithfield Industrial Estate
Aston Street
Shifnal
Shropshire TF11 8DT
Tel: 0952-462800. Fax. 0952-462801

Type of business: Courier Service
Total investment cost (exc. working capital) £14,000
BFA membership: Early development

Hornets Network Ltd
26 High Street
Merstham
Surrey RH1 3EA
Tel: 07374-4211

Type of business: Despatch service

Intacab Ltd
Service House
West Mayne
Basildon
Essex SS15 6RW
Tel: 0268-415891. Fax. 0268-541154

Type of business: Passenger transport
Total investment cost (exc. working capital) £40,000

Interlink Express Parcels
Brunswick Court
Brunswick Square
Bristol BS2 8PE
Tel: 0272-426900

Type of business: Delivery serivces
BFA membership: Full

Nexday Ltd
Sunrise House
Bedford Road
Northampton NN1 5NW
Tel: 0604-234134. Fax. 0604-231057

Type of business: Express parcel delivery services
Total investment cost (exc. working capital) £9,100
BFA membership: Early development

Panic Link Ltd
Control Sortation Centre
Melbourne Road
Lount
Leics LE6 5RS
Tel: 0530-411111. Fax. 0530-417423

Type of business: Delivery services
Total investment cost (exc. working capital) £20,000-£50,000

TNT Express (UK) Ltd
TNT House
Abeles Way
Atherstone
Warks CV9 2RY
Tel: 0827-303030. Fax. 0827-301301

Type of business: Delivery services
Total investment cost (exc. working capital) £4,500
BFA membership: Full

Transam Express Courier Parcels Ltd
Creswicke House
9 Small Street
The Centre
Bristol BS1 1DB
Tel: 0272-277641

Type of business: Express parcels services
Total investment cost (exc. working capital) £12,000
BFA membership: Early development

Quick Printing/Graphic Design

AlphaGraphics Printshops Of The Future (UK) Ltd
Ryedale Building
58-60 Piccadilly
York YO1 1NX
Tel: 0904-611344. Fax. 0904-646298

Type of business: Quick printing
Total investment cost (exc. working capital) £140,000
BFA membership: Early development

EuroSpeedy Printing Centres (SW) Ltd
Smythen Street
Exeter
Devon EX1 1BN
Tel: 0392-436254. Fax. 0392-410250

Type of business: Quick printing
Total investment cost (exc. working capital) £65,000

Kalamazoo Franchising Ltd
Northfield
Birmingham B31 2RW
Tel: 021-411-2345. Fax. 021-411-2145

Type of business: Quick printing
Total investment cost (exc. working capital) £101,103

Kall-Kwik Printing
Kall-Kwik House
106 Pembroke Road
Ruislip Middlx HA4 8NW
Tel: 0895-632700. Fax. 0895-678267

Type of business: Quick printing
Total investment cost (exc. working capital) £67,500
BFA membership: Full

PDC International Plc
1 Church Lane
East Grinstead
West Sussex RH19 3AZ
Tel: 0342-315321. Fax. 0342-327117

Type of business: Quick printing
Total investment cost (exc. working capital) £56,000
BFA membership: Full

PIP Printing
FranPrint Ltd
Black Arrow House
2 Chandos Road
London NW10 6NF
Tel: 081-965-0700. Fax. 081-961-8831

Type of business: Quick printing
Total investment cost (exc. working capital) £67,500
BFA membership: Full

Printdesigns Ltd
Reliance Works
Chester Road
Kelsall
Cheshire CW6 ORJ
Tel: 0829-52095. or 52552.
Fax. 0829-51589

Type of business: Graphic design and print
Total investment cost (exc. working capital) £76,000
BFA membership: Early development

The Print Machine Ltd
71 South Street
Bishops Stortford
Hertsm CM23 3AL
Tel: 0279-505290

Type of business: Quick printing
Total investment cost (exc. working capital) £36,000

Prontaprint Plc
Coniscliffe House
Coniscliffe Road
Darlington DL3 7EX
Tel: 0325-483333. Fax. 0325-488665

Type of business: Quick printing
Ready cash requirement: £30,000
BFA membership: Full

Retailing - Beauty Products/ Toiletries

The Barry 'M' Shop
1 Bittacy Business Centre
Bittacy Hill
Mill Hill East
London NW7 1BA
Tel: 081-349-2992

Type of business: Retailers of beauty products

Body and Face Place (The)
Alan Paul Plc
Alan Paul House
164 New Chester Road
Birkenhead
Merseyside L64 9BG
Tel: 051-666-1496. Fax. 051-666-1459

Type of business: Retailers of natural beauty products
Total investment cost (exc. working capital) £65,000
BFA membership: Full

Body Reform
Natural Beauty Products Ltd
Western Avenue
Bridgend Industrial Estate
Bridgend
Mid Glamorgan CF31 3RT
Tel: 0656-766566. Fax. 0656-50456

Body Shop International Plc
Nairn House
Dominion Way
Rustington
West Sussex BN16 3LR
Tel: 0903-776151

Type of business: Natural beauty products

Copy Cats Ltd
46 Kansas Avenue
Salford Quays
Greater Manchester M5 2GL
Tel: 061-872-4114. Fax. 061-872-4129

Type of business: Retail fragrance and cosmetic bar
Total investment cost (exc. working capital) £10,000

Goodebodies Natural Beauty International Body Centres Ltd
Osborne House
20 Victoria Avenue
Harrogate
North Yorks HG1 5QY
Tel: 0423-500206. Fax. 0423-505334

Type of business: Natural Beauty products retailers
Total investment cost (exc. working capital) £51,500

Herbal World
Suite 16-17 Teme Street
Tenbury Wells
Worcs WR15 8AA
Tel: 0584-811515. Fax. 0584-811530

Type of business: Retailers of natural beauty and aromatherapy products
Total investment cost (exc. working capital) £60,000
BFA membership: Early development

Nectar Cosmetics Ltd
Carrickfergus Industrial Estate
Belfast Road
Carrickfergus
Northern Ireland BT38 8PH
Tel: 09603-69133. Fax. 09603-62892

Type of business: Retailers of natural beauty products
Total investment cost (exc. working capital) £60,000-£70,000
BFA membership: Full

Secret Garden Plc
153 Regent STreet
London W1
Tel: 071-439-3101. Fax. 071-43- 0642

Type of business: Aromatherapy and natural skin care retailers
Total investment cost (exc. working capital) £50,000
BFA membership: Early development

The Soap Shop Ltd
44 Sidwell Street
Exeter EX4 6NS
Tel: 0392-215682

Type of business: Retailers of environment-friendly cleaning products and toiletries
Total investment cost (exc. working capital) £30,000
BFA membership: Early development

Yves Rocher (London) Ltd
664 Victoria Road
South Ruislip
Middx HA4 ONY
Tel: 081-845-1222. Fax. 081-845-1023

Type of business: Retailing of natural beauty products
BFA membership: Full

Convenience Stores/Confectioners/Health Foods/Grocery

Beanfreaks Ltd
3 St. Mark Street
Cardiff CF1 2AF
Tel: 0222-222678

Type of business: Health food retailing

Bellina
31 Knightsdale Road
Ipswich
Suffolk IP1 4JJ
Tel: 0473-47444

Type of business: Retailing of Belgian chocolates
BFA membership: Associate

Circle C Stores
24 Fitzalan Road
Roffey
Horsham
West Sussex RH13 6AA
Tel: 0403-210450. Fax. 0403-68359

Type of business: Convenience stores
Total investment cost (exc. working capital) £80,000
BFA membership: Full

Circle K
Fareham Point
Wickham Road
Fareham
Hants PO16 7BU
Tel: 0329-822666

Type of business: Convenience stores
BFA membership: Full

Holland & Barrett
Canada Road
Byfleet
Surrey KT14 7JL
Tel: 09323-36022

Type of business: Retailing of health foods
BFA membership: Full

The Late Late Supershop (UK) Ltd
132-152 Powis Street
Woolwich
London SE18 6NL
Tel: 081-854-2000. Fax. 081-316-1936

Type of business: Convenience stores
Total investment cost (exc. working capital) £100,000-£150,000
BFA membership: Full

Natural Life Health Foods Ltd
15 Queens Street
Salisbury
Wilts SP11EY
Tel: 02407-3643. Fax. 0722-411086

Type of business: Retailers of health foods
Total investment cost (exc. working capital) £40,000-£70,000

Rusts Ltd
17 Covingham Square
Swindon
Wilts SN3 5AA
Tel: 0793-25331. Fax. 0793-481280

Type of business: Convenience stores
Total investment cost (exc. working capital) £70,000-£90,000
BFA membership: Early development

Scoop-A-Market
Bonnington Road Lane
Edinburgh EH6 5PX
Tel: 031-555-0545. Fax. 031-555-0550

Type of business: retailing of loose food items
Total investment cost (exc. working capital) £17,000

Thorntons
Derwent Street
Belper
Derbyshire DE5 1WP
Tel: 077-382-4181

Type of business: Retailing of confectionery
BFA membership: Full

Weigh and Save
3rd Floor Bridgewater House
Whitmarsh Street
Manchester M1 6LU
Tel: 061-236-7374

Type of business: Retail grocery
BFA membership: Full

Dry Cleaners

Euroclean
13 The Office Village
4 Romford Road
London E15 4BZ
Tel: 081-519-3045. Fax. 081-519-5873

Type of business: Dry cleaning
Total investment cost (exc. working capital) £80,000
BFA membership: Full

Muggins (UK) Ltd
JLA Group
Meadowcroft Lane
Halifax Road
Ripponden
West Yorkshire HX6 4AJ
Tel: 0422-822282. Fax. 04222-824390

Type of business: Dry cleaning and home cleaning services
Total investment cost (exc. working capital) £75,000-£85,000
BFA membership: Early development

Fashion

Bow Belles
Bow Belles
Brunswick Suite
Colwick Park
Nottingham NG2 4BH

Type of business: Hire of bridal wear

Bumpsadaisy Ltd
3 The Bayer Building
211 Lower Bristol Road
Bath BA2 7DQ
Tel: 0225-444188. Fax. 0225-444192

Type of business: Retailing and hire of maternity wear (home or shop based)
Total investment cost (exc. working capital) £23,320 (shop), £5,000 (home based)

Cinderella Designer Gowns Ltd
Lochrin
Coatbridge ML5 3SS
Tel: 0236-40957. Fax. 0236-35911

Type of business: Ladies dress hire
Total investment cost (exc. working capital) £9,500

Clarks Shoes Ltd
P.O. Box 106
40 High Street
Street
Somerset BA16 OYA
Tel: 0458-43131

Type of business: Shoe retailers
Total investment cost (exc. working capital) £85,000
BFA membership: Full

Clothesline
248 Seaward Street
Glasgow G41 1NG
Tel: 041-429-1433. Fax. 041-429 -5516

Type of business: Retailers of ladies casual fashions at discounted prices
Total investment cost (exc. working capital) £20,000
BFA membership: Associate

Coppernob
95 Great Portland Street
London W1N 5RA
Tel: 049-481-5158/5159

Type of business: ladies fashion

Dash
P.O. Box 5
Rowdell Road
Northolt
Middx UB5 5QT
Tel: 081-845-7777

Type of business: Retailing of fashion leisure wear
BFA membership: Associate

Just for the Night
80 Sandridge Road
St.Albans
Herts AL1 4AR
Tel: 0727-40759

Type of business: Ladies evening dress hire
Ready cash requirement: £13,000

Levi Shop
Levi Strauss (UK) Ltd
Moulton Park Industrial Estate
Northampton NN3 1OQ
Tel: 0604-790436

Type of business: Retailers of casual wear

Mamanbebe
40 Station Road Industrial Estate
Hailsham
East Sussex BN27 2EW
Tel: 0323-442121. Fax. 0323-442061
Type of business: Nursery/fashion retailing
Total investment cost (exc. working capital) £30,000

Pronuptia de Paris (Youngs Franchise Ltd)
70-78 York Way
Kings Cross
London N1 9AG
Tel: 081-0278-0343

Type of business: Bridal wear

Snips in Fashion
Eurobe Ltd
Station Approach
St.Mary Cray Station
Orpington
Kent BR5 2NB
Tel: 0689-22722. Fax. 0689-76517

Type of business: Fashion retailers
Total investment cost (exc. working capital) £20,000
BFA membership: Full

Tie Rack Plc
Capital Interchange Way
Brentford
Middx TW8 OEX
Tel: 081-995-1344. Fax. 081-995-0352

Type of business: Retailers of ties and accessories
Total investment cost (exc. working capital) £50,000
BFA membership: Full

Young's Formal Wear
(Young's Franchise Ltd)
70-78 York Way
Kings Cross
London N1 9AG
Tel: 081-278-0343

Type of business: Men's formal wear

Interior Furnishings

Apollo Window Blinds Ltd
Johnstone Avenue
Glasglow G52 4YH
Tel: 041-810-3021. Fax. 041-883-6577

Type of business: Window blind and curtain retailing. Blind manufacturing.
Total investment cost (exc. working capital) £29,000
BFA membership: Full

The Blind Spot (Franchising) Ltd
805 Lincoln Road
Peterborough PE1 3HG
Tel: 0733-312913. Fax. 0733-557688

Type of business: Retailers and manufacturers of made-to-measure window blinds
Total investment cost (exc. working capital) £30,000-£50,000

Carpetlink Ltd
63-65 Boughton
Chester CH3 5AF
Tel: 0244-319349

Type of business: Retailing of carpets

Colour Counsellors Ltd
3 Dovedale Studios
465 Battersea Park Road
London SW11 4LR
Tel. 01-978-5023 Fax. 01-924-3008

Type of business: interior design and supplies
Total investment cost (exc. working capital): £12,000
BFA membership: full

Curtain Dream
30 Nesfield Street
Bradford
West Yorks BD1 3ET
Tel. 0274-840840

Type of business: retailers of curtains and soft furnishings

Decorating Systems (Scotland) Ltd
Alva Industrial Estate
Clackmannanshire
Scotland FK12 5DQ
Tel. 0800-838582 Fax. 0259-69434

Type of business: van-based interior design service
Total investment cost (exc. working capital): £10,900 - £13,900

Home Choose Carpets
Jubilee House
Jubilee Court
Dersingham
King's Lynn PE33 6HH
Tel. 0485-43021

Type of business: van based sales of carpet

Pictures/framing

Athena
Pentos Retailing Group Ltd
Berwick House
Livery Street
Birmingham B3 2PB
Tel. 021-236-6886 Fax. 021-233-3804

Type of business: retailers of cards, posters, prints, frames, gifts
Total investment cost (exc. working capital): £90,000

Fastframe Franchises Ltd
International Centre
Netherton Park
Stannington
Northumberland NE61 6EF
Tel. 067089-697/797 Fax. 067089-792

Type of business: picture framing
Total investment cost (exc. working capital): £49,000
BFA membership: full

The Frame Factory Franchise Ltd
67 Vivian Avenue
Hendon
London NW4 3XE
Tel. 01-202-2499 Fax. 01-202-1235

Type of business: retail framing
Total investment cost (exc. working capital): £28,000

Original Art Shops Ltd
12 Southchurch Road
Southend-on-Sea
Essex SS1 2NE
Tel. 0702-460391

Type of business: retailers of pictures and framing
Total investment cost (exc. working capital): £40,000
BFA membership: full

Travel agencies

Exchange Travel (Agency) Ltd
Exchange House
Parker Road
Hastings
East Sussex TN34 3UB
Tel. 0424-423571 Fax. 0424-420515

Type of business: travel agency
Total investment cost (exc. working capital): £40,000
BFA membership: full

Video Rental

Moviebank (The)
The Automated Retailer Co Ltd
21 Greycaine Road
Bushey Mill Lane
Watford WD2 4QT
Tel. 0923-55923 Fax. 0923-35417

Type of business: automated video rental library
Total investment cost (exc. working capital): £8,125
BFA membership: early development

Vidoe Cube (UK) Ltd
23 Harley House
Marylebone Road
London NW1 5HE
Tel. 01-224-3060 Fax. 01-224-2061

Type of business: automated video rental library
Total investment cost (exc. working capital): £55,000

Other

Bike
31 Kensington Church Street
London W8 4LL
Tel. 01-376-2711

Type of business: retailing of cycles and accessories

Capricci
CMT International
Bridge House
Saltcotes Road
Lytham St. Annes
Lancs FY8 4HN
Tel. 0253-733656 Fax. 0253-733656

Type of business: retailers of luggage, leathergoods and accessories
Total investment cost (exc. working capital): £20,000

Compleat Franchise Services Ltd
Enterprise House
Buckingham Road
Aylesbury
Bucks HP19 3QQ
Tel. 0296-433113 Fax. 0296-26102

Type of business: cookware and houseware retailing
Total investment cost (exc. working capital): £55,000

Computerland Europe SA
Windsor Crown House
7 Windsor Road
Slough
Berks SL1 2DX
Tel. 0753-512123

Type of business: retailers of computers and software
BFA membership: rull

Crown Optical Centre
Crown Eyeglass Plc
Glenfield Park
Northrop Avenue
Blackburn
Lancs BB1 5QF
Tel. 0254-51535 Fax. 0254-680241

Type of business: eye centres
Total investment cost (exc. working capital): £20,000
BFA membership: full

Descamps Ltd
197 Sloane Street
London SW1X 9QX
Tel. 01-235-3903

Type of business: retailers of up-market household linen
Total investment cost (exc. working capital): £60,000 - £100,000
BFA membership: early development

Fires and Things
Heat House
4 Brighton Road
Horsham
West Sussex RH13 5BA
Tel. 0403-56227 Fax. 0403-58583

Type of business: retailing of fires and fireplaces
Total investment cost (exc. working capital): £25,000
BFA membership: associate

The Flower Express
20 Theresa Avenue
Bishopstown
Bristol B57 9EP
Tel 0272-428669

Type of business: retailers of flowers

Flower Stop Ltd
35 Cranleigh Close
Sanderstead
Surrey CR2 9LH
Tel. 01-651-6415

Type of business: retail photo developing and printing

In-Style Optical Centres
Home Optical Services Ltd
50 Houghton Avenue
Bacup
Lancs OL13 9RD
Tel. 061-655-3105

Type of business: eye centres
Total investment cost (exc. working capital): £15,000

Insport
1d Saxeway Chartridge Lane
Chartridge
Chesham
Bucks HP5
Tel. 0494-791277 Fax. 0494-792083

Type of business: retailers of sport equipment and clothing
Total investment cost (exc. working capital): £60,000

Inter-Teddy Worldwide Ltd
13 Manor Court
Leigham Avenue
London SW16 2DH
Tel. 01-664-6063

Type of business: retailers of gift-wrapped teddy bears

Knobs & Knockers Franchising Ltd
Hathaway House
7d Woodfield Road
London W9 2EA
Tel. 01-289-4764 Fax. 01-289-0343

Type of business: retailers of brass fittings and home accessories
Total investment cost (exc. working capital): £80,000 - £90,000
BFA membership: full

Kwik-Silver Print (Franchising) Ltd
263 Commercial Road
Portsmouth
Hampshire PO1 4BP
Tel. 0705-730205 Fax. 0705-738941

Type of business: photographic developing and printing
Total investment cost (exc. working capital): £15,000

Mainly Marines
6 Trojan Way
Croydon CR0 4XL
Tel. 01-681-8421

Type of business: retailing of aquatic products
BFA membership: associate

Memories Plc
5 Cambridge Street
Manchester M1 5GF
Tel. 061-236-4487 Fax. 061-236-4495

Type of business: photographic studios
Total investment cost (exc. working capital): £40,000
BFA membership: early

The Open Fire Centres
Cattespoole Mill
Tardebigge
Nr Bromsgrove
Worcs B60 1LZ
Tel. 021-445-5550 Fax. 021-445-6174

Type of business: retailers of fireplaces
Total investment cost (exc. working capital): £18,000
BFA membership: early development

Pandel Tiles
Proctor & Lavender Ltd
Unit 38
Forge Lane
Minworth Industrial Park
Sutton Coldfield
West Midlands B76 8AH
Tel. 021-351-5391 Fax. 021-351-4810

Type of business: retailers of ceramic tiles
Total investment cost (exc. working capital): £10,000

Phone-In (UK) Ltd
Enterprise House
Valley Street North
Darlington
Co. Durham DL1 5GY
Tel. 0325-483859 Fax. 0325-481330

Type of business: retailers of phones and other telecommunications equipment.
Total investment cost (exc. working capital): £28,000

Robin Hood Golf Centre
196-202 Robin Hood Lane
Hall Green
Birmingham B28 0LG
Tel. 021-778-4161 Fax. 021-777-7544

Type of business: retail golf centres
Total investment cost (exc. working capital): £35,000 - £40,000

Ryman
Pentos Retailing Group Ltd
35 Livery Street
Birmingham B3 2PB
Tel. 021-236-6886 Fax. 021-233-3804

Type of business: retail stationers
Total investment cost (exc. working capital): £120,000

Singer
91 Colman Road
Leicester LE5 4LE
Tel. 0533-769471

Type of business: retailing of sewing machines, etc.
BFA membership: full

Snappy Snaps (UK) Ltd
11-12 Glenthorne Mews
115 Glenthorne Road
London W6 0LJ
Tel. 01-741-7474 Fax. 01-748-3849

Type of business: retail photo processing
Total investment cost (exc. working capital): £68,000
BFA membership: associate

Tandy
Intertan (UK) Ltd
Tandy Centre
Leamore Lane
Walsall WS2 7PS
Tel. 0922-710000

Type of business: retailers of hi-fi and electrical products

Body Sense Ltd
The Chestnuts
18 East Street
Farnham
Surrey GU9 7SD
Tel. 0252-733121 Fax. 0252-733670

Type of business: body toning salons
Total investment cost (exc. working capital): £36,000

Splash Dance
143a North Street
Romford
Essex RM1 1ES
Tel. 0708-730431

Type of business: water work-out fitness classes

Sweatbox UK Ltd
10 Barnstaple Close
Thorpe Bay
Essex SS1 3PD
Tel. 0702-582469/349340

Type of business: keep-fit classes with associated merchandise
Total investment cost (exc. working capital): £20,000

APPENDIX 3

THE CONSTITUTION AND THE RULES AND BY-LAWS OF THE ASSOCIATION

1. **NAME**
The name of the Association shall be The Independent Kall-Kwik Franchise Owners Association (The Association, or IKKFOA).

2. **ADDRESS**
The Address of the Association shall be that of the Chairman, for the time being, of the Association.

3. **AIMS AND OBJECTS**
The Aims and Objects of the Association are:

(a) To maintain and improve the facilities and effectiveness of the Kall-Kwik system for the benefit of Members.
(b) To provide a platform, through its Committee, for joint liaison between Kall-Kwik Printing and Members on all matters of general and mutual interest necessary to achieve (a) above.
(c) To promote social contact and discourse between Members on all matters of common concern and interest.
(d) To act, through its Committee, upon any other matter to protect the general interests of all Members.

4. **CONSTITUTION**
(a) The Constitution of the Association shall consist of an Elected Committee of sufficient numbers and geographical distribution to represent the Membership, with a Chairman, Secretary and Treasurer.
(b) The Committee and its Officers shall be elected and/or appointed as specifically provided for in clauses 9, 10, 12, 13 and 14.
(c) The classes of Membership and their eligibility to vote shall be as specifically provided for in Clauses 5, 6, 7 and 8.

5. **MEMBERS**
(a) A Member of the Association shall be any person who is a Franchisee signatory or co-signatory to a Kall-Kwik Printing Franchise Agreement (Agreement) and is operational (Member).
(b) Any Member may attend, and speak at, any General, Special or Social Meeting of the Association, but may vote only as specifically provided for in Clause 8.
(c) Membership of the Association is automatic and shall be open to any person as defined in (a) above who wishes to support and participate in the activities of the Association.

6. **FOUNDING MEMBERS**

(a) A Founding Member shall be any Member who was operational prior to 1st June 1981, whose name appears in the list of Founding Members in the Member's Handbook.

(b) All provisions as for Members shall apply to Founding Members.

(c) Founding Members may be requested to participate in the activities of the Committee as provided for in Clause 15(b).

7 **ASSOCIATE MEMBERS**

(a) Associate Membership shall be open to any person otherwise qualified as in Clause 5(a) above who has completed the Kall-Kwik Franchisees Training Course but has not yet become operational (Associate Member).

(b) The provisions of Clause 5(b) above shall apply to Associate Members.

8. **VOTING MEMBERS**

(a) A voting member of the Association shall be a member whose subscription to IKKFOA is current (Voting Member) as provided for in Clause 21 (a)(b)(c)(d)(e).

(b) Where there is more than one Member co-signatory to an Agreement all such co-signatory Members shall appoint one of them as Voting Member.

(c) A Member who is a signatory or co-signatory to more than one Agreement may act as Voting Member for each of the Agreements, subject also to the provisions of (a) and (b) above.

(d) For the purposes of conducting the Association's business the Voting Member shall be the unit of membership with one Voting Member only per Agreement.

(e) Only Voting Members shall make nominations or propose or second resolutions, or vote at meetings or in ballots.

9. **MANAGEMENT BY ELECTED COMMITTEE**

(a) The affairs of the Association shall be managed and conducted by a representative Committee consisting of five Elected Members, who may also appoint an additional Member as provided for in (c) below. (Committee) (Committee Members).

(b) There shall be a minimum of one and a maximum of two Committee Members elected from each of three representative regions: UK North, UK South and Greater London as defined in Clause 11 below.

(c) The Elected Committee Members shall have the power at any time, to appoint by unanimous vote, an additional Member to serve on the Committee for a term of up to twelve months.

(d) The Committee shall have the power to do any of the things necessary to achieve the Aims and Objects of the Association bearing in mind always the requests and resolutions of the Voting Membership and of the Annual General Meeting and Special Meetings.

(e) A minimum of three Committee Members, of which one shall be the Chairman, shall constitute a quorum.

(f) All disciplinary matters regarding Committee Members shall be decided by majority vote of all members of the committee.

10. ELIGIBILITY TO SERVE ON COMMITTEE

To be eligible for nomination and election, or appointment to, and to serve on, the Committee a Member:

(a) shall be a Voting Member.
(b) shall not be a member who is a co-signatory to an Agreement to which a current committee member is also a co-signatory.
(c) shall have been operational for a minimum period of twelve months prior to the time at which, if elected, the member would commence serving the term.
(d) shall not be in unreasonable breach of the Agreement.
(e) shall not be a signatory or co-signatory to any non Kall-Kwik franchise agreement, or be directly connected or associated with any other franchise business, or with any business which, in the majority opinion of all Committee Members, is or may be potentially competitive with other Members, or may create a conflict of interest.

11. REPRESENTATIVE REGIONS

The Representative Regions as stated in Clause 9(b) above shall be defined for the time being as:

(a) UK North: the counties of Gloucester, Warwick, Northampton, Cambridge and Lincoln, and all areas of the United Kingdom to the north and north west of those counties.
(b) UK South: all areas of the United Kingdom (excluding Greater London) to the south of the area defined in (a) above.
(c) Greater London: the area contained within the M25 Orbital Motorway.
(d) The Committee may re-define the boundaries above from time to time as they deem appropriate, as the number and distribution of the members' locations changes, in order to maintain approximately equal numbers of members in each region. Such redefining shall be stated at the time of notifying members of forthcoming elections.

12. NOMINATION AND ELECTION OF COMMITTEE MEMBERS

(a) Nominations shall be received and elections held for Committee Members at the Annual General Meeting.
(b) Notice of elections for each region shall be given to members one month prior to the AGM.
(c) Nominees shall be proposed and seconded by Voting Members and shall confirm their willingness to serve if elected.
(d) Any Voting Member may propose or second the nomination of a Member from their region. Nominations may be made in writing to the Chairman prior to the AGM. or from the floor of the meeting.
(e) Committee Members shall be elected by a simple majority of votes cast by voting members.
(f) In making nominations members should aim to achieve a representative mix of Member's: length of membership; metropolitan or provincial locations; and geographical distribution.

13. **PERIOD OF SERVICE ON COMMITTEE**

(a) Committee Members shall be elected to serve for a term from the date of their election to the date of the next but one AGM. - aproximately two years (Term).

(b) Committee Members may offer themselves for re-election for a second Term but may serve only for a maximum of two consecutive Terms at one time, except as provided for in (d) below.

(c) Former Committee Members who have previously served two consecutive Terms may be nominated for election after the elapse of a further Term.

(d) A Committee Member who is nominated as Chairman during a second consecutive term, with not more than one year remaining to serve at the time of such nomination, may be nominated and elected at the end of that second consecutive term to serve for one further year, or until the next AGM, as a representative Member in the office of Chairman.

(e) In the event of the resignation or termination of office of a committee Member, the Committee shall be empowered to co-opt by majority vote of all Committee Members a Voting Member to represent that region until the next AGM, when an election shall be held to confirm that appointed member, or to receive and elect other nominations to complete the original Term of office remaining of one year.

14. **COMMITTEE OFFICERS**

The Committee shall appoint at each AGM:

(a) A Committee Member to served as Chairman for the ensuing year until the next AGM. The appointment shall be submitted to the meeting for the members approval.

(b) A Committee Member to serve as Secretary until the next AGM.

(c) A Committee Member or Voting Member to serve as Treasurer until the next AGM.

15. **COMMITTEE MEETINGS AND RESPONSIBILTIES**

(a) The Committee shall meet regularly to discuss and take action on matters raised by Members of general concern to all Members.

(b) The Committee shall meet at approximately six monthly intervals with all Past Chairmen and Founding Members, qualified under the provisions of Clause 8 and Clause 10(e), to discuss matters of general policy concerning The Association.

(c) The Committee shall arrange regular meetings with the Management of Kall-Kwik Printing to raise and discuss matters of interest to the membership.

(d) The Committee shall not deal with matters which are solely of a personal or individual nature relating to a Member's Agreement and shall encourage continuing direct dialogue by Members within the framework of the established relationship and of their Agreement. The Committee may however offer assistance, if so requested by a Member or by Kall-Kwik Printing, if in the longer term there is failure to resolve such matters satisfactorily.

(e) Members should keep the Committee informed, where appropriate, of individual matters of concern to them in order that the Committee may coordinate a general interest approach if similar individual situations are being experienced by other Members.

16. SUB-COMMITTEES

(a) The Committee may co-opt Members and/or appoint Sub-Committees of Members with specialised knowledge or interests, to advise or act on special projects on behalf of the Association.

(b) The Committee shall be empowered to seek the advice of outside specialists from time to time as it may see fit, to provide for the needs of the Association Membership, and to disburse fees or remuneration to such specialists as provided for in Clause 22.

17. ANNUAL GENERAL MEETING

(a) The Annual General Meeting of the Association (AGM) shall be held each year at the Annual Kall-Kwik Printing Conference.

(b) The Agenda for the AGM shall include: The Chairman's Report and Summary of the Committee's proceedings for the year; the minutes of the previous AGM and matters arising; a summary of the Associations accounts; elections and appointments; and any other business.

(c) Notice of the Meeting, the Agenda, and Notes on the above shall be circulated to all Members not less than two weeks prior to the AGM.

(d) Only Members and their spouses may attend the AGM.

18. SPECIAL MEETINGS AND POSTAL BALLOTS

(a) The Chairman may at any time for any purpose call a Special Meeting or hold a Special Postal Ballot, and shall do so forthwith upon the majority request of all of the Committee, or upon the requisition in writing of twenty Voting Members, stating the purpose for which the Special Meeting/Ballot is called.

(b) No business other than that for which a Special Meeting/Ballot is called shall be transacted at such a Meeting or Ballot.

(c) A minimum of twenty one days notice shall be given of a Special Meeting or fourteen days for the return of a Postal Ballot.

(d) A majority of two thirds of Voting Members present at a Special Meeting or of votes received in a Postal Ballot shall be required to pass any resolution so proposed except as provided for in Clause 24.

(e) Only Members and their spouses may attend Special Meetings.

19. SOCIAL MEETINGS

(a) The Chairman may arrange at any time, at the request of the Committee or of Members, Social Meetings for the purpose of furthering social contact, discourse and understanding between Members, regionally and nationally.

(b) The Committee may appoint, or authorise sub-committees of members to arrange and conduct such Social Meetings on behalf of the Association.

(c) Any Member or Associate Member and their spouse and family may attend any Social Meeting and may bring with them non-members as their guests. Non-member guests shall be the sole responsibility of their member host(s).

20. RESOLUTIONS

(a) Any Resolution, other than Resolutions provided for by Clause 24, may be proposed or seconded by a Voting Member at the AGM, or in writing to the Chairman at any time prior to the AGM, or in accordance with the provisions of Clause 18 relating to Special Meetings.

(b) A majority of Voting Members present at the AGM shall be required to pass a Resolution.

(c) In the event of a tied vote, the Chairman shall make a casting vote.

21. SUBSCRIPTIONS

(a) An annual Subscription shall be paid for each Agreement by each Voting Member due on 1st January of each year covering the ensuing year to 31st December.

(b) The amount of the full annual Subscription shall be fixed each year, by the Voting Membership at the AGM, for the following year based on the estimated amount required to cover the Association's administrative expenditures.

(c) The Subscription payable by Voting Members in their first year of operation shall be one-half of the full annual subscription.

(d) A Voting Member who is serving on the Committee shall have the Subscription waived for the calendar year(s) for which the Member so serves.

(e) The Committee may also, at its discretion, by majority vote waive the Subscription for a period, of any Member in recognition of services rendered by that Member, or in other special circumstances as it may see fit. Any Member whose Subscription is so waived may be a Voting Member not withstanding the provisions of Clause 8(a).

(f) Subscriptions, or any balances held by the Association shall remain the property of Voting Members, and shall be expended by the Committee only in accordance with the authorisation of Voting Members as provided for in Clause 22.

(g) In the event of the winding up or dissolution of the Association, any balance of Subscriptions held in the Association's accounts, after all outstanding expenditures have been paid, shall be returned to Voting Members pro-rata, on the basis of one full part or half part for each full or half Subscription paid by the Voting Members for the current and previous calendar year.

22. EXPENDITURES

(a) Subscriptions shall be used solely to cover necessary expenditures, only as specifically authorised by the Committee, incurred in the administration of the Association's Committee, Annual, Special and Social Meetings and other affairs, including reimbursement of direct out-of-pocket costs of

Members attending committee meetings, printing, postage, telephone and fees.

(b) Any single expenditure in excess of £200 may only be authorised by a Resolution and vote of the Association.

23. ACCOUNTS

(a) The Association's Accounts shall be maintained by the Treasurer appointed under the provisions of Clause 14(c).

(b) A current bank account shall be maintained with the Chairman and/or Treasurer as signatories.

(c) A deposit account, subject to sufficient interim balance of funds, shall be maintained.

(d) A full record itemising all receipts and expenditures shall be kept and Accounts approved annually by the Committee prior to the AGM.

(e) The Treasurer shall present a summary of the Accounts to all Voting Members at the AGM.

24. CHANGES TO THE CONSTITUTION, RULES AND BY-LAWS

(a) Any Resolution to amend the Constitution, Rules and By-Laws of the Association shall be proposed by a number of Voting Members equal to not less than one-sixth of the total number of Voting Members at the time of the making of the Resolution(s).

(b) Such Resolution(s) shall be sent to the Chairman, together with, as appropriate, accompanying Notes and explanation of the purposes of the Resolution by the proposers.

(c) The Chairman shall circulate copies of the Resolution and Notes, together with the Committee's comments to all Voting Members for their consideration.

(d) A vote on the Resolution(s) shall be taken at the next AGM, or may be taken previously at a Special Meeting or Postal Ballot under the provisions of Clause 18(a) (b) and (e) with not less than twenty eight days notice of any such meeting or return of the ballot.

(e) A vote by Voting Members of a number in favour of not less than two-thirds of the total number of Voting Members of the Association at the time of the ballot shall be required to approve any amendments to the Consitution, Rules and By-Laws.

25. RULES

(a) A copy of these Rules and By-Laws shall be circulated to all Members by the Secretary.

(b) The Secretarty shall change the Rule Book within twenty eight days of any meeting or ballot in strict accordance with the wording of the accepted amendments and shall circulate notice of such changes to all Members.

26. **CONDUCT OF MEMBERS**

(a) All Members of the Association shall be bound by these Rules and By-Laws and such other Rules and By-Laws as shall be made from time to time.

(b) Members, who in the opinion of the Committee have behaved in a manner prejudicial to the welfare and interests of the Association and its Membership may, by majority vote of all of the Committee, be suspended or expelled from the Association, after having not less than fourteen days notice of the complaint made and an opportunity of being heard in explanation of defence.

APPENDIX 4

Franchise agreement – short form

By John Adams and K. V. Prichard Jones

REPRINTED FROM FRANCHISING: PRACTICE AND PRECEDENTS IN BUSINESS FORMAT FRANCHISING BY KIND PERMISSION OF THE PUBLISHERS, BUTTERWORTHS

Dated .... 19........

1 Parties

.... whose [registered office *or* principal place of business] is at (*address*) ('the Franchisor') (1)

.... whose [registered office *or* principal place of business] is at (*address*) ('the Franchisee') (2)

2 Definitions

The following terms shall have the following meanings:

2.1 'Advertising Contribution': ....% of Gross Turnover (as defined in clause [3.12] of the Conditions] of the Business

2.2 'Business': the use (for mutual benefit) of the Mark and the Know-How in the business of trading under the Permitted Name in the style and manner stipulated by the Franchisor for (*insert details of Business to be carried out*)

2.3 'Conditions': the Standard Conditions and Special Conditions (if any) annexed to this Agreement which shall be deemed to be incorporated in this Agreement in their entirety

2.4 'Continuing Fees': the franchise fees of ....% of Gross Turnover (as defined in clause [3.12] of the Conditions) of the Business

2.5 'Financial Year': each year during the Term ending on the .... (*year end date*)

2.6 'Initial Fee': the initial franchise fee of £.......... (........pounds)

2.7 'Know-How': the operational systems and methods of the Franchisor as divulged to the Franchisee from time to time during the Term

2.8 'Location': the premises shortly described as .... or such other premises as are approved by the Franchisor during the Term

2.9 'Manual': the confidential written systems of and regulations for the operation of the Business issued and amended by the Franchisor from time to time during the Term incorporating part of the Know-How and deemed to form part of this Agreement (Serial Number ....)

2.10 'Mark': the [Legend] [and design] and the logos associated with the same and any additional or substitute Marks which the Franchisor shall deem suitable for the Business during the Term

2.11 'Minimum Package':

2.11:1 The equipment products literature stock of all types and

2.11:2 The minimum staff levels [at the location] stipulated in the manual from time to time during the Term

2.12 'Payment Dates':

2.12:1 For the Initial Fee: on the signing of this Agreement

2.12:2 For the Advertising Contributions and the Continuing Fees: the [tenth] day of each [calendar month] during the Term in respect of the Business during the immediately preceding calendar month

2.13 'Permitted Name': the permitted business name of the Franchisee which shall be '........'

2.14 'Term': .... years from .... 19....... (the Commencement Date) and expiring on .... 19....... (the Expiry Date) unless sooner determined as provided in the Conditions

2.15 'Territory': the geographical area of (*insert description of area*) [and shown edged red on the map annexed to this Agreement]

3 The Right

In consideration of the payment of the Initial Fee the Insurance Premium the Advertising Contribution and the Continuing Fees by the Franchisee to the Franchisor and of and subject to the agreements on the part of the Franchisee in this Agreement the Franchisor grants to the Franchisee the right of using the Mark and the Know-How only:

3.1 In the Business

3.2 At and from the Location

3.3 Within the Territory

3.4 For the Term

3.5 Under the Permitted Name

3.6 In accordance with the Manual

Dated ....day of .... 19........

Signed by .... (*name of director*) for and on behalf of .... (*name of Franchisor*)

Signed by .... (*name of director*) for and on behalf of .... (*name of Franchisee*)

STANDARD CONDITIONS

1 Title

The Franchisor warrants that it is the beneficial owner of the Mark and Know-How

2 Franchisor's obligations

The Franchisor agrees as follows:

2.1 Training
To provide within 90 days of this date at a place chosen by the Franchisor training in the conduct of the Business for one director of the Franchisee and all the initial employees of the Franchisee the cost of which is included in the Initial Fee
2.2 Manual
To issue the Franchisee with the Manual and to update it (provided the same shall remain the property of the Franchisor)
2.3 Advertising
To undertake an advertising and promotional programme for the Mark in selected areas of the British Isles in such manner as it considers appropriate using the Advertising Contribution
2.4 Advertising bank account
To pay the Advertising Contribution (together with similar contributions from [stores *or* outlets] owned by the Franchisor) into a separate bank account of the Franchisor maintained for that purpose only
2.5 Expenses
To issue to the Franchisee an account of the total expenditure by the Franchisor on advertising and promotion in each Financial Year of the term provided that the Franchisor shall be entitled to recoup at any time from the total of the Advertising Contribution from all its franchisees in any year any excess of such expenditure over the total of receipts of the Advertising Contributions in previous or future years
2.6 Exclusive
Not to undertake on its own behalf nor to grant any franchise to any other person or entity in respect of the Business in the Territory (subject as appears later in these Conditions)
2.7 Information
Throughout the Term to consider and respond to all reasonable requests from the Franchisee for information and assistance concerning the Business
2.8 Supply Conditions
To procure that products for the Business shall be supplied to the Franchisee by the Franchisor or its approved suppliers on the same terms as those supplies to [stores *or* outlets] operated by the Franchisor itself in the United Kingdom
[2.9 Additional sales
To permit the Franchisee to sell such equipment and similar items in addition to the Minimum Package in order to satisfy specific orders or demand subject to the prior approval by the Franchisor of such equipment and other items]

3 Franchisee's obligations
The Franchisee agrees throughout the Term:
3.1 Training first
3.1:1 Not to commence the Business until [one director of] the Franchisee and all its senior employees have received training from and have been approved as competent by the Franchisor

3.1:2 To notify the Franchisor whenever it employs new staff in the Business

3.1:3 Not to permit any person to be employed in the Business unless such person is first trained and approved as competent by the Franchisor

3.1:4 To procure that all its executives and employees attend further training during the Term when required by the Franchisor

3.2 Registered user

Where necessary to become the registered user of the Mark or to execute on demand from the Franchisor such formal licence for records purposes as may be required in the United Kingdom

3.3 Authority

To display at the Location and on all stationery and any literature used by the Franchisee the text stipulated in the Manual from time to time disclosing that the Franchisee is licensed by the Franchisor and is not a branch or agent of the Franchisor

3.4 Mark

3.4:1 Constantly to protect and promote the goodwill attached to the Mark (which the Franchisee acknowledges is of great value)

3.4:2 To hold any additional goodwill generated by the Franchisee for the Mark or the Permitted Name as bare trustee for the Franchisor

3.4:3 Not to cause or permit any damage to the Mark or the title of the Franchisor to it or assist others to do so

3.4:4 Not to use the Mark the Know-How or the Permitted Name except directly in the Business

3.4:5 Not to use the Mark the Know-How or the Permitted Name in any manner after the Term or other sooner determination of the Agreement

3.4:6 Not to use the Mark or any derivation of the same in the corporate name (if any) of the Franchisee

3.5 Secrecy

Not at any time during or after the Term:

3.5:1 to divulge to any third party any information concerning the Business the Franchisor the Know-How or any other systems or methods of the Franchisor used in the Business (especially that contained in the Manual)

3.5:2 to copy in any way in any part of the Manual

3.6 Disclosure

Not to employ any person in the Business until that person has signed a non-disclosure undertaking in the form approved by the Franchisor from time to time

3.7 Volume

To use its best endeavours to achieve the greatest volume of business for the Business at the Location consistent with good service to the public

3.8 No other business

Not without the prior approval of the Franchisor:

3.8:1 to permit any other business venture to operate or trade at or from the Location

3.8:2 to extend the scope or range of the Business at the Location

3.8:3 to engage directly or indirectly in any other business other than the Business

3.9 No illegal use

Not to engage in any activities in the Business which may be contrary to law or governments or other regulations

3.10 Payments

To pay the Initial Fee the Continuing Fees and the Advertising Contribution (without demand deduction or set-off) to the Franchisor (or as it directs) on each of the Payment Dates (time being of the essence)

3.11 VAT contingency

Whenever applicable to pay to the Franchisor VAT or any other tax or duty replacing the same during the Term charged or calculated on the amount of the Initial Fee the Continuing Fees and the Advertising Contribution

3.12 Calculations

To calculate the Continuing Fees and the Advertising Contribution on the gross turnover of the Business arising directly or indirectly from the conduct of the Business in the Territory during each calendar week of the Term (and for any period less than a complete calendar week) and gross turnover shall include

3.12:1 all credit sales of whatever nature whether or not the Franchisee has received payment of the outstanding accounts by the Payment Date relevant to the week when such credit sales were made

3.12:2 all cash sales of whatever nature made but not invoiced by the Franchisee in each week

3.12:3 all services performed and business dealings whatsoever (other than purchases) made or conducted in the Territory by the Business during each week

But shall exclude

3.12:4 any VAT

3.12:5 any customer refunds or credits arising from the supply of defective goods or services or the like provided that such refunds or credits shall only be deducted from gross turnover in the calendar week in which they are paid or allowed to the customer

3.13 Service report

On each Monday of each week to post by first-class mail (or by electronic means if required by the Franchisor) to the Franchisor complete and accurate statements in the form approved by the Franchisor in the Manual) of the sales and services performed by the Business since the last such Payment Date

3.14 Accurate accounts

To keep accurate books and accounts in respect of the Business in accordance with good accountancy custom in the United Kingdom and the standards set out in the Manual and to:

3.14:1 Accountants
have them audited at the expense of Franchisee once a year during the Term by the firm of Chartered Accountants nominated by the Franchisor

3.14:2 Audit
submit the whole of such audited accounts to the Franchisor within three months of the end of such year

3.14:3 Custody
keep them for not less than [3] years

3.14:4 Inspection
permit the Franchisor to inspect and take copies (at the expense of the Franchisor) of any financial information or records it requires (on reasonable prior notice in the event of inspection after normal business hours)

3.14:5 Financial Year
procure that each financial year or period of the Business shall be the same as the Financial Year

3.15 Discrepancies

In the event of discrepancies (amounting in total to more than [2%] per year of gross sales) in any such books or accounts to permit accountants nominated by the Franchisor but at the expense of the Franchisee to undertake audits of the same in each year of the Term of the Franchisor (at intervals at the discretion of the Franchisor) on reasonable notice and during normal business hours

3.16 VAT report

Within 14 days of submission or receipt to supply to the Franchisor a copy of each VAT return and/or assessment in respect of the Business

3.17 Conduct of the Business

Not to conduct the Business except:

3.17:1 Standards
In respect of services to the standards and quality and in the standard style and by the methods stipulated in the Manual from time to time

3.17:2 Regulations
In confirmity with all relevant government or other regulations

3.17:3 Financial systems
Under proper and comprehensive financial systems and controls as approved or stipulated by the Franchisor

3.17:4 Venue
At or from the Location or such other venue first approved by the Franchisor

3.17:5 Inside Territory
Inside the Territory

[3.17:6 Equipment
With the equipment part of the Minimum Package in good and reliable condition]

[3.17:7 Staff
With the staff part of the minimum package at full complement and fully trained and approved by the Franchisor]

3.17:8 Dealerships
In accordance with the rules and regulations of any dealership or distributorship arrangements for any of the equipment or products dealt in by the Business

3.18 Insurance policy

3.18:1 To maintain and pay all premiums in respect of a comprehensive insurance policy (in terms approved by the Franchisor) issued by an insurer nominated by the Franchisor in respect of the Location for all items stored there and for the business

3.18:2 To note on such policy that:

3.18:2.1 the Franchisor shall be covered by such policy in respect of all claims arising from activities at the Location or in the Business or of the Franchisee which are risks covered by such policy

3.18:2.2 the insurer shall notify the Franchisor in the event of any late premium payment by the Franchisee

3.19 Inspection of Premises

To permit the Franchisor or its representatives to inspect the Location at any time during the Term

3.20 Right notices

To affix such patent copyright or trade mark ownership notices to any stationery or literature used by the Franchisee in the Business as the Franchisor may require from time to time

3.21 Infringement indemnity

To indemnify the Franchisor from:

3.21:1 any alleged unauthorised use or infringement of any patent trade mark copyright or other intellectual property (other than the Mark and Know-How) by the Franchisee

3.21:2 any claim by any third party in respect of the conduct of the Business or the conduct or neglect of the Franchisee

3.21:3 any infringement by the Franchisee of any relevant regulations

3.22 Infringement notice

To notify the Franchisor of any suspected infringement of the intellectual property or other rights of the Franchisor and to take such reasonable action thereupon as the Franchisor directs at the expense of the Franchisor

3.23 Payment

Not to purchase any supplies [courses] products equipment or literature for the Business except from the Franchisor or (with the consent of the Franchisor) its approved suppliers to ensure even standards of quality of products and services from all the franchisees of the Franchisor and:

3.23:1 to pay the Franchisor for any equipment stationery or other items so purchased within 21 days of dispatch by the Franchisor

3.23:2 to pay promptly any other suppliers of the Franchisee in accordance with their usual terms and conditions

3.24 No sub-franchise

Not to grant any sub-franchise in respect of the Mark the Know-How or the Business

3.25 Promotions

3.25:1 To advertise the Business in the Territory in accordance with the requirements of the Franchisor set out in the Manual from time to time

3.25:2 (As part of such obligation) to expend not less than ......% of the gross turnover of the Business in each Financial Year upon local advertising and promotional activities

3.25:3 To participate in such promotional activities for the Business in the Territory as the Franchisor requires during the Term

3.26 Assignment

Not to assign transfer or otherwise deal with the Right or this Agreement or the Business in any way without the prior approval of the Franchisor which shall not be unreasonably withheld in the following circumstances:

3.26:1 if the proposed assignee is acceptable to the Franchisor and shall agree to be bound by the terms and conditions of the standard franchise agreement used by the Franchisor at the time of such proposed assignment for the residue of the Term and

3.26:2 if the Franchisee shall pay to the Franchisor the reasonable costs and expenses incurred by the Franchisor in the assessment of each proposed assignee

3.27 Director reliance

(As the Right has been granted to the Franchisee by the Franchisor in reliance upon the quality of the directors and shareholders of the Franchisee) not to permit any change in the same without the prior approval of the Franchisor which shall not be unreasonably withheld subject to the provisions in sub-clauses [3.26:1 and 3.26:2) of these conditions

3.28 Prices

3.28:1 Not to charge any customer any prices in excess of those stipulated in the Manual from time to time

3.28:2 Not to sell any items or provide any services to any person or entity associated with the Franchisee or its shareholders except at prices usually charged by the Franchisee to its non-connected customers

3.29 No competition

And for a period of [two] years afterwards:

3.29:1 Not to engage directly or indirectly in any capacity in any business venture competitive with or likely to damage the surviving goodwill of the Business in the Territory or in any territory any business venture competitive with any business of the other franchisee of the Franchisor

3.29:2 Not to solicit the customers or former customers of the Business with the intent of taking their custom

3.29:3 Not to employ any employee or former employees who were employed in the Business by the Franchisee or by the Franchisor or any other franchisee of the Franchisor

and to procure that all directors and shareholders of the Franchisee enter into direct covenants of similar content with the Franchisor

3.30 Grant back

To notify the Franchisor and provide full details of any improvements in the methods systems products or programmes described by the Franchisor in the Manual or employed in the Business and to permit the Franchisor to incorporate free of charge any such improvements in its Manual for the benefit of the Franchisor and all its franchisees.

[3.31 Premises

3.31:1 To maintain the Location in good decorative repair and condition

3.31:2 To alter the exterior and interior decoration signs and furnishings of the Location when required to do so by the Franchisor in accordance with any amendments it may make to the house style of the Business

3.31:3 To observe and perform all its obligations under any lease or tenancy of the Location]

4 Expiry procedure

On expiry or termination of this Agreement the Franchisee agrees:

4.1 Not to endeavour to surrender the telephones used in the Business nor to hinder the transfer of such telephones to such person as the Franchisor directs

4.2 To return to the Franchisor all stationery used in the Business

4.3 To return to the Franchisor all publicity promotional and advertising material

4.4 To return to the Franchisor the Manual in good condition and without having made any copy of the Manual

4.5 To sign such notification of cessation of use of the Mark as is necessary for recording at the Trade Marks Registry

4.6 To cease carrying on the Business immediately

4.7 (When the Franchisee is the tenant or lessee of the Franchisor at the Location) to surrender to the Franchisor the relevant tenancy agreement or lease immediately upon such expiry or termination and to vacate the Location immediately

5 Expiry financial procedure

The Franchisee agrees:

5.1 Four weeks prior to the expiry of the Term or three weeks after receipt of notice of termination of this Agreement to furnish to the Franchisor a complete and accurate up-to-date list of customers of the Business with estimates of turnover of the Business to such expiry or termination date and
5.2 Thereupon to pay the Continuing Fees and the Advertising Contribution on the estimated Gross Turnover to such date and
5.3 Not later than the first Friday after such date to pay to the Franchisor any additional amount of the Continuing Fees and the Advertising Contribution calculated on actual gross turnover of the Business to such date

6 Miscellaneous

It is further agreed between the parties:

6.1 Reservation of rights

6.1.1 All the rights not specifically and expressly granted to the Franchisee in this Agreement are reserved to the Franchisor

6.1:2 The Franchisor may grant a licence to any entity to manufacture any products in the Territory or elsewhere for use in connection with the Business or displaying the Mark or for other purposes (except in competition with the Franchisee in the Territory) without any liability to the Franchisee

6.2 Interest

Without prejudice to the rights of the Franchisor and the condition that the Initial Fee the Advertising Contribution and the Continuing Fees are paid on time (time being of the essence) all sums due to the Franchisor which are not paid on the due date shall bear interest from day to day at the annual rate of ....% over the current Bank plc daily base interest rate with a minimum of ......%

6.3 Payment not on time

In the event that the Franchisee fails to pay any money due to the Franchisor on time the Franchisor may

6.3:1 cease immediately to take orders from and to deliver goods and services to the Franchisee

6.3:2 afterwards impose whatever credit limit it considers appropriate in respect of the Business of the Franchisee

6.4 Receipt

The receipt of money by the Franchisor shall not prevent either of the parties questioning the correctness of any statement in respect of that money

6.5 Force majeure

Both parties shall be released from their respective obligations in the event of national emergency war prohibitive governmental regulations or if any other cause beyond the control of the parties shall render performance of the Agreement impossible provided that this clause shall only have effect at the discretion of the Franchisor except when such event renders performance impossible for a continuous period of [12] calendar months

6.6 Severance

In the event that any provision of this agreement or these Conditions is declared by any judicial or other competent authority to be void voidable illegal or otherwise unenforceable [or indications of the same are received by either of the parties from any relevant competent authority] [the parties shall amend that provision in such reasonable manner as achieves the intention of the parties without illegality or the Franchisor may sever the offending provision from the same at its discretion *or* the remaining provisions of this Agreement shall remain in full force and effect unless the Franchisor in the Franchisor's discretion decides that the effect of such declaration is to defeat the original intention of the parties in which event the Franchisor shall be entitled to terminate this Agreement by [30] days' notice to the Franchisee and the provisions of clause [4] shall apply accordingly]

6.7 Low sales

The Franchisor may terminate this Agreement in the event that reasonably substantial turnover (which shall be calculated by the Franchisor on the basis of demographic and socio-economic data in respect of the Territory and the performance of its other franchisees) arising from the Business at the Location is not achieved within two years of the Commencement Date of the Agreement or for a continuous period of twelve months at any time afterwards during the Term provided that the Franchisor shall have the right (but not the duty):

6.7:1 then to appoint management personnel to supervise the Business at the expense of the Business to assist the Franchisor to increase sales and/or

6.7:2 to reduce the area of the Territory in proportion to such sales

6.8 New outlets

6.8:1 In the event that the Franchisor decides that the Territory is sufficiently large geographically and has a sufficiently large population to justify one or more further outlets for the Business in the Territory it may notify the Franchisee of such decision and on receipt of such notice the Franchisee shall have the right to open such further outlet elsewhere than at the Location in an area of the Territory nominated by the Franchisor) provided that the Franchisee informs the Franchisor within 90 days of such notice of its agreement to do so

6.8:2 In the event that the Franchisee fails to notify the Franchisor of such agreement within 90 days or fails to open such further outlet in the Territory within six months of such notice the Franchisor shall have the right to reduce the Territory to enable it to provide an exclusive area in which a new franchisee may trade using the Mark and the Know-How without liability to the Franchisee

6.9 Prior obligations

The expiration or termination of this Agreement shall not relieve either of the parties of their respective prior obligations or impair or prejudice their respective rights against the other

6.10 Discretion
No decision exercise of discretion judgement opinion or approval of any matter mentioned in this Agreement or arising from it shall be deemed to have been made by the Franchisor except if in writing and shall be at its sole discretion unless otherwise expressly provided in this Agreement or these Conditions

6.1 Notice

6.11:1 Any notice to be served on either of the parties by the other shall be sent by prepaid recorded delivery or registered post (as the case may be) or by telex or by electronic mail and shall be deemed to have been received by the addressee within 72 hours of posting or 24 hours if sent by telex or by electronic mail to the correct telex or electronic mail number of the addressee

6.11:2 Each of the parties shall notify the other of any change of address or number as soon as practicable and in any event within 48 hours of such change

6.12 No agency
The parties are not partners or joint venturers nor is the Franchisee able to act as the agent or to pledge the credit of the Franchisor in any way

6.13 Whole agreement
The Franchisee acknowledges that this Agreement and these Conditions contain the whole agreement between the parties and it had not relied upon any oral or written representations made to it by the Franchisor or its employees or agents and has made its own independent investigations into all matters relevant to the Business

6.14 Breach procedure
In the event that the Franchise fails to observe or perform any of its obligations under this Agreement or these Conditions in any way then the Franchisor may terminate this Agreement on 30 days' written notice and

6.14:1 notwithstanding such notice period if the breach complained of its incapable of remedy this Agreement shall terminate absolutely on service of such notice

6.14:2 in every other case if the breach complained of is remedied to the satisfaction of the Franchisor within the notice period this Agreement shall not terminate

6.14:3 no waiver of any breach of those obligations shall constitute a waiver of any further or continuing breach of the same

6.15 Insolvency
If the Franchisee enters into liquidation or suffers a receiver to be appointed to it or to any of its assets or makes a composition with any of its creditors (or the equivalent in Scotland) the Franchisor may at any time afterwards terminate this Agreement on notice with immediate effect and:

6.15:1 no creditor agent representative or trustee of the Franchisee shall have the right to use the Mark or the Know-How or continue the Business without the prior consent of the Franchisor

6.15:2 until payment of all money due to the Franchisor from the Franchisee on any account the Franchisor shall have a lien on any of the stock literature or other products held by the Franchisee

6.16 Assignment

The Franchisor may assign charge or otherwise deal with this Agreement in any way

6.17 Renewal option

The Franchisee shall have the option to extend the Term for a further period of .... years commencing on the day following the Expiry Date subject to the following:

6.17:1 service of notice of extension by the Franchisee on the Franchisor not later than ...... calendar months prior to the Expiry Date and

6.17:2 payment by the Franchisee to the Franchisor not later than two calendar months prior to the Expiry Date of a renewal fee of ......% of gross turnover of the Business during 12 calendar months prior to the first day of the calendar month in which such notice is served or the then current Initial Fee charged by the Franchisor to its franchisees (whichever is the less) and

6.17:3 proper performance and observance by the Franchisee of all its obligations under this Agreement throughout the Term and

6.17:4 execution by the Franchisee of a new franchise agreement in the standard form used by the Franchisor at the time of service of such notice in respect of the further period of .... years without any option to review

6.18 Further extension

In the event that any regulation requires the Franchisor to extend the Term beyond the period of a further .... years as mentioned in clause [6.17] of these Conditions then the same provisions and procedure as set out there shall apply to any such subsequent extension.

6.19 Death or incapacity

6.19:1 In the event of the death of an individual Franchisee the personal representatives of the Franchisee shall have six calendar months from the date of death to notify the franchisor of their decision

6.19:1.1 to continue the Business whereupon such personal representatives shall be deemed to be proposed assignees of the Business or

6.19:1.2 to assign the Business to any of the heirs of the Franchisee or to a third party

whereupon the provisions set out in subclauses [3.26:1 and 3.26:2] of these Conditions shall apply

6.19:2 In the event of the incapacity of [the Franchisee *or* .... (*the key director of the Franchise*)] at any time or after such death (but prior to any such decision by such personal representatives) the

Franchisor shall have the right (but not the duty) to appoint management personnel to supervise the conduct of the Business (at the expense of the Business) to ensure that the Business shall operate in a satisfactory manner to preserve the goodwill of the Mark pending the recovery of the Franchisee or such decision

6.19:3 If so requested by the Franchisee (or the personal representatives of the Franchisee) the Franchisor may act as a non-exclusive agent for the sale of the Business and in such event shall be paid its expenses and fees as follows:

6.19:3.1 in the event that the assigneee is found by the franchisee [3%] of the sale price of the Business (including any lease premium and fixtures and fittings) or

6.19:3.2 in the event that the assignee is found by the Franchisor [5%] of such sale price

6.20 Headings

Headings contained in these Conditions are for reference purposes only and shall not be incorporated in the Agreement or these Conditions and shall not be deemed to be any indication of the meaning of the clauses and sub-clauses to which they relate

6.21 Proper law

English law only shall apply to this Agreement in every particular (including formation) and the English Courts shall have sole jurisdiction to which the parties exclusively submit

BURGER KING RESTAURANT FRANCHISE AGREEMENT

CONTENTS

SPECIMEN

THIS AGREEMENT is made the

day of between
Burger King Corporation a Florida Corporation ("BKC") &
of

("Franchisee") and
and
of
("Principal (s)")

INTRODUCTION

A. BKC is the registered proprietor of certain trade marks ("Burger King Marks") in the United Kingdom in respect of certain products and goods which are prepared and / or sold in the operation of a Burger King restaurant.

B. BKC has developed a distinctive and comprehensive restaurant format and operating system, including the Burger King Marks, a recognised restaurant design, equipment system, colour scheme and style of building, signs, copyright materials, slogans, uniforms, standards, specifications and procedures of operation, quality and uniformity of products and services offered, and procedures for inventory control and management (the "Burger King System") and is engaged in the business of operating, and granting franchises to operate, Burger King restaurants using the Burger King System and Burger King Marks.

C. BKC has established a reputation and image with the public as to the quality of product and services available at Burger King restaurants, which reputation and image have been and continue to be unique benefits to BKC and its franchisees.

D. Franchisee recognises the benefits to be derived from being identified with and receiving a franchise from BKC and being able to utilise the Burger King System and the Burger King Marks.

NOW, IT IS HEREBY AGREED AS FOLLOWS:

1. FRANCHISE GRANT: TERM AND LOCATION

1.1 BKC grants to FRANCHISEE and FRANCHISEE accepts a franchise to use the Burger King System and the Burger King Marks only in the operation of a Burger King Restaurant ("Franchised Restaurant") at

____

____

all fully described in Exhibit "A" ("Premises"). The term of this Agreement shall commence on the date the Franchised Restaurant opens for business (the "Commencement Date") and shall end on the expiry date of the lease referred to in Exhibit A but shall not exceed twenty (20) years. Franchisee agrees to operate the Franchised Restaurant at the Premises for the entire Term in accordance with the terms of this Agreement. This franchise is granted for these Premises only and no area, market or territorial rights are granted to the FRANCHISEE

2. FRANCHISE FEE

In consideration of the rights granted above, FRANCHISEE shall on or before the date of this Agreement pay to BKC the sum of... which shall be fully earned on the signing of this Agreement.

3. FRANCHISEE REPRESENTATIONS

3.1 FRANCHISEE warrants that all persons having an interest in FRANCHISEE and / or the Franchised Restaurant (whether directly, beneficially or contingently) have been disclosed to BKC in the Agreement, pursuant to which FRANCHISEE and BKC are entering into this Agreement. If FRANCHISEE is designated in the Agreement as the individual responsible for the day - to - day operation of the Franchised Restaurant, then FRANCHISEE will devote his full - time to the operation of the Franchised Restaurant. If under the terms of the Agreement FRANCHISEE is permitted to entrust the management of the Franchised Premises to a Manager (as defined in the Agreement), FRANCHISEE shall maintain in its employ such Manager who (i) successfully completes the required BKC training programme; (ii) is approved by BKC; (iii) lives within a reasonable travel distance of the Franchised Restaurant; (iv) will devote full - time and efforts in the operation of the Franchised Restaurant. If the Manager is no longer employed in that capacity, FRANCHISEE shall immediately give notice to BKC of such employment change and within a reasonable time thereafter, FRANCHISEE shall present for approval by BKC the name (s) and qualifications of those candidate (s) nominated to succeed the former Manager.

3.2 If at any time during the Term of this Agreement FRANCHISEE operates five (5) or more Burger King Restaurants (including the Franchised Restaurant), on demand from BKC, FRANCHISEE shall, in addition to complying with the requirements for a Manager, maintain in its employ, on a full - time basis one (1) individual ("Area Manager") for every four such restaurants who shall have successfully completed BKC's training as a district manager.

3.3 FRANCHISEE agrees that it has not and will not hereafter, directly or indirectly, avoid the direct operation requirements set forth herein through entry into a Management Agreement or other such arrangements with persons other than the Manager or Area Manager. FRANCHISEE shall furnish to BKC with such evidence as BKC may reasonably request from time to time for the purpose of assuring BKC that the management of the Franchised Restaurant is as stated herein and in the Conversion Agreement.

3.4 FRANCHISEE acknowledges that there are many factors which may affect the number of Managers and Area Managers to operate FRANCHISEE'S Burger King Restaurants and that FRANCHISEE'S employment of the minimum number of Managers and Area Manager's specified herein does not, by itself, assure compliance with the operating standards contained herein and in BKC's Operations Manual (defined below).

10th January 1990
(Standard, Non-conversion Edition)

4. STANDARDS AND UNIFORMITY OF OPERATION

OPERATING MANUAL

4.1 The FRANCHISEE acknowledges that the close personal relationship between the FRANCHISEE and BKC and strict adherence to the Burger King System are fundamental to this franchise. Accordingly the FRANCHISEE shall (subject to obtaining any necessary consents) at all times comply with the standardised design, data equipment system, colour scheme, style of building and signage, uniform standards, specifications and procedures of operation, quality and uniformity of product and service from time to time contained in BKC's Operations Manual and other manuals describing the Burger King System (collectively, "the Manual"). The FRANCHISEES shall at all times keep the Manual at the Franchised Restaurant and all changes or additions made by BKC shall be inserted upon receipt. In the event of any conflict between the Manual kept at the Franchised Restaurant and the master copy maintained by BKC, the master copy shall prevail.

4.2 The FRANCHISEE shall accept and comply with such modifications and additions to the Manual as BKC may from time to time, in exercising its judgement in good faith, believe to be desirable. BKC shall give reasonable notice prior to the introduction of such modifications and additions. The contents of the Manual are confidential and proprietary to BKC and may be used by FRANCHISEE only in connection with the operations of the Franchised Restaurant and other franchised Burger King Restaurants held by the Franchisee. The Manual and other specifications, standards and operating procedures communicated in writing to the Franchisee shall be deemed a part of this Agreement.

IMPROVEMENTS

4.3 FRANCHISEE shall notify BKC of any potential improvements or new features which it identifies as capable of benefiting the Burger King System. FRANCHISEE shall not use potential improvements or new features at the Franchised Restaurant until authorised by BKC. BKC may evaluate such potential improvement or new feature in its own restaurants. BKC may without payment of any royalty to FRANCHISEE introduce any such improvement or new feature into the Burger King System for the benefit of BKC and other franchisees and FRANCHISEE grants to BKC a non-exclusive licence in respect thereof for such purpose.

BUILDING & PREMISES

4.4 As regards both the interior and the exterior of the Premises:

4.4.1 The Premises shall (subject to obtaining any necessary consents) be constructed and improved in the manner authorised and approved by BKC and the appearance of the Premises shall not thereafter be altered except as may be approved in writing by BKC. FRANCHISEE shall at its own expense maintain the building and premises in good condition and in accordance with the requirements of any lease or licence under which the Premises are held and in compliance with all applicable laws and the requirements of any relevant authority or undertaking and the Manual, relating to health and safety or to any other matter whatsoever. Without prejudice to the foregoing, FRANCHISEE shall undertake repairs and replacements requested by BKC within such reasonable time as may be specified by BKC. All obligations in this sub-clause 4.4.1 are subject to the requirements of any competent local authority or other body.

4.4.2 FRANCHISEE shall on an ongoing basis improve and alter the interior of the Premises to conform to BKC's national or local plans specifications and standards for new or remodelled Burger King restaurants, as such plans specifications and standards may from time to time be reasonably changed and defined by the Manual ("Current Image"). FRANCHISEE shall remodel the exterior of the Franchised Restaruant and the Premises at least once every seven (7) years from the date of this Agreement (including any extension of the Term) to ensure conformity with the then Current Image for the exterior. BKC shall act reasonably as regards the costs and timing of changes to the Current Image.

SIGNS

4.5 The Burger King Marks shall (subject to obtaining any necessary consents) only be erected and displayed on the Premises in the manner and in such locations as are authorised by BKC. FRANCHISEE agrees to display and maintain in good condition and repair signs reflecting the then Current Image and shall not place additional signs or posters or advertising materials on the Premises without the prior written consent of BKC. Only signs procured in compliance with sub-clausse 4.11 may by utilised at the Premises. FRANCHISEE shall within a reasonable time of a request by BKC discontinue the use of and destroy any such signs as are declared obsolete by BKC.

EQUIPMENT

4.6 Only equipment procured in accordance with sub-clause 4.11 shall be use in the Franchised Restaurants. The equipment shall be maintained in a condition conforming to the requirements of the Manual and shall be replaced as the equipment becomes obsolete or inoperable or as otherwise required by the Manual, with equipment conforming to such criteria and standards as are then approved for use in the Burger King System. If BKC determined that additional or replacement equipment is needed because of a change in menu items or method of preparation or service or because of health or safety considerations, FRANCHISEE shall install the additional or replacement equipment within the reasonable time specified by BKC, provided the cost is not excessive in relation to the business.

MENU AND SERVICE

4.7 All menu items which BKC from time to time deem appropriate shall be served, and no items (whether of food or otherwise) which are not set forth in the Manual or otherwise authorised and approved by BKC in writing, shall be served, advertised or promoted. FRANCHISEE shall only sell the approved menu items by retail from and through the Franchised Restaurant and shall not sell such items for redistribution or resale, nor unless required by the Manual, by the delivery service. Notwithstanding the above, FRANCHISEE may resell to any Franchisee under the Burger King System any product or thing which the FRANCHISEE is required to stock or sell. FRANCHISEE shall adhere to all specifications contained in the Manual or as otherwise prescribed by BKC regarding ingredients, methods of storage, preparation and service, weight and dimensions of products served, and standards of cleanliness and sanitation. All food, drink and other items will be served and sold in packing procured in accordance with sub-clause 4.11. hereof.

4.8. FRANCHISEE shall at all times stock any third-party branded item which from time to time shall form part of the presentation and offering of the Burger King System in the United Kingdom.

4.9. FRANCHISEE shall, as directed by the Manual, purchase exclusively from BKC or from such other source or sources as BKC may from time to time specify, such food items BKC may specify which are (a) poultry, red meat, fish or potato products or buns and (b) which are either manufactured to particular specifications laid down by BKC or sold under one or more of the Burger King Marks.

4.10. FRANCHISEE shall procure all other food and drink items and all consumable items used in the storage, preparation, cooking and sale of menu items (including cooking oil, spices, relishes and packaging materials), in accordance with sub-clause 4.11. hereof.

4.11. All items required to be purchased in accordance with this sub-clause shall comply with all such specifications as are from time to time laid down in the Manual. In addition, BKC may from time to time nominate one or more suppliers authorised to supply any one or more of such items. FRANCHISEE in such case shall purchase exclusively from such nominated supplier or suppliers. Should the FRANCHISEE propose an alternative supplier BKC shall evaluate such supplier against its current criteria and within ninety (90) days either approve or disapprove the supplier, giving reasons. FRANCHISEE agrees that in the interests of effective quality control, BKC may require suppliers to the Burger King System to have national coverage or to be capable of supplying entire system requirements in relation to the particular product or products in question.

SALES BETWEEN FRANCHISEES

4.12. Notwithstanding anything in this Agreement FRANCHISEE shall be free to sell to or purchase from any other franchisee under the Burger King System any item required for use in the Franchised Premises provided:

the product has been procured in accordance with all relevant provisions of this Agreement and

the product is delivered to the purchasing franchisee in a safe and hygienic condition and has at all times been stored and handled in accordance with BKC's specifications (if any) for that product.

PAYMENT

4.13. FRANCHISEE shall pay for all items purchased from BKC or its Associated Companies (defined in Clause 17.1 hereof) in accordance with the standard credit terms which they from time to time operate.

HOURS OF OPERATION

4.14. The Franchised Restaurant shall be fully open for business during the minimum hours of   to   seven (7) days a week, fifty-two (52) weeks a year, unless otherwise authorised or directed by BKC. The Franchised Restaurant may be closed for up to three (3) days per year if FRANCHISEE desires.

UNIFORMS

4.15. All personnel within the Franchised Restaurant shall wear only uniforms of such design colour and material as are from time to time specified by the Manual and procured in accordance with sub-clause 4.11.

ADVERTISING AND PROMOTIONAL MATERIALS

4.16. Only those advertising and promotional materials or items which are authorised from time to time by BKC in writing prior to use shall be used, sold or distributed and no display or use of the Burger King Marks shall be made without the prior written approval of BKC. All materials on which Burger King Marks are used must include the designation R or such other designation as BKC may specify.

COMPLIANCE WITH LAWS AND HYGIENE STANDARDS

4.17. In all matters relating to health, safety and hygiene FRANCHISEE shall at all times conduct the operation at the Franchised Premises strictly in accordance with all requirements of the law, any competent authority and the Manual. In the event of conflicting standards FRANCHISEE shall comply with the highest standard required.

4.18. FRANCHISEE shall participate in any self-audit scheme which may from time to time form part of the Burger King System.

4.19. FRANCHISEE shall immediately notify BKC of any actual or suspected occurance of any serious communicable disease or infection at or among staff or customers at the Franchised Restaurant.

RIGHT OF ENTRY; INSPECTION AND CLOSURE

4.20. BKC shall have the unrestricted right to enter the Franchised Restaurant to conduct such reasonable activities as it deems necessary to ascertain compliance with this Agreement. The inspections may be conducted without prior notice at any time when FRANCHISEE or any one of its responsible employees or representatives is at the Franchised Restaurant. The inspections shall be performed in a manner which minimises interference with the operation of the Franchised Restaurant. BKC may require the removal of any items which do not comply with this Agreement at the Franchisee's cost. In the event that BKC identifies, or reasonably suspects the existence of, any significant risk to health or safety in any aspect of the operation at the Franchised Premises, BKC may require FRANCHISEE immediately to close the Franchised Premises until the hazard has been eliminated. BKC shall specify the grounds for taking such action and such steps if any as it believes are necessary to eliminate the hazard and shall co-operate with FRANCHISEE to enable FRANCHISEE to re-open Franchised Premises as soon as possible. BKC shall inform FRANCHISEE and FRANCHISEE'S restaurant manager immediately it decides the store must be closed.

5. SERVICES AVAILABLE TO FRANCHISEE

5.1 BKC agrees periodically to advise and consult with FRANCHISEE in connection with the operation of the Franchised Restaurant and to provide free of charge to FRANCHISEE:

5.1.1. a pre-opening training programme conducted at BKC training facilities and / or Burger King restaurants in the United Kingdom and / or the Franchised Restaurant (but the Franchisee shall bear the cost of items per clause 7.2).

5.1.2. pre-opening and opening supervision and assistance by personnel of BKC at the Franchised Restaurant for such period of time as BKC, in its discretion, deems appropriate,

5.1.3. an opening promotional programme as specified in the Agreement pursuant to which this Agreement is entered into,

5.1.4. BKC's Manual, a copy of which will be loaned to FRANCHISEE for the Term of this Agreement,

5.1.5. such merchandising, marketing and advertising research data and advice as may be developed from time to time by BKC and deemed by it to be helpful in the operation of a Burger King Restaurant,

5.1.6. communication of new developments, techniques and improvements of BKC in food preparation, equipment, food products, packaging, service and restaurant management which are relevant to the operation of a Burger King Restaurant.

6. RESTAURANT SITE

6.1. The Premises shall be used exclusively as a Burger King Restaurant. In the event of the building being damaged or destroyed by fire or any other peril, or required to be repaired or altered by any competent , authority

FRANCHISEE shall at its own expense repair or reconstruct the building within a reasonable time to reflect the then Current Image of Burger King restaurants, having first submitted to BKC all plans and specifications related thereto for prior approval. If the cost of meeting Current Image exceeds the cost of reinstatement to the previous image of the Premises and for that reason alone the insurance moneys are insufficient, FRANCHISEE may reinstate the Premises to their original image. Where the Premises are insured by a person other than FRANCHISEE FRANCHISEE'S obligation shall be limited to taking such steps as are reasonably available to the FRANCHISEE to procure that any insurance moneys are laid out in accordance with this sub clause.

7. TRAINING

7.1. The FRANCHISEE or the Operating Partner and / or Manager and / or Area Manager employed by FRANCHISEE shall undertake and complete continuing training programmes in the United Kingom as may from time to time be reasonably required by BKC to ensure compliance with current operational standards.

7.2. The FRANCHISEE shall be responsible for the cost of all travel and living expenses, salaries and insurance and any other personal expenses.

7.3. Any new Manager employed by FRANCHISEE shall within ninety (90) days after commencing his duties in the Franchised Restaurant be approved byBKC and shall have successfully completed initial franchisee training.

7.4. FRANCHISEE shall implement a training programme for employees in accordance with training standards and procedures from time to time prescribed by BKC and (without prejudice to any other obligation in this Agreement) shall at all times staff the Franchised Restaurant to meet the reasonable requirements of the Manual.

8. ROYALTY & ADVERTISING CONTRIBUTION

8.1. BKC shall lay periods ("Accounting Periods") which may be of four (4) or five (5) weeks duration. The FRANCHISEE shall not later than the tenth (10th) day following each Accounting Period deliver to BKC a return of Gross Sales for the Accounting Period and pay to BKC by way of royalty for the use of the Burger King System and the Burger King Marks a royalty equal to 4% of Gross Sales for the preceding Accounting Period.

8.2. In addition, FRANCHISEE shall pay to BKC by the tenth (10th) day of each Accounting Period an amount equal to 4% of Gross Sales in respect of the preceeding Accounting Period. This sum, less direct administrative expenses, will be used for advertising, sales promotion and public relations on a national and / or local basis including creative, production, media and clearance costs of advertising and sales promotion materials, and those market research expenditures directly related to the development and evaluation of the effectiveness of advertising and sales promotion. Contributions from suppliers to marketing expenditures shall be added to any moneys received under this Clause 8.2. The allocation and timing of such expenditure shall be at the sole discretion of BKC. BKC shall provide an annual audited statement of receipts and expenditures in accordance with this clause 8.2.

8.3. The term "Gross Sales" includes all sums charged by FRANCHISEE for goods, merchandise or services sold at or from the Franchised Restaurant including, for the avoidance of doubt, all unauthorised sales. The sale of Burger King products away from the Franchised Restaurant is not authorised, but should any such sales be approved in the future, they will be included within the definition of Gross Sales. Gross Sales exclude any value added tax, and cash received as payment in credit transactions where the extension of credit itself has already been included in the figure upon which the royalty and advertising contribution is computed.

8.4. All payments under this Agreement shall be made in such place and in such manner as BKC may reasonably designate. Until further notice all payments shall be made to Burgerking (U.K.) Limited in England and in sterling. Should FRANCHISEE fail to make the return of Gross Sales within the period stipulated, FRANCHISEE shall pay to BKC by way of royalty and Advertising Contribution a sum equal to eight (8) percent of Gross Sales last reported, subject to adjustment as and when the actual amount of Goods Turnover is establiched.

8.5. Any late payment shall attract interest from the date of default until payment on a daily basis at 2% over National Westminster Bank's sterling base rate (or that of such other major clearing bank as BKC may designate) for the time being in force, or such interest rate as the U.K. courts may from time to time be authorised to apply, whichever is the higher.

9. ACCOUNTING PROCEDURES: RIGHT OF AUDIT

9.1. FRANCHISEE agrees to keep true accurate and complete records of his Gross Sales in such form as BKC may from time to time rerquire and to furnish BKC with a Gross Sales Statement in the format prescribed by BKC within fourteen (14) days of the end of each Accounting Period. In addition, FRANCHISEE shall retain for a period of at least six (6) years and upon request submit to BKC copies of all value added tax returns and supporting data and records relating to sales made at and from the Franchises Restaurant and such other records as BKC may reasonably from time to time request.

9.2. BKC shall have the right to examine or audit all records relating to Gross Sales. If at any time the FRANCHISEE is shown to have understated Gross Sales in respect of any period, FRANCHISEE shall within fifteen days of receipt of a demand pay to BKC the balance of the royalty and advertising contribution due in respect of such period plus interest thereon in accordance whith clause 8.5. of this Agreement from the date such payments were originally due; and in addition if such understatement is greater than 5 per cent of actual Gross Sales, the FRANCHISEE shall reimburse to BKC all costs of investigation including professional fees, an allocation of overheads, travel, lodging and wages, reasonably incurred.

9.3. BKC shall hold all information provided under this clause confidential unless required by a competent authority to disclose it.

10. LIMITATIONS OF FRANCHISE

TRADE MARKS, TRADE NAMES, SERVICE MARKS AND TRADE SECRETS

10.1. FRANCHISEE acknowledges that all rights, title, and interest to the Burger King System and the Burger King Marks, belong and shall continue to belong solely to BKC, and FRANCHISEE disclaims any right or interest therein or in the goodwill derived therefrom. FRANCHISEE agrees that all materials loaned or made available to him but not to the general public by or at the direction of BKC at any time relating to the Burger King System, including, without limitation, the Manual in its entirety, financial information, marketing strategy and marketing programmes, are to be considered trade secrets of BKC and shall both during and after the Term be kept condidential and shall be used by the FRANCHISEE only in connection with the operation of the Franchised Restaurant and other franchised Burger King Restaurants. FRANCHISEE agrees not to divulge any of the trade secrets to any person other than his employees and then only to the extent necessary for the operation of the Franchised Restaurant, and shall not permit any person to reproduce or copy the Manual or any part thereof or any other trade secrets of BKC. FRANCHISEE shall use reasonable endeavours to safeguard the Manual and any other trade secrets of BKC. The above obligations shall not extend to any information which is or comes into the public domain unless this is caused by the neglect or breach of this Agreement by the FRANCHISEE.

10.2. FRANCHISEE acknowledges that at the date of this Agreement he has no right to any of the Burger King Marks or the Burger King System except as licensed by this Agreement or any other Franchise Agreement issued by BKC to FRANCHISEE. FRANCHISEE shall immediately notify BKC of all infringements or imitations of the Burger King Marks which come to his attention, or challenges to FRANCHISEE'S use of any of the Burger King Marks and BKC shall exercise absolute discretion in deciding what action, if any, should be taken. The FRANCHISEE shall not be entitled to exercise any of the rights relating to trade or service mark infringement conferred on a registered user by the relevant trade mark legislation.

10.3. Neither before nor after the end of the Term shall FRANCHISEE use in his corporate, business or partnership name any of the Burger King Marks, or any slogan or copyright material used in the Burger King System, or any variation or abbreviation or words confusingly similar to any of the above.

10.4. This clause 10 applies to any Principal named in this Agreement as it applies to the Franchisee.

INDEPENDENT CONTRACTOR

10.5. FRANCHISEE is an independent contractor and is not an agent, partner, joint venturer or employee of BKC, and no fiduciary relationship exists between the parties. FRANCHISEE shall not bind or obligate BKC in any way nor shall he represent that he has any right to do so. BKC shall have no control over the terms and conditions of employment of the FRANCHISEE's employees.

10.6. In all public records and in FRANCHISEE's relationships with other persons, on stationery and other business forms, FRANCHISEE shall indicate independent ownership of the Franchised Restaurant and that it is operated under a frachise granted by BKC. FRANCHISEE shall exhibit in the Franchised Restaurant in such places as may be designated by BKC a notice that the Franchised Restaurant is operated by an independent operator under licence from BKC.

11. UNFAIR COMPETITION

11.1. FRANCHISEE shall during the Term of the Agreement use his best and continuing efforts to promote and develop the business at the Franchised Premises.

11.2. The FRANCHISEE shall not during the Term and for one year thereafter (or if the FRANCHISEE shall sell the business, for one year following such sale) engage directly or indirectly nor to be employed in any fastfood, counterservice hamburger business which would compete with the Franchised Restaurant. Furthermore, the FRANCHISEE shall not during the Term engage directly or indirectly nor be employed in any fastfood, counter - service hamburger business in a location where such business would compete with any restaurant operating under the Burger King System.

11.3. The FRANCHISEE shall not during the Term acquire an interest in any fast food, counterservice hamburger undertaking which competes with the Burger King restaurant business where such interest is by its nature and size capable of enabling the FRANCHISEE to influence the economic conduct of such undertaking.

11.4. This clause applies to any Principal named in this Agreement as it applies to the Franchisee.

12. INSURANCE: INDEMNIFICATION

FRANCHISEE shall all times during the Term of this Agreement carry a comprehensive general liability insurance incorporating products liability (including contractual liability) and third-party liability in a form acceptable to BKC for an amount not less than five million pounds (£5,000,000.00) per occurence or for such increased amounts as BKC may reasonably from time to time request. Each policy shall name BKC and its Associated Companies as joint insured parties, shall provide that the policy cannot be cancelled without thirty (30) days' prior written notice to BKC and its Associated Companies and shall insure the contractual liability of FRANCHISEE under paragraph 12.4 below. Within 14 days after the Commencement Date FRANCHISEE shall furnish to BKC a certificate of insurance confirming that such cover is in effect. All policies shall be renewed and a renewal certificate of insurance mailed to Burgerking (U.K.) Limited or such other location as BKC may from time to time specify, within 14 days of renewal.

12.2. FRANCHISEE shall at all times during the Term maintain Employer's Liability insurance as required by law.

12.3. FRANCHISEE shall produce to BKC or Burgerking (U.K.) Limited upon demand evidence that all such policies are in full force and effect according to the above provisions.

12.4. FRANCHISEE is responsible for all losses or damages and contractual liabilities to third persons arising out of or in connection with the possession ownership or operation of the Franchised Restaurant, and for all claims or demands whatsoever, whether relating to injury illness or death or otherwise directly or indirectly resulting therefrom. FRANCHISEE shall defend, indemnify and hold BKC, Burgerking (U.K.) Limited, and BKC's Associated Companies, harmless of, from, and with respect to any such matters unless proven to result from the negligence of or defects in goods manufactured by BKC, Burgerking (U.K.) Limited, or BKC's Associated Companies. BKC shall notify FRANCHISEE of any claims, and FRANCHISEE shall be given the opportunity to assume the defence of the matter. If FRANCHISEE fails to assume the defence, BKC may defend the action in the manner it deems appropriate, and FRANCHISEE shall pay to BKC all costs including attorney's fees, incurred by BKC in effecting such defence, in addition to any sum which BKC may pay by reason of any settlement or judgment. BKC's right to indemnity under this agreement shall arise and be valid notwithstanding that joint or concurrent liability may be imposed on BKC by statute, regulation or other law.

13. TAXES, V.A.T.

13.1. All royalties, fees and other charges referred to in, or payable in accordance with, this Agreement are quoted exclusive of V.A.T. and the FRANCHISEE shall pay V.A.T. as required by law.

13.2. FRANCHISEE shall duly pay all charges rates or taxes associated with the occupation of the Franchised Premises, and shall pay V.A.T. upon any rental due in respect of the Franchised Premises if the landlords shall so require.

13.3. Where the law permits an election regarding the treatment of any supply or deemed supply under this Agreement for V.A.T. purposes, the FRANCHISEE shall make or join in any such election as the Frachisor may from time to time require.

14. ASSIGNMENT: RIGHT OF FIRST REFUSAL

14.1. FRANCHISEE shall not sell, assign, transfer or make any declaration of trust in respect of the Franchised Restaurant or this Agreement, or any beneficial interest therein, or permit any person to do so, without the prior written consent of BKC, except as expressly stated hereunder.

14.2 If FRANCHISEE wishes to dispose of the entire interest of FRANCHISEE in the Frachised Restaurant and this Agreement he shall give BKC a written letter of intent signed by the intending purchaser together with such information as BKC may reasonably request. BKC shall not unreasonably delay any such request.

14.3 Within 21days of the fulfilment of the above conditions, BKC shall notify FRANCHISEE whether it wishes to purchase at the price and upon the terms stated in the letter of intent and otherwise on fair and reasonable terms and such notice shall constitute a binding contract and BKC and Franchisee shall complete the sale and purchase with all reasonable speed and in any event within 28 days of BKC's notice, subject only to obtaining any necessary consents from landlords or others. In addition to the purchase price specified BKC shall pay to FRANCHISEE any VAT due thereon against receipt of a VAT invoice.

14.4. If BKC does not accept FRANCHISEE's offer to sell the Frachised Restaurant, FRANCHISEE may conclude the sale to the purchaser named in the said letter of intent at a price at least equal the price and subject to the terms stated in the letter of intent, subject to obtaining the prior written consent of BKC which shall not be unreasonably withheld or delayed, provided the Franchisee shall first have provided BKC with a duly completed application form together with such references as BKC shall reasonably require and the opportunity to interview the proposed assignee or such person as BKC may reasonably require. The sale to the proposed assignee must be completed within ninety (90) days of BKC's notice or such longer time as may be required to obtain the consent of any landlord or other person. The election by BKC not to exercise its right of first refusal as to any such offer shall not affect its right of first refusal as to any subsequent offer. Conditions imposed by BKC on such sale may include (but are not limited to) the following:

14.5.1 All obligations of FRANCHISEE to BKC or BKC's Associated Companies whether arising under this Agreement or otherwise, must be satisfied at the time of sale.

14.5.2 The purchaser shall prior to the sale being completed have agreed to an appropriate training schedule.

14.5.3 Approval by BKC of the terms and conditions of the contract of sale and purchase which affect the sufficiency of cash flow from the business after payment of debt service necessary for reinvestment in the business, for refurbishing, maintaining and remodelling the Premises in accordance with this Agreement.

14.5.4 FRANCHISEE shall pay to BKC the sum of two thousand pounds (£2,000.00) or BKC's then current franchise transfer fee, whichever is the higher, as a contribution towards the costs and expenses incurred by BKC in connection with the above.

ASSIGNMENT BY BKC

14.6 BKC may assign this Agreement to any person or company which acquires its Burger King business in the United Kingdom or a substantial part thereof, whether by outright acquisition or by way of a master franchise agreement. BKC may delegate the performance of any of its duties and the exercise of its rights hereunder to Burgerking (U.K.) Limited.

INTERNAL REORGANISATION OF FRANCHISEE

14.7 Notwithstanding the above, FRANCHISEE may following prior written notification to BKC assign this Agreement to any company of which FRANCHISEE owns and controls 100 per cent of all issued share capital, provided such company shall not previously have traded and provided further that FRANCHISEE shall remain jointly and severally with such company liable for the due performance of each and every covenant and condition in this Agreement.

14.8 CONTROL OF CORPORATE FRANCHISEE

14.8.1 Where the Franchisee is a limited company the Franchisor shall be entitled to terminate this Agreement if a change in control of the Franchisee occurs without prior written consent of the Franchisor. For these purposes a change in control shall occur only when

(a) the Franchisee ceases to be controlled by the Principal named in this Agreement, or

(b) if more than one person is named as Principal, when the Franchisee ceases to be controlled by one or more of the Principals named in the Agreement (but so that Principals may freely dispose of shares between themselves), or

(c) where the Franchisee ceases to be controlled by one or more persons whom the Franchisor has approved to control the Franchisee in place of the Principal or Principals.

14.8. 2. For these purposes a person shall be deemed to control the Franchisee where such person is a "parent undertaking" or "parent company" of the Franchisee in accordance with section 258 Companies Act, 1985, as inserted by s.21, Companies Act, 1989, or would be if such person were a company.

14.8.3 BKC shall not unreasonably withhold or delay its consent to a change in control of the Franchisee.

14.8.4 This sub-clause 14 (8) shall have no application to any Franchisee which is at the date of this Agreement or subsequently becomes listed on a recognised Stock Exchange or quoted on the Unlisted Securities Market or the Third Market or to any shares subject to a Business Expansion Scheme made under the Finance Act 1986 (as amended) at the date of this Agreement or to any company which is at the date of this Agreement and remains wholly-owned by such a company.

14.8.5 A change in control shall not be deemed to occur merely by reason of shares passing to personal representatives or to a surviving joint owner on the death of a shareholder.

15. DISPOSAL OF FRANCHISEE'S INTEREST ON DEATH

15.1 Clause 14 above shall apply to any sale by the personal representatives of any deceased person as it would apply to a sale by such person were he alive.

15.2 Should the personal representatives wish to transfer this Agreement and the Franchised Restaurant or the beneficial interest of the deceased therein to a spouse or child of the deceased entitled thereto under the Will or intestacy then BKC shall have no right of first refusal and BKC shall consent to such transfer to any such person who (i) meets BKC's criteria for Franchisee selection, and (ii) if the deceased personally managed the Franchised Premises, successfully undergoes Franchisee training.

15.3 Where the deceased was the FRANCHISEE, until the personal representatives of the deceased dispose of the Franchised Restaurant they shall operate it in all respects in accordance with this Agreement. If the personal representatives fail so to do, or if the personal representatives request BKC, BKC may, but shall be under no obligation to, appoint a manager to operate the Franchised Restaurant on behalf of the personal representatives. If such manager is provided, his liability and the liability of BKC shall be limited to exercising reasonable care in the management of the Franchised Restaurant. BKC shall be entitled to make a reasonable charge in respect of the provision of such manager and may withdraw his services at any time on giving not less than one month's notice.

15.4 Where the deceased was the FRANCHISEE, if the personal representatives of the deceased have not within a period of 18 months from the death of the deceased completed the disposal of the Franchised Restaurant, BKC may either terminate this Agreement by one month's notice or by notice elect to purchase the Franchised Restaurant and / or right title and interest of the personal representatives therein at their fair market value upon fair and upon reasonable terms to be agreed between the parties and failing agreement within one month of such notice either party may at any time apply to the President for the time being of the Institute of Chartered Accountants for the appointment of an expert who shall determine the terms and conditions of such sale as shall appear to him fair and reasonable in all circumstances. Following such determination the sale and purchase shall be completed within 28 days.

16. TERMINATION, AND EFFECTS OF TERMINATION

16.1 The occurrence of any of the following events shall constitute good cause for BKC, at its option and without prejudice to any other rights of the BKC, and without compensation to the Franchisee, to terminate this Agreement, such notice to be given in writing.

16.1.1 If the FRANCHISEE shall compound with its creditors or if any distress or execution is levied on the FRANCHISEE's goods or if the FRANCHISEE enters into liquidation whether compulsory or voluntary (save where it is for the purpose of amalgamation or reconstruction only while solvent) or if an administrator or administrative receiver or other receiver is appointed by a court over the whole or any part of the FRANCHISEE's undertaking or application is made to any court for any such appointment to be made, or being a partnership the FRANCHISEE is dissolved, or if any other steps are taken under any insolvency, bankruptcy, receivership, or moratorium laws from time to time in force, but so that the appointment of a receiver or manager in accordance with the terms of any mortgage charge or debenture shall for these purposes be disregarded;

16.1.2 If FRANCHISEE ceases to occupy the Premises;

16.1.3 If FRANCHISEE abandons the franchise relationship without the prior consent of BKC at any time during the Term of this Agreement. The cessation of operation of the Franchised Restaurant on the Premises (except for the purposes of repair cleaning refurbishment or remodelling or in compliance with the requirement of any competant authority) without the consent of BKC, whether the Premises remain vacant or are converted to another use, shall be considered abandonment of the franchise relationship.

16.1.4 If the FRANCHISEE knowingly challenges the validity of the Burger King Marks.

16.1.5 If the FRANCHISEE fails to remedy any of the following breaches within five days of service of a notice requiring FRANCHISEE to remedy the same: failure to operate the Franchise Restaurant in accordance with the operating standards contained in the Manual relating to product specification, cleanliness, health, and sanitation; the use of trade or service marks, slogans or promotional or advertising material not approved by BKC;

16.1.6 If the FRANCHISEE fails to pay any sum due hereunder within 10 days of a demand stating that he is in default;

16.1.7 If the FRANCHISEE makes any materially false statement in connection with any return of Gross Sales or in any other account required hereby other than a manifest and unintentional error;

16.1.8 If the FRANCHISEE commits any other material breach of the terms of this Agreement and fails to remedy the same within 30 days of service of a notice requiring him to do so or commits any material breach of the terms of this Agreement which is not capable of remedy;

16.1.9 If the FRANCHISEE commits persistent breaches of the terms of this Agreement (whether or not material in isolation) after written warning has been given, any three breaches occuring within the period of six months shall be deemed to constitute persistent breaches;

16.1.10 If the FRANCHISEE for any reason other than the act or default of BKC ceases to be entitled to remain registered as a registered user of any of the Burger King Marks;

16.1.11 If any events occur which are contrary to Clauses 14 or 15 hereof;

16.1.12 Sentencing of the FRANCHISEE or (in the case of a partnership) any person comprising the FRANCHISEE or any directors of a corporate FRANCHISEE to a term of imprisonment in excess of three years.

16.1.13 If the FRANCHISEE the Principal or (in the case of a partnership) any person comprising the FRANCHISEE engages in activities prohibited by clause 11 (unfair competition) or discloses any trade secrets of BKC in violation of Clause 10.

16.1.14 If the FRANCHISEE has knowingly made false misleading statements in order to obtain this Agreement.

16.1.15 If (in the case of a partnership) any of the above occurs in relation to any one or more of the persons who comprise the Franchisee.

16.2 Upon termination or expiry of this Agreement, FRANCHISEE's right to use the Burger King System, the

Burger King Marks, the trade secrets of BKC, BKC's promotional material and any other intellectual property rights of BKC contained in the M.O.D. Manual or used in the Burger King System, shall immediately terminate. On termination or expiry of this Agreement FRANCHISEE shall immediately return to BKC the Manual loaned to him together with all other material containing trade secrets.

16.3 BKC shall have the option upon termination or expiration of this Agreement to purchase some or all usable paper goods containers and printed menus packaging and other items bearing the Burger King Marks, restaurant equipment, furniture, fixtures and signs, at their market value.

16.4 FRANCHISEE agrees immediately upon termination or expiry of this Agreement to make such removals or changes in signs and the Premises as BKC shall request so as to distinguish the Premises from their former appearance and from any other Burger King Restaurant.

16.5 In the event FRANCHISEE fails to comply with the terms of sub-clause 16.2 - 16.4 inclusive, BKC shall have the right to enter the Premises to carry out such matters at FRANCHISEE's expense and to remove any items not returned by FRANCHISEE.

17. MISCELLANEOUS

INTERPRETATION

17.1 The introduction shall be considered a part of this Agreement. Paragraph headings are used only for convenience and do not form part of this Agreement. Where the context so admits, words importing any gender shall include any other gender; the singular shall include the plural and vice versa; where the FRANCHISEE consists of more than one person, physical or legal, covenants on the part of the FRANCHISEE shall be joint and several; references to value added tax include references to any tax replacing it; expressions used to define the parties in this Agreement shall include their successors in title, personal representatives and assigns; a covenant on the part of the FRANCHISEE or any person who may join in this Agreement as guarantor or surety not to do something includes a covenant not to permit others to do it; any right given to the BKC includes the right to do it through servants or agents or third-party contractors or to do it in conjunction with its servants, agents or third-party contractors and includes any necessary rights of access; where the FRANCHISEE covenants to do something, it shall be done at the FRANCHISEE's expense; to the extent of any inconsistency, this Agreement prevails over the Manual. The term "Associated Companies" as used in this Agreement shall mean companies which are the holding company or subsidiary of a given company or where both companies have the same holding company, and the terms "holding company" and "subsidiary" shall have the meaning ascribed to them in Section 736, Companies Act 1985.

17.2. Also for the avoidance of doubt, where the context so admits, the expressions "Burger King Marks" and "Burger King System" include any additions, deletions, or substitutions which BKC may from time to time in its absolute discretion determine to make, whether the same shall be trade or service marks or whether or not application for registration has been made by BKC.

NON-WAIVER

17.3 The failure of BKC to exercise any right or option given to it under this Agreement, or in any separate guarantee or other security, or to insist upon strict compliance by FRANCHISEE or any guarantor with the terms and conditions of this Agreement shall not constitute a waiver of any terms and conditions in this Agreement with respect to any other or any subsequent breach, nor a waiver by BKC of its right at any time thereafter to require exact and strict compliance with the terms and conditions of this Agreement.

RIGHTS CUMULATIVE

17.4. The rights and remedies set forth in this Agreement are cumulative and not mutually exclusive and are in addition to any other rights or remedies which may be granted by law or available in equity.

GOVERNING LAW, FORUM & COMPLIANCE

17.5. This Agreement shall be read and construed in accordance with English law. The English Courts shall have exclusive jurisdiction.

SEVERABILITY

17.6. BKC and FRANCHISEE agree that if any provision of this Agreement may be construed in two ways, one of which would render the provision illegal or otherwise voidable or unenforceable and the other of which would render the provision valid and enforceable, such provision shall have the meaning which renders it valid and enforceable. Subject to this, the provisions of this Agreement are severable and this Agreement shall be interpreted and enforced as if all invalid or unenforceable provisions were not contained in the Agreement and partially valid and enforceable provisions shall be enforced to the extent only that they are valid and enforceable.

NOTICES

17.7. All notices to BKC shall be in writing, and shall be handed delivered or sent by registered mail and until further notice shall be sent to Burgerking (U.K.) Limited at its registered office as agents for BKC.

17.8. All notices to FRANCHISEE shall be in writing and shall be hand delivered or sent by registered mail addressed to FRANCHISEE at the Franchised Restaurant or the FRANCHISEE's registered office or the FRANCHISEE's last known address or at the Premises. Such notices shall be validly served by Burgerking (U.K.) Limited as agent for BKC.

17.9. If sent by first class post notices shall be deemed delivered on the earlier of actual receipt or the third day after being posted.

MODIFICATIONS

17.10. This Agreement may only be modified or amended by a written document executed by a duly authorised person on behalf of the party against whom any such amendment or modification is sought to be enforced.

SURVIVAL OF TERMS

17.11 Any provisions of this Agreement which impose an obligation after termination or expiration of this Agreement shall survive the termination or expiration of this Agreement and remain binding on the parties.

ENTIRE AGREEMENT

17.12. This Agreement, together with the franchise application and lease or agreement for lease, and the Preliminary Agreement executed by BKC and the FRANCHISEE with regard to the Franchised Restaurant, constitute the entire agreement of the parties and supersedes all prior negotiations commitments, representations warranties, and undertaking of the parties (if any) with respect to the subject matter of this Agreement and to the Franchised Restaurant.

PRELIMINARY AGREEMENT

17.13. This Agreement is subject to the terms and conditions of the Agreement (if any) a copy of which is attached as Exhibit B. In the event of any conflict, the latter Agreement shall prevail.

INDEPENDENT ADVICE

17.14. FRANCHISEE AND THE PRINCIPAL EACH ACKNOWLEDGE THAT THEY HAVE BEEN ADVISED BY BKC OR ITS AGENTS TO TAKE PROFESSIONAL ADVICE ON ALL ASPECTS OF THIS AGREEMENT AND THE BURGER KING BUSINESS AND ACKNOWLEDGE THAT THEY HAVE TAKEN SUCH INDEPENDENT ADVICE AS THEY DEEM NECESSARY AND HAVE INDEPENDENTLY SATISFIED THEMSELVES ON ALL RELEVANT MATTERS BEFORE ENTERING INTO THIS AGREEMENT.

BURGER KING CORPORATION	WITNESSES
______________________	______________________
Duly authorised person	
	______________________

FRANCHISEE	WITNESSES
______________________	______________________
______________________	______________________

PRINCIPAL (S)	WITNESSES
______________________	______________________
______________________	______________________

EXHIBIT A

Description of the Premises which are the subject of the Franchise

as the same described in a lease / underlease dated day of 198
under which the Franchisee is the lessee

EXHIBIT B

Copy of the Preliminary Agreement attached

Index

In the following index, 'franchise' is abbreviated to 'fr', 'franchising to 'fr'ing', 'franchisor' to 'fr'or' and 'franchisee' to 'fr'ee'.